Teaching and Researching Speaking

APPLIED LINGUISTICS IN ACTION

General Editors:

Christopher N. Candlin and David R. Hall

Books published and forthcoming in this series include:

Teaching and Researching Speaking

Second Edition

Rebecca Hughes

Longman
is an imprint of

PEARSON

Harlow, England • London • New York • Boston • San Francisco • Toronto
Sydney • Tokyo • Singapore • Hong Kong • Seoul • Taipei • New Delhi
Cape Town • Madrid • Mexico City • Amsterdam • Munich • Paris • Milan

PEARSON EDUCATION LIMITED

Edinburgh Gate
Harlow CM20 2JE
United Kingdom
Tel: +44 (0)1279 623623
Fax: +44 (0)1279 431059
Website: www.pearsoned.co.uk

First edition published in Great Britain in 2002
Second edition published 2011

© Pearson Education Limited 2002, 2011

The right of Rebecca Hughes to be identified as author
of this work has been asserted by her in accordance
with the Copyright, Designs and Patents Act 1988.

Pearson Education is not responsible for the content of third party internet sites.

ISBN: 978-1-4082-0504-4

British Library Cataloguing in Publication Data
A CIP catalogue record for this book can be obtained from the British Library

Library of Congress Cataloging in Publication Data
Hughes, Rebecca.
    Teaching and researching speaking / Rebecca Hughes. – 2nd ed.
        p. cm. – (Applied linguistics in action series)
    Includes bibliographical references and index.
    ISBN 978-1-4082-0504-4 (pbk.)
    1. Oral communication–Study and teaching.   I. Title.
    P95.3.H84 2010
    808.5071–dc22
                                                                        2010031600

10   9   8   7   6   5   4   3   2   1
14   13   12   11   10

Set in 10.5/12pt Janson by 35
Printed and bound in Malayia, CTP-KHL

To my mother, Alyna Hughes, 1918–2009

Contents

Figure list

General Editors' Preface

Applied Linguistics *in Action*, as its name suggests, is a Series which focuses on the issues and challenges to teachers and researchers in a range of fields in Applied Linguistics and provides readers and users with the tools they need to carry out their own practice-related research.

The books in the Series provide the reader with clear, up-to-date, accessible and authoritative accounts of their chosen field within Applied Linguistics. Starting from a map of the landscape of the field, each book provides information on its main ideas and concepts, competing issues and unsolved questions. From there, readers can explore a range of practical applications of research into those issues and questions, and then take up the challenge of undertaking their own research, guided by the detailed and explicit research guides provided. Finally, each book has a section which provides a rich array of resources, information sources and further reading, as well as a key to the principal concepts of the field.

Questions the books in this innovative Series ask are those familiar to all teachers and researchers, whether very experienced or new to the fields of Applied Linguistics.

- What does research tell us, what doesn't it tell us and what should it tell us about the field? How is the field mapped and landscaped? What is its geography?

- How has research been applied and what interesting research possibilities does practice raise? What are the issues we need to explore and explain?

- What are the key researchable topics that practitioners can undertake? How can the research be turned into practical action?

- Where are the important resources that teachers and researchers need? Who has the information? How can it be accessed?

Each book in the Series has been carefully designed to be as accessible as possible, with built-in features to enable readers to find what they want quickly and to home in on the key issues and themes that concern them. The structure is to move from practice to theory and back to practice in a cycle of development of understanding of the field in question.

Each of the authors of books in the Series is an acknowledged authority, able to bring broad knowledge and experience to engage teachers and researchers in following up their own ideas, working with them to build further on *their* own experience.

The first editions of books in this series have attracted widespread praise for their authorship, their design, and their content, and have been widely used to support practice and research. The success of the series, and the realization that it needs to stay relevant in a world where new research is being conducted and published at a rapid rate, have prompted the commissioning of this second edition. This new edition has been thoroughly updated, with accounts of research that has appeared since the first edition and with the addition of other relevant additional material. We trust that students, teachers and researchers will continue to discover inspiration in these pages to underpin their own investigations.

Chris Candlin & David Hall
General Editors

Acknowledgements

I would like to thank all those who have helped me in the process of writing this book including:

My husband, Kieron O'Hara, for his immensely kind and practical support, as ever. My colleagues at the Centre for English Language Education and, in particular, Liz Hamp-Lyons for her illumination of some key points for me in the assessment chapter.

Chris Candlin and David Hall whose patience, and insightful comments, have been hugely appreciated.

To Dr Xu Jun, who acted as my editorial assistant in the closing stages of a substantially rewritten second edition, with all the complexities that that entails, I offer my particularly warm thanks.

I would like to pass on sincere gratitude to the editorial team at Longman.

I offer my thanks to everyone who has helped me, and any errors and omissions remaining should be placed at my door.

Publisher's Acknowledgements

We are grateful to the following for permission to reproduce copyright material:

Figures

Figure on page 70 from *Everyday Listening and Speaking*, Oxford University Press (Cunningham, S. and Moor, P. 1992), by permission of Oxford University Press; Figure 4.2 from *Automated Scoring of Spontaneous Speech Using SpeechRater v1.0*, Educational Testing Service (Xi, X., Higgins, D., Zechner, K. and Williamson, D.M. 2008) p. 29, reprinted by permission of Educational Testing Service, the copyright owner. However, these materials are provided in their entirety by Pearson Education. No endorsement of this publication by Educational Testing Service should be inferred; Figure 5.1 from Speaking whilst monitoring addresses for understanding, reprinted from *Journal of Memory and Language*, 50, pp. 72, 2004, Clark, H.H. and Krych, M.A., with permission from Elsevier.

Tables

Table 4.1 adapted from https://www.ets.org/Media/Tests/TOEFL/pdf/Independent_Speaking_Rubrics_2008.pdf, reprinted by permission of Educational Testing Service, the copyright owner. However, these materials are provided in their entirety by Pearson Education. No endorsement of this publication by Educational Testing Service should be inferred; Table 4.2 adapted from http://www.ielts.org/PDF/UOBDs_SpeakingFinal.pdf, reproduced with the kind permission of Cambridge ESOL.

Text

Quotes 3.2, 3.4, 4.4 from *Exploring Spoken English*, Cambridge University Press (Carter, R. and McCarthy, M. 1997); Quote 3.3 from *Discussions A-Z, Intermediate: A resource book of speaking activities*, Cambridge University Press (Wallwork, A. 1997); Quote 3.12 from *Making Polite Noises*, Evans

(Hargreaves, R. and Fletcher, M. 1979); Quote 3.16 from *Study Speaking: A course in spoken English for academic purposes*, Cambridge University Press (Lynch, T. and Anderson, K. 1992), reproduced with the permission of the author and the publisher; Quote 3.17 from *Barron's How to Prepare for the IELTS*, Barrons Educational Series Inc (Lougheed, L. 2006); Quote 4.17 from http://www.ets.org/toefl/ibt/scores/improve/speaking_familiar_fair, reprinted by permission of Educational Testing Service, the copyright owner. However, these materials are provided in their entirety by Pearson Education. No endorsement of this publication by Educational Testing Service should be inferred; Quote 4.18 from *International English Language Testing System Handbook*, IELTS (IELTS 2007), reproduced with the kind permission of Cambridge ESOL; Quote 4.19 from http://www.dcsf.gov.uk/curriculum_esol/tree/speaking/speaktocommunicate/e3/), reproduced under the terms of the Click-Use Licence; Extract 4.20 from http://www.cambridgeesol.org/exams/general-english/sfl/speaking-assessment.html, reproduced with the kind permission of Cambridge ESOL; Quote 4.21 from *Examples of Speaking Performances at CEF Levels A2 to C2*, University of Cambridge ESOL (Cambridge ESOL Examinations Research and Validation Group 2009), reproduced with the kind permission of Cambridge ESOL; Quote 5.6 and 5.7 from The clause as a locus of grammar and interaction, *Discourse Studies*, 7 (4–5), pp. 481–505 (Thompson, S.A. and Couper-Kuhlen, E. 2005), © 2005 by SAGE. Reprinted by permission of SAGE.

In some instances we have been unable to trace the owners of copyright material, and we would appreciate any information that would enable us to do so.

Introduction

Quote 0.1 The object of study in speech

It is often said that every true academic discipline must have its own corpus, a body of knowledge peculiarly its own and distinct from all other disciplines. To what extent does the field of speech today meet such a test? What can be defined as the corpus of speech?

(Auer, 1959: 22)

Who is this book for?

This book is intended for classroom professionals or higher degree students who need to have an up-to-date, detailed, and straightforward summary of current research and issues in the field of teaching and researching speaking. In part, the book aims to assist communication between students and practising teachers on the one hand, and theoreticians and researchers in applied linguistics on the other, by helping to position work on the skill of speaking in the context of classroom issues, and illuminate these from a variety of research perspectives.

In particular, this book aims to help the reader gain enough background knowledge to approach their own research project in the field with greater confidence. Therefore, rather than merely summarising ideas from academic texts and articles, the key concepts or issues are related to a range of research skills and processes which are commonly used to investigate them.

The structure of the book

There are four main sections to this book, each of which addresses key issues in the following areas:

Section I: This gives the background to and context for the present situation in teaching and researching speaking. Here there are two contextualising chapters, the first giving the historical background to research and attitudes to teaching speaking, the second summarising current research into the topic, current paradigms and issues in the field.

Section II: This gives a more detailed description of research applications, assessment and classroom issues. The first of three chapters in the section gives an overview of approaches and materials in the domain of teaching speaking and addresses the issue of how far 'real' speech is dealt with in the classroom. The next chapter deals with the assessment of speech and is followed by a final chapter summarising several approaches to researching speech through case-study material and reviewing trends in current mode-based research and possible new directions.

Section III: The first chapter in this section returns to the issue of the need for further research into the topic of speech in its own right. The next section provides further case studies and suggestions for a number of research projects capable of being carried out by classroom practitioners or students.

Section IV: The final section gives an overview of cross-disciplinary relationships, and research resources that are available both in traditional media such as print bibliographies and journals, and online resources, networks and sites that relate to teaching and researching speaking. There is a glossary of key terms at the end of the section.

Section

I

Issues in teaching and researching speaking

Chapter 1

Conceptual and historical background

This chapter will...

- investigate and describe some of the typical features of spoken discourse;
- provide a historical context for the attitudes to teaching and researching speech;
- begin to highlight some of the problems in teaching and researching speaking arising from attitudes to speech that have tended to prevail in linguistic theory.

1.1 Introduction

A central theme that this chapter discusses is the status of speech in society at different points in time and in linguistic theory and practice in particular. A significant issue which I will be addressing throughout this book is the fact that the spoken form gained primacy of status in language sciences in the twentieth century to the point where there was, and there remains, a merging in applied linguistic and wider research circles, of the concept of 'speaking' with 'language'. This has had an impact on how the form is assessed, taught, and researched, as later chapters will show.

The chapter tries to explain this process, why it is significant, and why, paradoxically, it has led to a lack of explicit attention within linguistic theory to the faculty of speech in its own right. The conceptual and historical overviews in this chapter are intended to provide an overview of some of the implications of this issue for the practice and theory of language teaching that the later chapters deal with in detail.

1.2   The skill of speaking

> **Quote 1.1**   An early plea for the teaching of speaking in its own right
>
> With regard indeed to the pronunciation of our tongue, the obstacles are great; and in the present state of things almost insuperable. But all this apparent difficulty arises from our utter neglect of examining and regulating our speech; as nothing has hitherto been done, either by individuals, or societies, towards a right method of teaching it.
>
> (Sheridan, 1781: v–vi)

1.2.1   Speaking is not a discrete skill

One of the central difficulties inherent in the study of speaking is that it overlaps with a considerable number of other areas and disciplines. How far, for instance, is the structure of a conversation culturally determined (also dealt with in pragmatics and ethnography)? How far are the grammar and vocabulary of speech different from other sorts of grammar (which is related also to the fields of syntax and semantics)? What are the critical factors in the stream of speech that make it intelligible (prosody, phonetics/phonemics)? This book attempts to carve out a niche for speaking in its own right whilst relating it from time to time for clarity to these distinct areas: the global or discourse level, the structural level and the level of speech production.

These three areas broadly relate to fairly stable areas of activity in linguistics of discourse, lexis and grammar, and phonology/phonetics and map on to, and overlap with, other threads of study in theoretical and applied linguistics. Some of the relationships are indicated in Figure 1.1.

1.2.2   Teaching speaking is not easily separated from other objectives

When the spoken language is the focus of classroom activity there are often other aims which the teacher might have. For instance, a task may be carried out to help the student gain awareness of, or to practise, some aspect of linguistic knowledge (whether a grammatical rule, or application of a phonemic regularity to which they have been introduced), or to develop productive skills (for example rhythm, intonation or vowel-to-vowel linking), or to raise awareness of some socio-linguistic or pragmatic point (for instance how to interrupt politely, respond to a compliment appropriately, or show that one has understood).

Figure 1.1   Levels and fields of research into speech and conversation

1.2.3   Teaching speaking versus using speaking to teach

A key question to ask, therefore, is whether a teacher is engaged in 'teaching the spoken form of a language' or 'teaching a language through speaking'. This distinction is important, although it may seem trivial at first sight. Spoken forms of language have been under-researched whether at the level of grammar or in broader genre-based studies. I will be arguing that this is due, in part, to attitudes to language data in linguistic theory. A teacher or materials writer may feel some confidence in dealing with stable written forms and genres – the essay, the business letter, or the laboratory report – and have a genuine understanding of the language appropriate to newer discourses, such as e-mail, texts, or chat room etiquette. However, the notion of how spoken genres are structured, and what forms are most typical of them, is difficult to establish. I will also be suggesting that this means there is a great deal of speaking going on in classrooms, but that this may be different from the effective teaching of speaking as a holistic skill. In particular, in Chapter 6, I will suggest that there has been too great a separation of form (grammar and vocabulary) and delivery (pronunciation and fluency). This has had the effect of dislocating the fundamental fabric of spoken mode – fluent intelligibility over a sophisticated range of styles and discourses – from other linguistic features. These are too often taught in isolation from the speaking skills needed to deliver them. A simple example to illustrate this would be the teaching of idioms for which timing, accurate and fluent delivery, and cultural knowledge of how to place them in a conversation, are all key requirements. They are presented as instances of informal conversational linguistic features but learners are generally taught them when they have a level of productive speech that is too low for them ever to achieve delivery without causing confusion. Far preferable would be to teach simple conversational strategies such as showing understanding with a filler such as 'mm' with effective timing of delivery and intonation.

1.2.4   Insights from speech corpora

The objectives in the speaking classroom may well change quite radically over the next ten years as insights emerging from corpora of natural speech and language processing combine to help us understand what speaking is actually like. Quotes 1.2 and 1.3 exemplify the approach. In the first, the prevalence of modal verbs in spoken academic discourse over written is highlighted as a finding from a corpus study. In the second, the authentic use of a word in a corpus of speech ('like') that is generally presented to the learner as a preposition is shown in contexts where it is used as a discourse marker to lead into reported speech or to show focus. Chapter 3 discusses the complex relationships between research findings such as these and the commercial publication of classroom materials.

Concept 1.1   **Corpus/corpora (pl.)/corpus linguistics**

At its most simple, a corpus (in linguistic contexts) is a collection of language samples. As such, a teacher's collection of photocopies of student essays might be regarded as a corpus. However, the term is strongly associated with the computer-aided analysis of language, and, in corpus linguistics, with the statistical analysis of word (and less often) structural frequencies. Just as the teacher might look through a collection of learners' essays before planning a class to see what common problems they were encountering, a corpus linguist can find patterns and frequencies in many million word samples of language. The collection of speech data for corpus design is a particular problem as large amounts of naturally occurring speech need to be both recorded and transcribed for the computer. This is a time-consuming (and difficult to automate) process and means that there has been a tendency for corpora to be biased in favour of the written mode.

1.2.5   Bringing the facets of speaking together

The human voice and the faculty of speech are inherently bound up with the projection of the self into the world. As a second language learner acquires a living language, a large number of aspects other than grammar

Quote 1.2 The authors of the *Longman Grammar of Spoken and Written English* on findings about speech that run counter to expectations

In many respects, the patterns of use described in the LGSWE will be surprising to materials writers, since they run directly counter to the patterns often found in ESL/EFL coursebooks. For example, progressive aspect verbs are the norm in most books that teach English conversation, in marked contrast to the language produced by speakers in actual conversation, where simple aspect verbs are more than 20 times more common than progressive aspect verbs. Similarly, most ESP/EAP instructors will be surprised to learn that modal verbs are much more common in conversation than in academic prose: in fact, only the modal *may* is used much more commonly in academic prose.

(Biber *et al.*, 1999: 46)

Quote 1.3 The authors of the *Cambridge Advanced Grammar of English* on what speech data can tell us about a word which is generally described as a preposition

Like can be placed in end position in order to qualify a preceding statement. It also indicates that the words chosen may not be appropriate:

> *Then she got out of the car all of a sudden **like**, and this bike hit her right in the back.*
> *It was a shattering, frightening experience **like**.*

Like is very commonly used (particularly among younger speakers) as a marker of reported speech, especially where the report involves a dramatic representation of somone's response or reaction:

> *So this bloke came up to me and **I'm like** 'Go away, I don't want to dance'.*
> *And my **mum's like** non-stop three or four times 'Come and tell your Grandma about your holiday'.*

(Carter and McCarthy, 2006: 101–2)

and vocabulary also need to be acquired for successful communication to take place. These relate to culture, social interaction, and the politeness norms that exist in the target language. To learn to communicate expertly in another language a speaker must change and expand identity as he or she learns the cultural, social, and even political factors, which go into language choices needed to speak appropriately with a new 'voice'. Therefore, while this book often treats the different 'layers' of speaking – discourse, grammar, and phonology – separately for the purposes of analysis, an underlying theme is that the teacher will ultimately need to help the student bring all these elements together into a new, unified, and appropriate means of communication on the journey from beginner to fluent speaker of another language.

1.3   The nature of speech in contrast to writing

Figures 1.2 and 1.3 provide a visual summary of some of the major, very general contrasts between the spoken and the written forms of language. Further information about the written form aimed at a similar audience to this book can be found in *Teaching and Researching Writing* (Hyland, 2009). The first diagram represents aspects that relate to how the two forms are generated: 'Aspects of production', and the second deals with tendencies in attitudes to the two forms: 'Social aspects'.

1.3.1   How speech reaches the world

When speech is considered in opposition to writing, several distinctive features become evident, particularly if the way it is produced is taken as the starting point (see Figure 1.2). Many of these features also affect the skill of listening, dealt with more fully in *Teaching and Researching Listening* (Rost, 2002).

Most important, and generally least considered in a linguistic discipline dominated by texts and recording of texts, is the fact that the spoken form of any language is fundamentally transient. When a word is spoken this event happens within the 'co-ordinates' of a particular place and moment and these can never be reduplicated, although we can now record the word via several different media.

A second, related, factor underpinning the nature of speech, and affecting the type of language choices that can be made, is its delivery via the oral/aural channel.

Concept 1.2   **Channel**

A term used to describe the physical means by which communication takes place. In terms of speaking there is the oral/aural channel and in terms of writing the visual/motoric channel. Discourse can be studied in terms of the effects of channel on the language. These include the constraints of speech processing in real time versus the capacity to reflect and edit that the written channel allows.

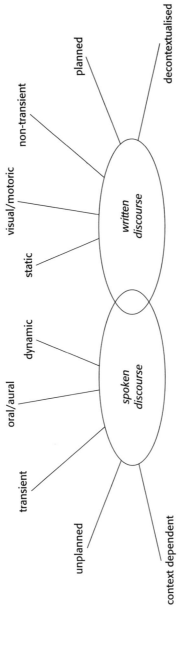

Figure 1.2 Aspects of production

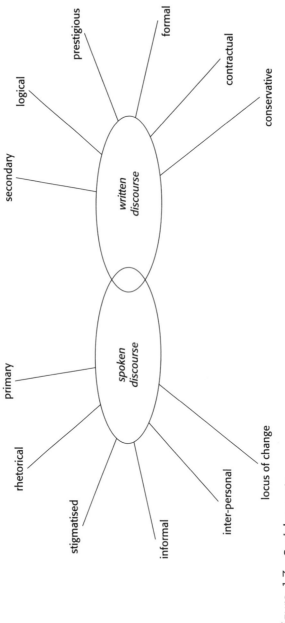

Figure 1.3 Social aspects

Whether in face-to-face situations or via televisual or other media, language which is spoken to be heard is (or should be) quite different from texts created to be read. One of the commonest problems in oral presentations is information overload for listeners as they try to process densely informative language that has been prepared via a written text. Several studies over a number of years have shown that speakers 'package' their information differently from writers whether at the level of the clause or through vocabulary choices (Chafe and Danielewicz, 1987; Biber, 2006) and subsequent chapters will look at these features in more detail.

Quotes 1.4 and 1.5   Language choices in speech as opposed to writing

Choosing lexical items is partly a matter of choosing aptly and explicitly, and partly a matter of choosing the appropriate level. In the first case, the deliberateness and editability inherent in writing lead to a more richly varied, less hedged, and more explicit use of words. Speakers are so strongly constrained by their need to produce language rapidly and by their inability to edit, that they are unable to imitate the lexical richness and explicitness of writing even when, as in lecturing, such qualities would be especially valued. In the second case, although the separate histories of spoken and written language have led to partially divergent vocabularies, it is not as hard for speakers to borrow liberally from the written lexicon, or conversely for writers to borrow from the spoken. Thus lectures that are more literary than conversations, and letters more conversational than academic papers. The constraints are not imposed by cognitive limitations, but by judgements of appropriateness.

(Chafe and Danielewicz, 1987: 94)

In contrast, previous research on university registers has found that mode differences are by far the most important in accounting for linguistic variation: spoken university registers are consistently different from written university registers in the use of a wide range of lexical and grammatical features (see, e.g., Biber, 2006, chap. 8). For example, verbal and clausal features are common in all spoken university registers and relatively rare in all written registers. In contrast, complex noun phrase features are common in all written university registers and relatively rare in all spoken registers. The results of previous 'multi-dimensional' analyses similarly show a fundamental divide between the spoken and written university registers (see, e.g., Biber, Conrad, Reppen, Byrd, & Helt, 2002): all spoken university registers, regardless of purpose, are 'involved', 'situated in reference', and characterized by the absence of 'impersonal' styles; in contrast, all written university registers, again regardless of purpose, are highly 'informational', 'elaborated in reference', and marked for 'impersonal' styles.

(Biber and Barbieri, 2007: 282)

Further salient aspects of the way speech is produced again relate to the transient and situated nature of the spoken channel. The vast bulk of spoken material is spontaneous, face-to-face, informal conversation. This kind of discourse is generally unplanned, dynamic and context dependent. A conversation may be guided by one speaker or another who wishes to deal with a particular topic; however, the vagaries of real-time contexts mean that most speech takes the form of a give and take, not only between speakers but also between the discourse and the context. The type of interesting study which can arise from this dynamism is how topics and topic change are managed by speakers, how speakers accommodate themselves to one another, how misunderstandings between speakers are 'repaired', how activity affects language produced, or how reference is made to new/old information within a conversation.

1.3.2 How speech is regarded

Figure 1.3 summarises some of the typical attitudes to speech, particularly as it is regarded in literate societies where the functions of spoken and written forms are generally clearly demarcated.

Although some theorists, for example Vachek (1973), have argued that the written form of language should be regarded as a separate and wholly independent language system, the spoken form has generally been regarded as the primary form of language upon which the written form is essentially dependent.

One of the reasons for this is that, in the absence of a pathological reason to prevent it, all humans develop the capacity for speech and it is only later in literate societies (and in the history of humankind) that the skill of writing develops. Hence, in Figure 1.3, the indication 'primary' versus 'secondary' for the spoken and written forms.

> **Quotes 1.6 and 1.7** Two different views of the 'transferability' of speech into writing
>
> It may sometimes happen that an utterance primarily intended for listening needs reading, and vice versa. . . . In such cases . . . transposition from the one into the other material is not done with the intention of expressing the given content by means of the other material; if it were so, the only possible accomplishment of the task would be to replace the spoken utterance with the written one or vice versa.
>
> (Vachek, 1966: 154)
>
> If a text is unintelligible when read aloud, it will also be unintelligible in writing, since the writing merely symbolises the spoken expression.
>
> (Halliday, 1989: 44)

The spoken form is very highly valued in linguistics and applied linguistics where it is regarded as the primary form of a language and the source of innovation and language change. In the realm of second language teaching there is also a high degree of attention paid to the skill of speaking. Indeed, to be a fluent *speaker* in a language is often the lay person's goal. The source of input in highly influential 'communicative approaches' is largely the spoken form, and there has been a conflation in linguistics of the term 'language' with 'speech' as if the two are entirely interchangeable.

This is due, in part, to the dominance of theories of first language acquisition that influenced theories of second language acquisition throughout the twentieth century. The spoken form is the basis for investigations in first language acquisition. Since no child learns to write before he or she learns to speak, the spoken mode is the only mode available for consideration and, therefore, in first language acquisition studies the issue of distinguishing 'language' from 'speech' is irrelevant. However, paradoxically, there is very little attention paid to speaking in its own right to be judged by its own distinctive criteria in the world of linguistics, or of language teaching. A survey of respected international journals in the field will find many more articles dealing explicitly with the written form than with the spoken. An internet search (Table 1.1) of scholarly activity using the key terms 'writing' and 'speaking' in the social sciences, arts and humanities suggests that there may be a growing attention to spoken mode, but that the balance remains strongly in favour of the written.

There is a similar 'invisibility' factor at work in the teaching and researching of the skill of listening (see also Rost (2002) in this series for further discussion of listening as a discrete skill).

This is not the place to debate at length the issue of the relative positions of the two forms – speech and writing – in the discipline of linguistics; however it is important to understand that the innate, universal human capacity for speech has led to its being regarded as the central form of interest to linguists. Therefore, even when theorists appear to pay no attention to actual instances of speech, fundamentally they are pursuing questions related to the primary language faculty. This faculty is the universal linguistic form: speech.

Table 1.1 Contrasting internet search results for 'writing' and 'speaking'

Key word	1990–2000	2000–2009
Writing	259,000	237,000
Speaking	16,500	29,200

(search date: 1 May 2009)

Ironically, however, although the spoken form takes pride of place in linguistic theory, its status is more ambiguous in society in general. The nature of and, therefore, the functions to which written language is put (most significantly its use as the medium of the binding contract and other legal functions), mean that it is generally held in higher esteem in literate society than the spoken form.

Speech is also quintessentially the form in which the inter-personal functions of language are carried out and the form is subject to the benefits and disadvantages that stem from the way it is produced, as detailed above and summarised in Figure 1.3. Therefore, whereas the tangible, non-ephemeral nature of writing lends it to logical and contractual functions in society, for example record keeping and legal tasks, the spoken form, being essentially more dependent on the time and place it is produced, is used for more informal or rhetorically based tasks. A powerful political speaker can sway an audience by oratorical devices in debate, but it is the written Act of Parliament that can be scrutinised and redrafted which eventually becomes law. Moreover, while you can be known verbally to all your friends and work colleagues by a first name quite different from the name on your passport, to change your name so that it becomes accepted on this legally recognised written document you must engage in an extensive legal process.

A final point to consider, but one of very great importance in terms of language change, is that the spoken form of a language tends to be the laboratory for linguistic innovation. New linguistic items, words and, less quickly, grammatical features tend to be generated in the spoken, rather than the written form of a language, as speakers accommodate their language behaviour to one another and fashions of speaking come and go. As new media such as text messaging on mobile phones, internet chat rooms, e-mail and other electronically delivered forms of writing emerge, this distinction between the speed of innovation in the oral/aural and the visual/motoric channels has become increasingly blurred. However, it is in the deeply interactive forms of language, where people affect one another's language judgements as they communicate in ways that are less restricted by stable, widely accepted conventions, that rapid alterations to language can take place. Despite new media (and in fact because of them in the case of the influences of the internet and other electronic media) speech remains the most important locus of change in a language.

To sum up, when speech is looked at both in terms of how it is produced and how it is regarded some of the paradoxes and difficulties involved in studying it come to the fore. This is particularly true when the form is looked at in comparison with the written. For the teacher and for the researcher the dynamic, ever-changing, inter-personally oriented and contextually defined nature of speech can be both a benefit and a drawback.

1.4   Where does speech fit in language studies?

I suggested above that there has tended to be a collapsing together in the discipline of linguistics of the concepts 'language faculty' and 'faculty of speech'. This in turn has clear repercussions on what comes under the scope of 'research into speaking' at the current time. For if language and speech are seen as indistinguishable one kind of research will be carried out, and if they are regarded as distinct areas for investigation then different kinds of research – ones that attend more to channel, mode and context – will be seen as appropriate.

One of the cornerstones underlying this issue is the paradigm set out by Noam Chomsky in the 1960s and which in turn has underpinned the greater part of second language acquisition studies, advances in grammatical models, and computer modelling in which a linguistic element is required. A central aspect to the discussion of speech is the dichotomy between the language faculty ('competence') and the way language is used in actual speech or writing ('performance'). Essentially, this division stemmed from Chomsky's questioning of how children can master language, and master it in such a way that, eventually, any speaker of a language can create and understand an infinite amount of discourse, most of it entirely new. See Concept 1.3 for further information.

Concept 1.3   **Competence versus performance**

Human beings do not have infinite brain power and cannot simply recognise and process each new example of language afresh. Therefore, Chomsky suggested that there must be an underlying, more basic, language capacity which could generate infinite sentences but was itself pared down enough to be within finite human abilities. This language faculty is what is referred to as 'competence'. Competence, the innate language potentials which all babies seem to be born with, contrasts with the samples of language which any individual baby might hear. Debate continues about the role of input in language acquisition, but, in terms of theory, the peculiarities of any particular speaker, sample of speech, or actual instantiation of a phoneme are categorised as 'performance'. Performance, it is argued, since it is open to the vagaries of individuals, is not really very useful to language theorists. Therefore, in this highly influential distinction, speech data have no place in 'pure' language science which is more interested in finding out about the nature of competence.

Concept 1.4   **Rationalism and empiricism in linguistics**

Rationalist and empiricist schools of thought are generally described in contrast to one another. As an empirical approach to something values real-world data a linguist of this persuasion takes it as fundamental that samples of language and 'Language' are inextricably linked. A rationalist, on the other hand, would suggest that we must look inside the brain or the mind in order to investigate 'Language' and, further, would propose the idea that examples of data from the real world are unhelpful and even misleading. The strong influence of the rationalist approach has clear implications for the study of the spoken form as it has tended to move the debate towards idealised and decontextualised examples which in turn fit better with the norms of writing than of speech.

The notion that humans have an innate, more recently articulated as a biological or genetic, language ability, which provides the basis for all language use no matter how seemingly diverse, developed in the twentieth century in opposition to earlier behaviourist models. These two opposing camps, one based on the notion of an innate cognitive model which sees the human child as 'pre-programmed' at birth to learn to speak, the other seeing learning as wholly dependent on an external stimulus, have a strong bearing on both the status of speech data in linguistic science and on theories of teaching language. The second half of the twentieth century saw the rationalist camp win the theoretical battle. See also Concepts 1.3, 1.4 and 1.5.

The rationalist model grew from dissatisfaction with the highly situated nature of earlier behaviourist explanations of language that relied entirely upon tangible, quantifiable data for input. The rationalist paradigm placed greater store on the logic of the underlying abstract system than on data, and particularly speech data.

Concept 1.5   **Behaviourism**

This concept is strongly associated with the American psychologist B. F. Skinner (1904–1990). The philosophy behind behaviourist models is that learning takes place through interaction with the world – through exposure to examples, through positive and negative stimuli, and trial and error – rather than from any inner faculty.

A great number of the important current issues in linguistics, therefore, relate to how much a researcher believes that the language system can usefully be abstracted away from the situatedness of speech described in previous sections. For example, in universal grammar studies or second language acquisition work a fundamental assumption is that it is not only acceptable, but also necessary to ignore most of the vagaries of real speech data (performance) in order to investigate more significant underlying inherent language faculties (competence). A language learner's speech in the target language may be analysed for patterns of grammatical use and misuse, but this will be investigated to provide evidence as to the state of their underlying linguistic knowledge.

At the other end of the spectrum, researchers in the fields of conversation or discourse analysis deal in the actual texture and dynamics of speech. They look at how language is delivered and how linguistic and paralinguistic mechanisms, for example eye contact, pausing or laughter, affect communication. Again, the findings of a particular study will be related to generalisations beyond the limitations of the data analysed, but scholars on this side of the discipline do not in general attempt to link their conclusions to an inherent mental capacity. In these fields there can be seen a swing of the pendulum in recent decades back towards a greater faith in data and against rationalist models. See also Concepts 1.6 and 1.7 for further information about conversation and discourse analysis.

It can be seen from the brief description of rationally versus empirically based approaches to language study (of which Chomskian rationalism and empirically grounded methods such as discourse and conversation analysis have been presented at each end of the spectrum) that the latter will have more direct and immediate relevance to studies of speech than the former. If a researcher does not believe that actual examples of speech (or writing) provide a sound basis for reaching conclusions about language, they will not give very much consideration to spoken data for their own sake.

Concept 1.6   **Conversation analysis (CA)**

Conversation analysis is a branch of linguistics which investigates the structure and social significance of patterns within conversational data. Conversation analysis shares many features with discourse analysis in that both are interested in structures beyond sentence level and the way stretches of language cohere and relate to one another. However, whereas discourse analysis, in its early forms at least, is concerned with 'rule-like' constraints on patterns of turns in conversation, conversation analysis tends to be more purely descriptive in nature and socio-linguistic in orientation.

Concept 1.7   Discourse analysis

Many influential ways of looking at language, for example, syntax, regard it as made up of sentences or clauses and investigate the relations between words inside these elements. Discourse analysis, however, is not interested in the relations between items at this level. Rather it looks beyond the sentence or the clause to see what patterns exist between longer sections of conversation or text. For instance, the pair of sentences, 'Good morning, it's a lovely day!' and 'Goodbye, see you later!' are individually well-formed, but said one after the other would be rather strange as an opening remark by one person and a response by another. Discourse analysts are interested in what constraints there may be on pairs of exchanges, in the typical patterns of initiation and response, or the organisation of talk more generally. Whereas CA only engages with spoken data, discourse analysis deals with both written and spoken mode. When written examples are the basis for the research, the term 'text analysis' will be used as synonymous with 'discourse analysis'.

Many individual studies have from time to time questioned the scope and role of performance data. For example, Berg (1997) took production errors in speech and in writing as the basis for an investigation of underlying regularities in the language system and in so doing moves from data towards theory. Equally, in the realm of data-driven linguistic research the growth of large corpora of the spoken word together with advances in the technology of storing and analysing corpora of speech data mean that there is a growing potential for generalisable conclusions to be made about patterns of speech and speech behaviour. In time, and with a growth of coherent research projects being carried out on them, these corpus-based generalisations may come to match the theoretically elegant conclusions of rationalist frameworks. Finally, cognitive and neurolinguistic approaches are pointing up fascinating insights about the processing demands of the spoken and written forms of a language. These emerging approaches are dealt with in Chapters 6 and 7.

1.4.1   Historical perspectives on speaking

The divisions between researchers who rely more heavily on data, and those who treat them with some suspicion did not spring into being in the middle of the twentieth century. Attitudes to the spoken form of language and its position in the curriculum have varied considerably through time, and in different cultures. The germ of the debate can be seen in classical philosophy and attitudes to rhetoric described below.

Furthermore, the status which is given to the faculty of speech in a particular society, or at a particular point in its history, is reflected in the position and emphasis placed on teaching the skill of speaking in the curriculum – something which is as true today as it was in earlier centuries. By looking at how the teaching and study of speech has varied through time a clearer perspective can be gained on how present attitudes fit into a bigger picture, and may point to the ways in which attitudes will change in future.

Attitudes to the spoken form of language have waxed and waned since earliest available records of how and why speaking was taught. These attitudes are usually linked to the ephemeral nature of speech production, and the fact that until very recently in the history of humanity, spoken language was directed at a present audience by a physically present speaker. In these key facts lie the strengths and weaknesses of the spoken form. On the one hand, its nature permits a speaker to convince, persuade, argue, or cajole using all the benefits of being physically in view of the listener through gesture, intonation, eye contact and so on. On the other, unless captured and recorded in some form, the spoken word is fundamentally transient in nature and cannot be checked or scrutinised after the event.

Whereas today the pedagogy of the spoken form tends to be overlooked in favour of the more stable and generally manageable written form, the following brief survey shows that at various times great emphasis has been placed on the teaching of speech.

1.4.2 Early attitudes to speech

As far back as ancient Egypt, the art of speaking has been connected to the skill of persuasion, and the ability to influence others by means of rhetoric. One of the earliest extended examples of written language is a five thousand year old papyrus containing advice on the topic of public speaking and disputation for an up-and-coming Egyptian politico: *The Instruction of Ptah-ho-tep and the Instruction of Kegemni* (Gunn, 1906).

With the ancient Greeks the systematisation of argument through speech began with Zeno of Elea (early in the fifth century BC) and reached its height in the teachings of Corax of Syracuse (around 460 BC) and the Sophists. Again, rather than learning the skill of speaking for its own sake, to improve one's own language or for any high-minded pedagogic objective, the impetus for this formalisation was practical, and, in particular at this time, related to the need to argue a case at law.

Given the strong link between the spoken form and the Sophists it is perhaps interesting that the word 'sophistry' has come to have the negative meaning it now has. The modern meaning of a deliberate use of false or misleading reasoning arose from the attack on the successful teaching of speaking techniques (or rhetorical tricks and devices) by higher-minded philosophers, most notably Plato. In the history of ideas, Plato has strong links with arguments based on idealised abstraction that resonate with a great deal of modern linguistic theory-driven approaches.

Quote 1.8 Attitudes to speaking in ancient Egypt

1. Be not proud because thou art learned; but discourse with the ignorant man, as with the sage. For no limit can be set to skill, neither is there any craftsman that possesseth full advantages. Fair speech is more rare than the emerald that is found by slave-maidens on the pebbles.
2. If thou find an arguer talking, one that is well disposed and wiser than thou, let thine arms fall, bend thy back, be not angry with him if he agree (?) not with thee. Refrain from speaking evilly; oppose him not at any time when he speaketh. If he address thee as one ignorant of the matter, thine humbleness shall bear away his contentions.
3. If thou find an arguer talking, thy fellow, one that is within thy reach, keep not silence when he saith aught that is evil; so shalt thou be wiser than he. Great will be the applause on the part of the listeners, and thy name shall be good in the knowledge of princes.
4. If thou find an arguer talking, a poor man, that is to say not thine equal, be not scornful toward him because he is lowly. Let him alone; then shall he confound himself. Question him not to please thine heart, neither pour out thy wrath upon him that is before thee; it is shameful to confuse a mean mind. If thou be about to do that which is in thine heart, overcome it as a thing rejected of princes.

(Gunn, 1906: 42–3)

Yet, away from the arena of law and individuals' disputation, the art of speaking continued to influence the history of the nation in major ways as central players in political life (most famously Demosthenes who remained synonymous with oratory and on the curriculum through to the Renaissance) combined powerful speech making with influential positions in public life. The most extensive 'textbook' to come down to us on the art of speaking at this time is Aristotle's *Rhetoric*, in which the teaching of speaking is divided into notions of the speaker, the audience and the matter of the speech. A great strength of this text was that it managed to synthesise theory and application and, to some extent, bring together the two sides in the style versus content, tricks of delivery versus serious seeking after truth argument that had held since Plato's attack on the Sophists.

The early Greek teachers of the art of speaking introduced key concepts that still underpin Western modes of disputation, such as the persuasive device of arguing from probability, the systematic structuring of speeches, and the art of swaying an audience through emotional appeal. However, the backlash against the spoken form, as superficial, transient and open to the ability of individuals to twist listeners' opinions through rhetorical devices, reflects the denigration that the spoken form has also tended to suffer from. This is particularly seen where the mode exists side by side with a more prestigious written discourse.

With the rise of Roman civilisation and scholars, for example Cicero (106–43 BC) and, later, Quintilian (AD 35–post 96), the theories of oratory of the Greeks were put to consistent, practical use in law and the political arena. However, the debate between the critics of empty rhetoric and proponents of oratory continued. Cicero did much to bridge the gap by emphasising both the need for appeal to the emotions, the sense of humour, and the ear of the listener, together with a deep and detailed understanding of the content being delivered. On the pragmatic side, he preferred to speak last in any debate so that his could be the final appeal to the emotions of the listeners, and he studied what particular combinations of phrases, rhythms and cadences were most effective in swaying the audience. However, in *De Oratore* he noted that the truly persuasive speaker needs to have an exceptional grasp of the topic, and that a good general education is the best starting point for a good speaker. Quintilian continued this tradition and was famous as an educator. His *Institutio Oratoria* provides a coherent teaching manual, placing great emphasis on the needs of the individual student.

Quote 1.9 Quintilian on pronunciation

Let him in the first place correct faults of pronunciation, if there be any, so that the words of the learner may be fully expressed and that every letter may be uttered with its proper sound. For we find inconvenience from the too great weakness or too great fullness of the sound of some letters. Some, as if too harsh for us, we utter but imperfectly or change them for others not altogether dissimilar, but, as it were, smoother.

(Quintilian, 1856/2006, I.11,4)

Interestingly, in the later Rome the need for individuals to plead their own case at law had declined. With the work of Quintilian, the emphasis shifts from the use of speech education to meet social and legal needs towards the teaching of rhetoric as an end in itself, and a valuable educational tool to allow individuals to reach their full potential.

It is in this change of emphasis from the teaching of speech as the basis of rhetorical devices towards speech as an educational adjunct that some of the subsequent influence of the classical tradition in Europe can be seen. The legacy of classical attitudes to speech in the Middle Ages and beyond was largely felt within the educational and, initially, religious context. An early solution to the 'style-versus-content' issue was the splitting up of the teaching programme into different areas, such as grammar (looking at the history and structure of language), logic (the arrangement of thoughts) and rhetoric that at this later stage came to be limited to the delivery of the thoughts. This, in turn, led in Elizabethan England and wider Renaissance Europe to an emphasis on language ornamentation for its own sake, quite divorced from any other educational or social need.

In classical attitudes to teaching speech several issues that remain pertinent today have their roots – for example:

- the relationship between speech delivery and style versus structure or content,
- the role of training versus the natural acquisition of speech,
- the position of speech in the curriculum, and in society,
- the influence of differences between individuals in speaking ability and how this affects the way they are regarded by others.

1.4.3 The eighteenth century and beyond

The following sections continue the historical thread, but look at some of these issues in the narrower context of language teaching as opposed to rhetoric or oratory. The history of language teaching in relation to speaking is developed further in Chapter 3.

> **Quote 1.10** The teaching of speech and social status in eighteenth-century Britain
>
> While the emphasis on correct grammar was even more pronounced in the eighteenth century, the promotion of 'good speech' was another expression of the same passion for accuracy of expression and stylistic elegance. There was considerable popular enthusiasm for instruction in the arts of 'polite conversation', public speaking, and elocution. Out-of-work actors and others with similar gifts had a field-day among the socially ambitious upper-middle classes, particularly in cities anxious to impress the metropolis with their accomplishments. . . .
>
> In spite of this interest in spoken language, it remained essentially 'extra-curricular' and made little impact on the basic education system.
>
> (Howatt, 1985: 76–7)

The beginning and end of the nineteenth century show a marked change in the status of speech in the language teaching process. This was brought about in the transition from 'grammar translation' methods which dominated language teaching in the early parts of the century in Europe to what came to be termed the 'Reform Movement' which arose around the 1880s.

Concept 1.8 **Grammar translation methods**

Although initially intended to simplify the language learning process and widen it from classical Greek and Latin, which had dominated the curriculum, these methods have come to be associated with all that current theories of language teaching abhor: a strong focus on isolated sentences, mechanical translation of sentences in and out of mother tongue, arcane and overly complex grammatical explanation, no place for real (spoken or written) communication.

Concept 1.9 **'Natural' or 'direct' methods**

Partly as a reaction to the 'grammar translation' approach, language teaching reformers at the end of the nineteenth and beginning of the twentieth century argued for a more natural approach to the teaching process. Critically in terms of the interest of this book, they placed the spoken form at the forefront of their pedagogy, generally insisting on mono-lingual speech-based interactions between student and teacher and focusing on matters arising from prompts in the learning context. At its most extreme the 'natural' or 'direct' methods led to 'total physical response' or 'TPR' approaches. In this the student responds through action to instructions given by the teacher in the target language. Fundamental to all the approaches is the primacy of speech, together with a move away from isolated sentences towards meaningful whole texts or interactions.

In the situational (and later functional) and audio-lingual methods developed later in the twentieth century, aided by the improvements in both colour publishing and digital technology, the emphasis on teaching and learning a language through the medium of speech remained at the heart of most teaching methodologies. However, it should be noted that although speech was used in these 'naturally' oriented teaching processes the actual forms used were very far from naturally occurring speech or indeed natural spoken communication. Typically, the interactions were highly constrained so that particular grammatical structures could be practised. Such structures were derived from standard formal grammars that were grounded in the norms of 'literate' writing.

Therefore, speech had a mixed status in language teaching through the first half of the twentieth century. The notion of 'speaking well' had dominated attitudes to the form from the very earliest teaching traditions associated with it, as noted in previous sections. The grammar translation methods which held sway through much of the nineteenth century were strongly associated with the written form and it was partly as a reaction to this that later movements adopted the oral medium with such enthusiasm. Nonetheless, the return to speech as the primary medium of instruction began a process that remains largely unresolved, that is to say, the simultaneous high regard for the spoken form and the lack of precise attention to the structure and peculiarities of this form beyond the classroom.

The 1960s with the influence of the work of Noam Chomsky, and the 1970s and 1980s with the growth of 'communicative' approaches, marked two distinct sea changes in the field of language teaching both of which did much to underpin present attitudes to the spoken form. While these two threads are brought into commonality by research in the field of second language acquisition, they have marked differences in the emphasis they placed on speech in their thinking. On the one hand, the transformational grammar movement internalised and made abstract the language system to such an extent that actual speech became something of an irrelevance. On the other, the tenets of the communicative movement held that language was acquired by meaningful and interesting communication in contexts which mimicked real communicative settings as closely as possible. Thus, for the latter school of thought to conceptualise speech as either simply the medium of instruction (as was the case with natural or direct methods) or as something largely irrelevant to the process of language study (as in the competence/performance distinction) was anathema. At its most extreme, the communicative approach sees the struggle to make and share meaning through the dynamic spoken form as the very engine of language acquisition. Nonetheless, the role of mode and the status of speech in language acquisition paradigms have been remarkably under-theorised.

Concept 1.10   **Communicative approaches**

Due to its wide and deep influence on the field of English language teaching, one often hears about the 'communicative approach'. However, it is perhaps useful to think of a variety of approaches which have changed and developed since the late 1970s in the UK and the USA, but all of which share common ground and ideology. Communicative approaches have been strongly associated with the work of Stephen Krashen in the USA on second language acquisition and, among others, Henry Widdowson in the UK. In particular communicative approaches:

- place high value on language in use (as opposed to abstract, isolated examples);

- assert that effective language acquisition (often opposed to language learning) only takes place through language use;
- aim to foster and develop the learner's communicative competence (as opposed to the more abstract concept of linguistic competence);
- regard errors as a natural part of the progression towards a greater understanding of the target language;
- link teaching methodologies to appropriate communicative tasks (rather than seeing classroom tasks as a means of practising a particular grammatical feature);
- tend to favour inductive, student-centred routes to understanding (rather than explicit, teacher-led explanations);
- place the learner at the centre of the learning process and assess progress in relation to factors affecting the individual (for example, levels of motivation).

The basic methods (for example, pair and group work) and beliefs (for instance that teachers should be facilitators of communication tasks rather than dominant 'lecturers' to students) of communicative language teaching have become the backbone of modern English language teaching since the 1970s. Task-based learning, the language awareness movement in the UK and the focus on form movement in America are all later responses to these fundamental tenets.

Summary

To sum up, this chapter aimed to place the teaching and research of speaking into a conceptual and historical context. In so doing, it drew attention to a fundamental issue in dealing with speech data: the status of instances of real speech within current theories of language, and in particular in the dominant research paradigm behind second language acquisition. The tendency to split off 'pure' linguistic theory from more descriptively or pedagogically oriented studies was discussed. I argued that this is because, generally speaking, linguistic theory gives little weight to the activity of speaking itself.

In this chapter, the threads of today's issues for teaching and researching speaking were also traced back to classical concerns with the division of form and content in the teaching of speech, and the long shadow cast by these ideas was described. In the concluding section, the issue of the status of speech in dominant second language teaching paradigms was noted. Within this section, I argued that there has been a tendency for speech to be both highly valued in the modern language teaching contexts and at the same time under-theorised and under-investigated as a faculty in its own right.

Further reading

Chapman, S. and Routledge, C. (eds) (2009). *Key Ideas in Linguistics and the Philosophy of Language*. Edinburgh: Edinburgh University Press. A title giving easily accessible information about the debates underlying the role of evidence versus abstraction in linguistic studies.

Cornbleet, S. and Carter, R. (2001). *The Language of Speech and Writing*. London: Routledge. An introductory activity-based text that raises awareness of the impact of the differences between speech and writing.

Horowitz, R. (2006). *Talking Texts: how speech and writing interact in school learning*. London: Routledge. A readable text on the differences between spoken and written language and some of the implications for teaching generally.

Howatt, A. P. R. and Widdowson, H. G. (2004). *History of English Language Teaching ELT*, 2nd edn. Oxford: Oxford University Press. A comprehensive history of language teaching.

Hughes, R. (1996). *English in Speech and Writing: investigating language and literature*. London: Routledge. Further discussion of the theoretical implications of the differences between speech and writing can be found in Chapter 6.

McCarthy, M. (1998). *Spoken Language and Applied Linguistics*. Cambridge: Cambridge University Press. Further discussion of the relationship between speech data and language teaching.

Chapter 2

The research space: paradigms and issues

This chapter will...

- describe some classical research paradigms as they relate to spoken mode and to analysing spoken data;
- discuss particular issues surrounding research into speaking;
- discuss the role and status of spoken data in language theory.

2.1 Introduction

This chapter begins with a brief introduction to research paradigms in general, and then discusses their usefulness and applicability in relation to researching speaking. In this chapter, I also address the question of the nature of spoken data and how this relates to the kind of research that is undertaken into spoken mode.

2.2 Classical research paradigms in relation to researching speaking

The research approaches dealt with in this book are, in general, empirically based. That is to say, they deal in real-world data of some kind – systematically recorded observations of classroom behaviour, transcripts of conversation, recordings of learners' utterances analysed for the occurrence of particular phonemes and so on. These data are gathered to investigate a central research question, often posed as a hypothesis, and are used as the basis of either a quantitative analysis (most often) or a qualitative analysis (less frequent apart from areas such as critical linguistics, socio-linguistics and ethnographically based work).

A second type of approach is a more theoretically oriented one. Here, rather than taking data as the starting point of an investigation, the researcher is primarily interested in theories, models, high-level concepts, and, crucially, the relationships between previous theories and ones that may emerge from a current investigation. In the context of extremely theoretically oriented work, for example philosophical logic (a discipline with a surprising amount of influence on linguistics), any real-world data are, if they are considered at all, seen as 'messy', subject to the vagaries of individual circumstances and irrelevant.

Different research approaches are often called 'paradigms' (see Concept 2.1) and these strongly influence how research is carried out. A paradigm functions as a framework or point of reference for both researchers and users of research output. It gives coherence to a study and links it to the work of others providing a shorthand by which it can be prepared and judged. If the researcher positions a study in, for example, an experimental paradigm he or she creates a set of expectations in his or her audience about the way the research will be conducted. These considerations affect how research is received.

Concept 2.1   **What is a paradigm?**

A paradigm is a framework for ideas which includes definitions of key terms and the relationships between them. The framework is coherent because the researcher assumes certain things as a starting point and new knowledge is absorbed into this mental 'map'. As noted in the previous chapter, in the US Noam Chomsky created a major shift in what people assumed about language when he conceptualised it as an inherent rule-governed system for which the human mind is hard-wired from birth, and also set up key concepts such as performance versus competence. This was in sharp contrast to pre-existing paradigms in American linguistics which had been strongly data-oriented/ethnographic in nature, and also contrasted to the European structuralist paradigms that had emerged after the work of Ferdinand de Saussure. This kind of change is referred to as a 'paradigm shift'.

Different disciplines work within different paradigms and even within the same academic department several paradigms can compete with one another. Most research outcomes make only small changes to the paradigm rather than altering it fundamentally – this is the nature of research findings generally. Paradigm shifts can and do occur when either a brilliant individual or a team compel others to change their mental map of a particular topic due to the strength of their findings or arguments.

Concept 2.2 **Empirical versus non-empirical approaches**

An empirical approach to a research project begins from situated questions and facts rather than decontextualised issues or questions of theory. Both kinds of approach can be used to deal with the same topic and the clearest differences between them lie in the methods used and what is regarded as a coherent approach and evidence. The less empirically motivated researcher in linguistics has traditionally been concerned with intuitions about language and the fit between new data and existing theory. The empirically oriented researcher will be more open to seeing patterns emerging from data and drawing conclusions from these that may challenge pre-existing ideas or intuitions. Both approaches will draw on theory and a pre-existing paradigm so the contrast is not so much between empirical and theoretical work but between the emphasis placed on data in terms of conclusions reached. All research needs to abstract away from particular instances of data in order to reach some coherent conclusion but empirically grounded work will retain stronger links to concrete examples and give these greater weight than non-empirically oriented research.

All paradigms orient towards a theory and towards data, but the balance between these will differ according to the tradition in which the academic is working. Academic research is meaningless if it is not embedded in the context of the work of others. This work is in turn framed within a paradigm that has a particular orientation towards data and theory. Different disciplines will also place different emphasis on the role of theory versus data. In linguistics, and particularly in the realm of spoken discourse, the relationship is quite complex and the locus of ongoing debate. At one end of the spectrum, an academic working in the field of syntax will aim to achieve an elegant, comprehensive and convincing description of a language feature such as negation in a particular language and relate this to current theories of negation generally. To be convincing the work will need to orient towards all previous work on negation and will tend to do this within a theoretically oriented paradigm. While examples will be used, the work will rarely be 'data driven' in the way that the work of a text or corpus linguist will be. At the other end of the spectrum, in computational linguistics there are academics developing models of grammar via automatic 'parsers' purely from massive numbers of examples in ways that allow syntactic categories and patterns in language to be described in a bottom-up fashion.

Table 2.1 gives an indication of how far, in general, some of the major branches of linguistics deal with situated data, whether they regard mode as relevant, or in contrast deal primarily with abstractions.

Table 2.1   **Branches of linguistics in relation to data and the relevance of mode**

Group 1 – Data driven or highly data informed

Computational linguistics	Phonetics
Discourse and conversational analysis	Socio-linguistics
Text and corpus linguistics	

Group 2 – Less data driven, but data and mode relevant to the analysis

Historical linguistics	Pragmatics
Lexicography	Psycholinguistics
Neurolinguistics	Second language acquisition
Phonology	

Group 3 – Theory driven, and mode generally not relevant

Morphology	Semantics
Philosophy of language	Syntax

The groupings shown in Table 2.1 should be regarded as broadly indicative and they are there to help situate a debate about the role of spoken data in language theory and, in turn, address the question of why there are few holistic theories of speech available. As an example, socio-linguistic research frequently draws its data from the spoken mode (for example, on the social marking carried by a particular phoneme or the speaking strategies of a particular racial group), but does not relate the findings to any broader theory of speech. It is important therefore to distinguish between research into speaking and research that uses speech data for a different research purpose.

There are reasons for the different status of data, and particularly speech data, in various branches of language studies. Linguistics as we know it today has a surprisingly short history and since the 1960s has been developing and positioning itself among several disciplines, newer and older than itself. In the early part of the twentieth century, what we call linguistics was termed the 'science of language'. It was primarily interested in concrete examples of language, and the study of the history of the development of a language or the comparison of different languages (philology and its branches) were the focus of its efforts. There was then a transition from what was a largely descriptive analytical discipline (and one that in its attention to detailed contrasts and taxonomies was akin to botanical science and related disciplines) to one that set great store on the need to theorise away from the messy, real-world data, to universal regularities or competencies. This process has led to particularly interesting and complex issues surrounding the attitude to speech data in language theory generally, and the next sections will deal with this further.

Concept 2.3   **The powerful influence of a compelling and coherent theory**

An interesting example to flesh out the differences between empirically oriented work and those that take theory as a starting point is research on rhythm in spoken language. The classical paradigm set up and developed by among others Pike (1945) and Abercrombie (1967) proposes that languages should be categorised in terms of two different rhythmic systems: syllable timing and stress timing. In the former kind of language every syllable has the same duration and in the latter syllable length varies so that a regular 'beat' is created by the words and phrases of the language. Spanish and French are, traditionally, categorised as syllable timed and English and Russian as stress timed languages. This very compelling idea of a binary contrast (nicely described as 'machine gun' (syllable timing) versus 'morse code' (stress timing) (Lloyd James, 1940)) has held sway with variations for nearly 70 years. This is despite the fact that researchers admit that when they measure and time samples of languages it is difficult to find data that consistently fit the theory. Very complex systems of metrics have been created (Low and Grabe (1995), Grabe and Low (2002)) to investigate speech rhythm, most of which begin from this binary contrast or refer back to it. More recently the idea of stress/syllable timing being less clear-cut categories towards which individual languages tend, rather than being their defining rhythmic characteristics, has emerged but the paradigm remains largely unshifted or at least still has currency.

2.3   Attitudes to speech data

Quote 2.1   Attitudes towards speech data in linguistics in the early 1980s

Methodologically, most contemporary linguists do not use actual speech as a source of data for the analysis of linguistic structure. They base this position in part on the argument that the phrasal breaks, such as restarts, found in actual speech give evidence of such defective performance that the data are useless for the study of competence.

(Goodwin, 1981: 12)

Quote 2.2 The status and usefulness of natural speech in linguistic theory

A record of natural speech will show numerous false starts, deviations from rules, changes of plan in mid-course, and so on. The problem for the linguist, as well as for the child learning the language, is to determine from the data of performance the underlying system of rules that has been mastered by the speaker–hearer and that he puts to use in actual performance.

(Chomsky, 1965: 5)

Even theoretically oriented work engages with data at some level. At its most basic the research is grounded in some real-world concepts, if not 'hard' data. When researchers think of empirical approaches in opposition to more theoretically oriented ones, it is a matter of what role the data are seen to have in the research process. In 'classical' theoretically oriented, scientific methods, the model or theory on which a study is based is not going to be fundamentally redefined by the outcomes of the research. Data which challenge the prevailing theory are likely to be set aside as 'blips' and more generally the phenomena being investigated will be selected in such a way that they will tend to fit in with the existing paradigm (see Concept 2.3 for an example of this).

These are particularly pressing issues for the researcher into speech for three reasons. First, unlike the written form, the building blocks of speech do not come to us in a clearly demarcated set of units. Our literate view of language means that it is a surprise to realise that the stream of speech is exactly that: there are no gaps between individual words. The process of understanding speech is highly dependent on an interpretive capacity on the part of the listener and this interpretive role is not one that the researcher can completely stand apart from when handling authentic data. Second, capturing and analysing speech depends largely on the written form and careful attention is needed to the relationship between the original data and its visual representation – the secondary data. Finally, as noted above, neat and clearly defined categories and patterns are extremely compelling and there can be a tendency to 'retrofit' speech data to pre-designated categories due to this. Research into spoken grammar shows this particularly clearly. The terminology of traditional pedagogic or prescriptive grammars struggles to describe the norms of the spoken mode.

Concept 2.4   **Finding words to describe the grammar of speech**

Traditional and/or pedagogic grammar provides a fairly consistent set of constructs, definitions and structural relations. A grammatical construct like 'relative clause' or 'noun phrase' is relatively stable and clearly defined – a researcher will find several hundred articles on the topics with ease.

Research into the grammar of spoken discourse has suggested that there are a number of constructions regularly used by speakers (for example, subject–verb ellipsis – 'Nice day' as opposed to 'It is a nice day' (Nariyama, 2004)) which do not fit into the norms of traditional grammar models, or items which have a high occurrence (for example, semi-modal verbs such as 'tend to' (Moore, 2007)) but which are presented as 'unusual' in standard grammars. Structures such as these that fall outside the standard definitions are less easy to handle for two reasons. First, by their nature they do not fall into the neat categories of the existing grammar model. Second, there will be no accepted terminology for the elements being described. Thus, a construction typical of spoken English such as the following, 'where he went wrong my mate Tony was not getting the car taxed before he went on his holiday', might be defined as a 'cleft' sentence, 'pre-posed', containing a 'left-shifted head' or other terms which may or may not mean exactly the same thing to everyone or overlap with one another exactly.

In the first part of the twentieth century, speech itself was difficult to capture, and even the advent of the tape recorder meant that gathering large samples of data and analysing them was a laborious process. The ability to record speech, and the comparatively recent growth in the power of the personal computer, has brought the possibility of large corpus studies to the office of the applied linguistics researcher. However, the complexities of capturing large quantities of spontaneous spoken data have meant that most corpora still depend for their input on the written mode. Insights from corpora that combine a balance of both spoken and written material are beginning to filter into the public domain in forms that can be used by the teaching community. See for instance Biber *et al.* (1999) *Longman Grammar of Spoken and Written English* or Carter and McCarthy (2006) *Cambridge Grammar of English*.

It is noticeable, however, that despite advances in the capturing and the analysis of speech data, research questions continue to be oriented towards areas other than finding out more about the nature of speech, *per se*. Considering the universality of the ability to speak across humankind there has been little attempt to draw together a unified theory of the process. Many disciplines value real speech data and place them at the heart of their theories. However, these approaches have tended to incorporate the spoken language into a theory that aims to describe or explain

> **Quote 2.3** The *Longman Grammar of Spoken and Written English* on surprises from corpus-based approaches to grammar
>
> [E]ven basic word classes – such as nouns, adjectives, verb, and adverbs – are far from evenly distributed across registers. Nouns and prepositional phrases are much more common in news than in conversation, whereas verbs and adverbs are much more common in conversation. These distributional patterns reflect differing functional priorities. For example, news texts have an informational focus, frequently using nouns to refer to people and things in the world. . . . In contrast, the interpersonal focus of conversation results in frequent use of verbs to narrate events and to present personal attitudes, while the online production and context dependent circumstances of conversation make it more appropriate to use pronouns instead of nouns.
>
> (Biber *et al.*, 1999: 11)

something else. For instance, second language acquisition (SLA) gives high importance to the effect of spoken input on the learner but the elements under discussion have tended to be the learner's inherent capacity for language learning, the closeness or distance between a target language and current utterances, how their first language affects their second, and so on.

Notable exceptions such as Levelt's seminal work *Speaking: from intention to articulation* (Levelt, 1989) fall outside what is considered core work in applied linguistics, coming under the umbrella of psycholinguistics. Even here work stops largely at the point of utterance and does not pursue the important issues of interaction, the influence of intonation and prosody, turn-taking and so on; nor how these features might relate to one another in a process of communication that is unique to the spoken mode. In language acquisition, research with an interest in bridging some of these gaps began to emerge in the early years of this century (see for instance, Judit Komos' readable *Speech Production and Second Language Acquisition* (Komos, 2006)).

2.4 The applicability of research approaches and frameworks to the study of speech

The previous sections have argued that care is needed in researching speaking due in three respects. These were the strong influence of a literate view of the form, the tendency to tidy speech data and to abstract away from the messiness of real-world, situated, talk in context, and the tendency to use speech data as the basis for research into some aspect of language other than the spoken mode in its own right. Here we look at the implications of these points, and what research into speaking *per se* may, in due course, emerge as.

Hand in hand with a removal of the object of study to the theoretical, unsituated, or abstract level is a convenient merging of the construct 'speech' with 'language'. It is convenient because it permits the models in question to use isolated examples closer to the norms of formal, published written mode and ignore deviant, ill-formed and difficult to parse forms which might come under debate if real-world examples of speech (and, indeed, writing) were the basis for the model. Secondly, such abstract approaches permit the theorist to ignore sound-based meaning-bearing elements of language, such as intonation, which are again less easy to formalise than text-based elements.

Much of a person's identity and communicative force is carried by the vocal pattern that we associate with them, and many of the affective aspects of language reach the world via the slightest changes in voice quality. In teaching spoken language one might imagine these aspects would be seen as of highest importance. However, since most abstract language paradigms do not take into account or try to account for aspects of the dynamic, interpersonally oriented mode that is speech, the focus tends to fall on structural input, disengaged both from its discourse context and from its meaning-bearing 'music'. In contrast to this, work that is ongoing in computer science and human–computer interaction is keen to better understand and incorporate findings about the links between commun-icative impact, affect, and prosody (for instance, Partala and Surakka (2004)). It will be interesting with the growth of multi-modal corpora and new techniques for searching these how far the findings of computer science, corpus linguistics, and the language classroom can be combined to provide insights that are eventually applicable to the spoken language curriculum.

The development of functional magnetic resonance imaging 'fMRI' technology linguistic research developed in the early years of this century has had an interesting effect on the study of spoken language. The capacity to link brain function to particular spoken stimuli has meant researchers can now build hypotheses to investigate questions about links between oral/aural input and events in the brain. The reason that this is a step change in the field is that earlier neurolinguistic work depended on making links between spoken events in the outside world and possible brain activity. This was often done by contrasting brain-damaged and non-brain-damaged speech performance. While this approach remains valid, the capacity to map and link spoken events and normal brain activity is an exciting new development for linguistics.

Concept 2.5   Functional magnetic resonance imaging (fMRI) and language

fMRI is a method by which activity in different parts of the brain can be shown as an image. The process is non-invasive as it scans from outside the body and analyses differences in blood flow. Changes in blood flow cause measurable fluctuations in oxygen levels and in turn its magnetic properties. The scanner translates these into data that are mapped on to particular areas in the brain. The assumption is that blood flow and neural activity happen hand in hand and therefore these images represent the physical location of the brain's response to particular stimuli.

Work in this field on language developed rapidly from around 2000 and the process has been used for a wide variety of studies ranging from vocabulary (Ellis *et al.*, 2006) to emotional responses to language (Beaucousin *et al.*, 2007).

2.5   Levels of analysis

One of the difficulties in researching speech is the fact that, unlike written texts, the notion of a freestanding genre or clearly delimited sample to be investigated does not readily lend itself to speech. Whereas the researcher into writing can start, if they wish, from a relatively well-defined set of texts that clearly fit into a category (newspaper language, popular fiction, advertising texts, academic writing and so on), the researcher into speech will generally find no such helpful categories to hand. Writing presents itself in front of the researcher through the materiality of its visual medium. The researcher into speech must usually look beyond the discourse to the context in order to delimit the data under investigation and to ensure they are, for instance, comparing like with like.

The issue can be best understood by looking at a stretch of talk, and thinking about the different levels and perspectives through which it could be investigated.

Figure 2.1 shows a brief extract from interviews conducted to create a corpus of Singaporean English. The corpus was created primarily for the purposes of research into prosodic features. It presents a readily accessible set of transcripts alongside digital audio files of the original speech data. This leads to a preliminary, overarching comment that the transcript and the spoken data are not the same thing and should not be conflated. Researchers into speaking all need to reach a carefully thought out position in relation to the visible recording of their data in the written form as this is rarely a neutral process. This can be understood in terms of a metaphor of degrees of magnification. The sample provided captures a number of aspects of talk: socio-pragmatic relationships (interviewer/subject, lecturer/student),

secs	spraker	
00	I	Where do they live in America?
01	S	Los Angeles and erm San Francisco.
04	I	Do you like it there?
06	S	Yeah . . . well not as much as Australia, because like you know in the States
10		it's more like erm a place to visit . . .
13		not so much a place to stay . . . yeah and to live in.
16	I	You don't think that you [could live in Los Angeles.
17	S	[No.
19		No no no definitely not.

Figure 2.1   **Extract from National Institute of Education Singapore Corpus of Spoken Singaporean English (available online with digital audio file at *http://videoweb.nie.edu.sg/phonetic/niecsse/f15/f15-f-tr.htm*)**

structural features (turns, questions/answers, clauses) and acoustic data relating to the stream of speech (temporal information in seconds, onset of overlapping talk). However, these are only a small subset of features that may interest the researcher. At a level of higher magnification, someone might wish to represent relative loudness or pitch movement in individual words. The greater the acoustic information being captured, the greater the efforts involved in transcription. There is therefore always a relationship between the 'magnification' (level of detail captured in a transcription of speech) and the research focus. A researcher may make a very simple initial transcript showing no data such as overlapping talk or pauses if they are primarily interested in finding instances of a particular type of interaction (jokes, for example) and then increase the level of detail for those extracts. Taken seriously transcription is a powerful research tool and can reflect the perspectives and needs of the researcher. As it is never an entirely neutral process, it is good practice for the individual transcriber to cross-refer with other researchers when difficulties of interpretation arise or when new categories of talk are being investigated. O'Connell and Kowal (2009) provide a thoughtful summary of the development of transcription systems and issues to consider. The most commonly used system is often referred to as the 'Jefferson method' after the linguist Gail Jefferson who developed this. A definitive overview can be seen in Jefferson (2004). Setting on one side this methodological preliminary issue, the extract shown in Figure 2.1 could be the object of study at many levels and the following sections deal with each of these.

2.5.1   Analysing speaking skills at the level of discourse and social interaction

Discourse-level studies are interested in questions of how speakers interact with one another (for example, how they know when it is their turn to speak), and how talk is organised in particular kinds of patterns over long stretches of language (for example, how speakers structure their talk for listeners so that they can follow changes in topic easily). At a wider level, researchers are often also interested in how, through talk, social features are expressed, such as identity, shared knowledge, or power relations. In the extract in Figure 2.1, the speakers are a lecturer (male) and a student (female). Their interaction takes place in a semi-formal interview setting. Their relationships, gender, and the interview context influence how they behave to one another conversationally. For instance, it is more likely that the lecturer/interviewer will initiate talk in this setting and it is likely that more of his discourse will be in the form of questions. Many disciplines outside linguistics are becoming increasingly interested in discourse analysis because of the insights it can give about how participants in a spoken interaction behave. For instance, researchers in the medical sciences may be interested in how to understand patient and practitioner relationships better in order to enhance training in communication for professionals and therefore the efficacy of treatment (see Salter *et al.* (2007) for an example of this work). Similarly, a wide-ranging recent summary of applications of linguistic analysis in the realm of business studies can be found in Bargiela-Chiappini *et al.* (2007).

During the 1970s and 1980s the main concern in the field was to consider where the discourse level of language fitted in with current views of language, and to what extent regularities or even 'rules' of interaction could be uncovered. This focus on rule-based paradigms reflected the dominant model for language that had grown up in the USA. Seminal work was carried out in America by conversational analysts who developed highly sophisticated systems for representing language features which had previously been studied very little, for example laughter or pauses or apparently trivial utterances, such as 'uh huh' or 'oh' (e.g. Schegloff, 1981). This detailed investigation into the mechanics of conversation led to concepts such as 'openings', 'closings', 'pair parts', 'formulaic exchanges' or the 'transition-relevance point' (TRP).

Concept 2.6   **Transition-relevance point (TRP)**

This is a moment in speaking when several linguistic features combine to signal to an interlocutor that they could take over the speaker role. In Anglophone cultures these tend to be the ends of clauses and are signalled by pitch, intonation, pace, micro-pausing as well as extra-linguistic features such as gaze. Next time you are in a free-flowing conversation you might like to stand back (or better still record a conversation) and see how speakers know that they can begin to speak without seeming to interrupt one another. For many learners of a language, ability to speak is not the factor which isolates them in a conversation. Rather it is the inability to 'read' the moments when they might be able to begin to speak.

In the UK key features of the structuring of discourse were investigated and notions such as 'discourse markers', 'transactions' and 'exchanges' were developed.

Concept 2.7   **Discourse markers**

These are words 'outside' clauses which carry little or no meaning in their own right but signal something to the listener about the structure or organisation of the talk, for example 'right' or 'ok' in English. As well as logical relations, discourse markers can signal more subtle aspects of talk: 'well' can indicate reservation or hesitation; 'now' can indicate a change in topic; 'actually' can mean many things including difference of opinion or correction or even defensiveness (cf. English cooking is very good. English cooking is very good, actually.). Because learners are usually taught a form of the language which is strongly influenced by written mode, spoken discourse markers are not given high prominence in a syllabus, if they are taught explicitly at all. This can leave a learner floundering both in terms of listening to conversation and taking part.

Both discourse analysis and conversation analysis have links to sociolinguistics in that they prefer not to deal with samples of language in isolation, and conversation analysis in particular is interested in the relations between interlocutors. Discourse analysis, however, has traditionally tended to concentrate on longer sections of language and focused on interrelations between different sections of text. Within this, the discourse analyst is interested in how speakers carry out functions of language and the choices made by them in different contexts.

In terms of the application of some of the main ideas of conversation and discourse analysis, but with a stronger focus on the former, Brown and Yule (1983) *Teaching the Spoken Language: an approach based on the analysis of conversational English* provided something of a bridge between the schools of thought outlined above and more practically classroom-oriented applications. Interestingly, despite the crucial aspects of speech that discourse-level studies have uncovered they have, overall, been very slow to trickle down into classroom teaching and published teaching materials in general. There have been books for teachers on the topic (for example, McCarthy, 1991, *Discourse Analysis for Language Teachers* or Evelyn Hatch's, 1992, very different *Discourse and Language Education*). Carter, Hughes and McCarthy (2000) attempts to bring some of the complexities of spoken grammar in discourse to the classroom via grammar materials. Chapter 3 deals with this more fully.

Discourse analysis in the UK does have strong incidental links to the classroom, however, in that much of the most influential early work (for example, Sinclair and Coulthard, 1975) was carried out on classroom interaction. These classic studies, which generated some of the fundamental categories of discourse analysis, were based on teacher–pupil talk.

During the 1990s and beyond there was increasing interest in the telecommunications and computing world that discourse analysis would solve problems of automation of human–computer understanding. This area has not achieved the early promise – humans are still constrained to limited lexical choices and clear talk in these contexts rather than the system being able to adjust to spontaneous talk. Nevertheless, it will be interesting to see what twenty-first-century discourse and conversation analysis can offer other disciplines and users wanting to apply the insights of linguistics to real-world applications.

The relationship between psychology and speech behaviour is another thread to research into global aspects of speech, and one which again links in with the bigger questions of how spoken language data relate to underlying linguistic systems, whether neurological, biological or genetic. Whereas discourse or conversation analysts will describe patterns of speech behaviour in order to uncover regularities in the organisation of spoken discourse, and will see these patterns as of interest in themselves, the psychologist will generally regard utterances as a source of evidence of mental or behavioural processes. So, for example, whereas a discourse or conversation analyst may look at a feature such as patterns of repetition in speech and see how far they can generalise about lexical repetition in its own right, the psychologist would investigate how such repetitions relate to how humans process complex utterances, or the timing and levels of pre-planning. For example, Clark and Wasow (1998) investigated a typical pattern of repetition, either PRONOUN + PAUSE/FILLER + PRONOUN (I uh I (think) . . .) or ARTICLE + PAUSE/FILLER + ARTICLE (The uh the (problem) . . .) and suggested that the different stages in this pattern related to the way in which speakers committed themselves to an utterance. They proposed that these items were an integral part of the underlying psychological processes by which utterances reach the world.

In terms of teaching languages, the fields of higher-level studies into speech described here open up several questions and ways forward, particularly in relation to uncovering differences between cultures in terms of how conversation is organised. This in turn can help learners and teachers understand potential pitfalls in language interaction that are not due to any grammatical mistake but different pragmatic and cultural expectations.

2.5.2 The research space at the level of language choices: grammar and vocabulary

A prominent strand of work on grammar and lexis that takes into account spoken mode has been developed through corpus studies. Douglas Biber's work, and most notably his influential *Variation Across Speech and Writing* (Biber, 1988), gives a strongly data-oriented analysis of a wide variety of spoken and written sources, concluding that certain grammatical features cluster together to make up the distinctive style of a spoken or written genre. These features in turn map on to dimensions of contrast, such as whether the language is concerned with conveying information or is more inter-personally oriented. Rather than suggesting a simple binary division between speech and writing, Biber suggested that there were patterns of probability among language features that show statistical regularity in how they co-occur in spoken and written genres.

There have been two major strands of work developed from this approach: applications of the register analysis in discrete fields and genres, and more theoretical and detailed insights about general language features. In terms of the former, this has been taken forward in, for instance, Douglas Biber's own work on English for special purposes including university writing and speaking (Biber, 2006), and with colleagues on English language assessment (Biber *et al.*, 2004), and the large body of work around the Michigan Corpus of Spoken Academic English ('MICASE'). In terms of the latter there has been, for instance, some work on language change as a feature capable of being investigated through corpora (see Concept 2.8 describing the process known as 'grammaticalisation').

Concept 2.8   **Grammaticalisation**

This is a concept associated with the study of language change. It is based on an underlying idea that words in a language can be categorised as primarily carrying semantic meaning or as primarily carrying out syntactic functions. The verb 'walk' would be in the first category and the verb 'have' would be in both categories. It has a lexical meaning when used in the sentence 'I have a brother' and has less semantic load when used in its auxiliary functions, as in 'I have broken my arm'. At different phases in the evolution of a language, words can change from lexical to grammatical functions and this process is called grammaticalisation. An example that is often given is the expansion of the lexical word 'back' as part of the body into an adverbial to indicate past time as in 'Back then . . .'. Lindquist and Mair (2004) provide a collection of research papers on what is also termed 'historical corpus linguistics'.

Early corpus-based work helped to inform research into speech on detailed aspects such as tenses (Aarts and Meyer, 1995), vocabulary (Stenström, 1990), clauses (Nelson, 1997), and ellipsis (Meyer, 1995). More recently, work has involved broader questions of the extent of generalisability and applicability of findings (for example, Conrad (2000), Mindt (2002), Baldwin *et al.* (2005)). Academics also began working on bridging the gap between corpus findings and the classroom (e.g. Johns, 1991; Tribble and Jones, 1990; Knowles, 1990; and most relevantly for the spoken mode, Svartvik, 1991) as soon as large corpora of speech became readily available. More recently scholars have focused attention on the interrelations between second language acquisition theories, or approaches to teaching, and the grammatical frequencies found in corpora (for example, Biber and Reppen (2002), Anderson (2007), Barbieri and Eckhardt (2007)). However, while these can provide some interesting ideas for classroom activities, there is still a gap between findings on the realities of grammatical and lexical choices in spontaneous talk, and what is presented in published material.

On the other hand, for the teacher or researcher starting out in research into spoken mode, gaining access to spoken corpora has become relatively straightforward. These resources range from sampling a larger corpus on-line (for example, the British National Corpus at: *http://sara.natcorp.ox.ac.uk/lookup.html*) to ordering a corpus or a sample on a CD-ROM (for example via ICAME at *http://www.hd.uib.no/icame/newcd.htm*) to gaining full access for scholarly work either via the corpus designers or publishers associated with the project. For further details, see Chapter 9.

Quote 2.4 **The linearity of speech and how grammar is conceptualised**

One fundamental difference between spoken and written language has to do with the 'linearity' of speaking in time, in that the temporal structure of speaking is inherently the outcome of an interactive process between speaker and listener. But despite the status of 'linearity' as one of Saussure's fundamental principles, in practice little more than lip-service is paid to the temporality of spoken language, which is treated as having few if any consequences for syntactic analysis. It is trivial to point out that a structuralist definition of the sentence is incompatible with an on-line model of syntax processing. A structuralist analysis, even of ostensibly spoken language, is carried out not from a real-time emergence perspective but as if it were – like a written text – a finished product.

(Auer, 2009)

Another area of work on spoken grammar looks at the interface between prosody and syntax. In the latter decades of the twentieth century, there were some notable attempts to set aside descriptive and prescriptive grammars and to incorporate prosodic elements into the analysis of the form. David Brazil's (1995) *A Grammar of Speech* was particularly unusual because the linear nature of speech production is taken seriously and talk is described in terms of having 'purpose'. It is interesting to note that, although Brazil's book is highly regarded, the teaching profession as a whole has found it difficult to assimilate many of the principles that underpin the work. The class text on pronunciation for advanced learners of English also by David Brazil (Brazil, 1994) presents a similar unification of discourse-level and other meaning-bearing language features. Hence, in many ways Brazil's work represents one of the most consistent attempts to look at the spoken form on its own terms.

Klein and Purdue (1992) *Utterance Structure: developing grammars again* was another exception to the rule. In this deliberately provocative and stimulating work the authors take issue with many of the assumptions of second language acquisition and base their analysis on the notion that learner utterances are a language to be studied in their own right (rather than in relation to a 'target' language). The book is of particular interest to the researcher into speech because it takes a strongly empirical (data-oriented) stand and builds the discussion on real utterances. However, the researcher new to speech research studies, reading either of these books, should realise that while both of them are fascinating neither of them have succeeded in becoming centrally accepted into the inner circle of applied linguistics, partly due to their (intentional) lack of overlap with the theories underlying the field more generally.

During the last decade of the twentieth century and first decade of the following one, a growing trend in the research into spoken grammar has been the field known as interactional linguistics. This is a highly relevant area for the researcher interested in approaching spoken data in terms of the dynamic and 'real time' aspects that tend to be lost when the spoken form is examined entirely through the lens of the written mode (see also Quote 2.4).

Concept 2.9   **Interactional linguistics**

This is a branch of linguistics that is closely related to conversation analysis. Whereas CA analyses speech data to better understand patterns of talk and the social aspects of talk that are revealed by interactions between participants, IL uses many of the same methods of analysis but the emphasis is on insights about language itself that can be gained from examining talk in interaction.

Work in IL has a strong connection with the Santa Barbara Corpus of Spoken English and the development of this by John Du Bois and colleagues was something of a catalyst for work at the interface between discourse and grammar. A bibliography of work in the area can be found at *http://www.linguistics.ucsb.edu/faculty/sathomps/bibliographies/bibliog-interactional-linguistics.htm* and the approach has been used to allow better understanding of grammatical variation that appears sensitive to interactional context (for example, how talk is organised around repetition (Bybee, (2006), syntactic constraints on offers of assistance (Curl, 2006) and so on).

Interactional linguistics is closely related to conversation analysis and approaches the emergent nature of grammatical elements from that perspective. There is also work on the interface between prosody and syntax that is aligned towards the experimental paradigm, for example Grosjean (1983) and Grosjean and Hirt (1996) which looked at the issue of how listeners predict the end of a clause from acoustic information earlier in the clause; or Marsi *et al.* (2002) who carried out work on this area in text-to-speech recognition.

2.5.3   The research space at the level of speech production: fluency and pronunciation

Traditionally, in the mid to late twentieth century, a great deal of research into phonology was undertaken to find evidence of an underlying system. This was generally carried out in relation to the model of language that tended to dominate at that time, and to an extent still does: the transformational or the universal grammar paradigm (see, for example, Nestor and Vogel (2007), *Prosodic Phonology*). Within this paradigm, some consideration was given to the interplay between the different levels, and the direction of influence between them. However, the aim of the work was generally to find evidence of internal language knowledge rather than to describe the system for any applied purpose. For example, Berg and Hassan (1996) examined speaker errors in three languages but were less interested in classifying or explaining the errors than in gaining insight into the 'mapping' or hierarchical conceptualisation of speakers' linguistic knowledge in the three cases.

In contrast to this approach, work into pedagogically related phonology has been carried out within a much less theoretically oriented, and generally an experimentally based, framework. Experimental-style research into the teaching of pronunciation is an area that can provide clearly relevant results for the classroom and Derwing and Monro (2005) provide a good summary of the research and teaching interface in this area. Keeping up to date with these kinds of results can help teachers plan the balance of the speaking syllabus, and can also account for contrasts between student progress in and outside the classroom, for example, if a student appears to be making good progress in pronunciation in controlled circumstances but remains difficult to understand when producing longer sections of speech.

In contrast, and at a more theoretical level, an emergent area in research of prosody has been studies of English spoken as a lingua franca (Concept 2.10). This work emerged during the early years of this century and is an area that has provided lively debate about standards, ownership of the language, and the balance between intelligibility versus a native speaker model in teaching speaking. Work such as Jenkins (2000) crystallised some of these ideas and a readable summary of the issues can be found in Pickering (2006). Chapter 6 returns to this topic in detail.

Concept 2.10   Lingua franca, intelligibility, and common core features

A lingua franca is a form of language used as a common one between speakers of different languages. It is, by its nature, associated with particular domains where people need to use language to talk to people they are unfamiliar with and to carry out functions beyond the family and other local domains. Latin was a dominant lingua franca in mediaeval Europe where it was used for religious and scholarly purposes alongside local 'mother tongue' languages. English is currently often used as a common language for business, academic and other purposes and a branch of applied linguistics research is on 'ELF' or English as a lingua franca (Seidlhofer, 2001). This work relates to discussions surrounding the importance of intelligibility over accuracy (as defined by Anglophone norms), and what common core of grammar and vocabulary is required for users to carry out communicative functions in what is their second or third language.

Summary

This chapter reviewed some classical approaches to the research process and addressed the particular problems for the researcher working with spoken forms of language. Beside the issue of the lack of extensive work on the spoken form in its own right, I raised the question of the role of speech data in language theory generally, and of the attitude to situated spoken discourse as the basis for generalisations about language. In relation to research based around teaching the spoken form, the further issue of the cultural and pragmatic problems raised by real speech data was aired.

Further reading

McEnery, A., Xiao, R., and Tono, Y. (2005). *Corpus-based Language Studies*. London: Routledge. A comprehensive and practically oriented overview of corpus-based language study, including summary of debates around using corpora and case studies of spoken corpora and language-teaching projects.

Paltridge, B. and Phakiti, A. (eds). (2010). *Continuum Companion to Research Methods in Applied Linguistics*. New York/London: Continuum. An up-to-date general handbook for the novice researcher that contains overviews of approaches such as conversation analysis and many others.

Szczepek-Reed, B. (2007). *Prosodic Orientation in English Conversation*. Basingstoke: Palgrave Macmillan. A highly readable title reporting research at the interface between prosody and conversational interaction.

ten Have, P. (2007). *Doing Conversation Analysis*. London: Sage Publications. A practically oriented introduction to conversation analysis.

Wennerstrom, A. (2001). *The Music of Everyday Speech*. New York: Oxford.

II Issues for teaching and assessing speaking

Chapter 3

Approaches, materials and the issue of 'real' speech

This chapter will...

- look at the issues involved in dealing with authentic speech in the classroom, particularly in the context of materials development and attitudes to the spoken form;

- give an overview of the development of approaches seen in published materials over the last few decades and relate these to some of the changes in the approaches to language teaching generally;

- present some examples of more recent approaches with commentary in relation to the influence of international tests of speaking, and balancing authenticity against the practicalities of the classroom.

3.1 Introduction

What is the overriding objective of a speaking component in a language-teaching syllabus? It seems a tautology to suggest that it is to enable the student to speak the target language. However, that simple objective is actually quite complex when authentic speech in context is given a central role. As teachers and researchers, we have preconceptions about the spoken form that influence our beliefs about it. These affect how we think about speech at the level of interaction, at the level of language choices and in what we think it means to be a 'fluent' speaker. Speaking is 'primary' as noted in Chapter 1, but messy and difficult to define, it is fundamental to language learning but open to the vagaries of individual use and context. The production of teaching materials and the handling of speaking in the language classroom show these tensions particularly clearly.

3.2   What are our models and standards when we teach speaking?

The attitudes to the spoken form of language expressed in Quotes 3.1 and 3.2 represent two widely differing schools of thought on the topic of speech. Both recognise the distinctive features of spoken discourse but contain markedly different value-judgements about the implications of those distinctive characteristics. In the case of Quote 3.1 there is a sense of 'high' and 'low' register being the main distinguishing feature between the spoken and written forms of language. The notion of a minimal level of structure and vocabulary, 'slurred' and elliptical forms, and commonplace or everyday discourse as opposed to high-flown or literary style being the norm for speech means that it is not something to be taken as a model for correct, acceptable language use in all circumstances. In this view, therefore, although the spoken form is unique, the features that go to make up that uniqueness may not be something entirely desirable for the learner to emulate, or for the teacher to introduce into the classroom.

Quotes 3.1 and 3.2   Two different perspectives on spoken grammar

In spoken language, grammar and vocabulary are reduced to a minimum. The words used often have special or hidden meaning born of some shared experience which an outsider would fail to grasp. The speaker makes much use of elided and slurred forms in the familiar pattern of their ordinary everyday speech. Utterances are typically short and often elliptical.... Short and rugged homespun words are usually more powerful and expressive than elaborate and high-flown words. Constructions that occur commonly in speech are not necessarily acceptable in formal and dignified writing.

(Yungzhong, 1985: 15)

... [S]poken grammars have uniquely special qualities that distinguish them from written ones, wherever we look in our corpus, at whatever level of grammatical category. In our work, too, we have expressed the view that language pedagogy that claims to support the teaching and learning of speaking skills does itself a disservice if it ignores what we know about the spoken language. Whatever else may be the result of imaginative methodologies for eliciting spoken language in the second-language classroom, there can be little hope for a natural spoken output on the part of language learners if the input is stubbornly rooted in models that owe their origin and shape to the written languages. Even much corpus-based grammatical insight...has been heavily biased towards evidence gleaned from written sources.

(Carter and McCarthy, 1997)

Figure 3.1   Spoken data in theoretically oriented models of grammar

In the case of the second quotation, the term 'uniquely special qualities' of speech, and the plea for more investigation of the form in its own right, imply that it is to be viewed as at least on a par with the traditionally more prestigious written form. Moreover, far from being a rather reduced and 'low' form of language the spoken form is presented as having a rich and diverse grammar of its own. In this school of thought, then, the spoken form is a neglected source of subtle language choices for the learner, and a form needing to be brought closer to the heart of language descriptions and into the 'menu' of language choices made available to learners (see also Figures 3.1 and 3.2).

The two different approaches outlined above represent the end points of a continuum of attitudes about the spoken form. On the one hand teaching forms that are unique to the spoken mode are seen as a marginal activity, rather as idioms or colloquialisms are introduced into the syllabus – something to enliven a lesson, but not regarded as an essential part of a student's structural knowledge. On the other hand, the spoken form is seen as a neglected source of richly diverse language choices that should be central to the teacher's repertoire of vocabulary and grammar structures to introduce a learner to.

In the debates surrounding models for teaching spoken grammar or pronunciation the role of authentic speech data is fundamental. Two books which can be used to exemplify the implications of deciding how far to

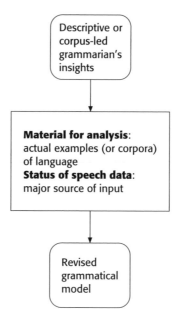

Figure 3.2   Spoken data in descriptively oriented models of grammar

incorporate real and contextualised data were published in the same year: Adrian Wallwork's (1997) resource book for speaking activities, *Discussions A–Z* and Carter and McCarthy's (1997) *Exploring Spoken English*. Wallwork's book is an extremely teacher-friendly, photocopiable resource book (see Quote 3.3), with a better than usual range of diverse, engaging and often witty topics and visual stimuli for discussion work. Its aim is to engender discussion and it meets this aim extremely well. These are materials to be handled by a teacher experienced in group work as there is little guidance for the novice, but they will almost inevitably get students talking.

The nature of discussion is dealt with briefly in the introduction but beyond that the material is simply there to function as a prompt rather than to raise awareness about matters such as the nature of interactions during discussion, cultural differences between discussions in different contexts or any socio-linguistic issues underlying debate or argument. In this sense, the book is solidly in the tradition of the past forty years in language teaching, which holds that it is imperative for the student to engage in activities that generate speech, and that such activities will promote language acquisition through processes similar to first language development.

In contrast, a book such as *Exploring Spoken English* focuses on the processes of talk and uses these as starting points for discussion (see Quote 3.4). As a classroom text it will be less easily incorporated into the standard language-learning context, since it requires advanced competence on the part of students and a high degree of confidence in handling language awareness-raising tasks on the part of the teacher. On the other hand, it provides an excellent set of resources, with accompanying audio material, of the realities of spoken interaction.

These two books are interesting examples at the two extremes of distinctive perspectives on the role of speech in the classroom context. The

---

Quote 3.3 Are you a good lover?

1. *Love* is an art which needs to be learned if it is to be practised well.
2. You can *love* someone too much.
3. A man and woman can be really good friends without being in *love*.
4. Women have deeper relationships with same-sex friends than men.
5. Men are more attracted to women who are hard to get.
6. Women should never make the first move.
7. You cannot be truly in *love* with two people at the same time.
8. You should only have eyes for your *lover*.
9. It is impossible to *love* and be wise.
10. *Love* can never be forever.

A kiss is just a kiss?
While the language of love-making may be universal when two people are from the same culture, the act of kissing can mean very different things in different parts of the world.

In China for example, kissing someone in public is seen as unhygienic and repulsive. In Japan, it may be tolerated, but only if the couple stand with bodies well apart and lips shut tight. And the Inuits of Alaska wouldn't dream of doing anything more oral than rubbing noses – not out of any moral scruples but because Inuit women tend to use their mouths for more everyday tasks such as cleaning oil lamps and chewing animal hides to soften them up.

Even if your intentions aren't amorous, you can still run into trouble. Many a foreigner has come unstuck when greeting a friend who is Dutch (mandatory three cheek-pecks) or French (two only).

1. Men kissing each other is disgusting.
2. Shaking hands is the best way to greet someone.
3. Kissing relatives is always embarrassing.
4. Scenes from films which show lovers kissing should be cut.
5. Couples should not be allowed to kiss in the street, on the bus, at the cinema, at school, at work.

(A. Wallwork, *Discussions A–Z Intermediate*, Cambridge University Press, 1997) former represents a classroom tool that will encourage lively and engaging speaking events to emerge and be sustained. These spoken interactions are in themselves the object of the classroom event. In assessing the success or failure of the section of a lesson based on these materials, a significant aspect would be the quantity of speech generated and the balance of the speech events between different class members. Conversely, the awareness-raising nature of material based on analysing actual speaker interactions will be judged not so much by the quantity of speech the student produces when engaging with the tasks and examples, but the depth of their understanding of why speakers use the language they do in a particular generic and social context.

Quote 3.4 Cooking rice

Activity
The text examined in this unit was recorded in the kitchen of a family home; all the participants are members of the same family. Here are some brief conversational exchanges. Would you expect to find conversations such as this in a family kitchen?:

   A: Would you like a biscuit?
   B: I beg your pardon.
   A: Would you like a biscuit?
   B: Oh, yes please. Thank you very much.
   A: I didn't know you used boiling water to make rice.
   B: You don't have to use boiling water but it is reckoned to be quicker.

Write short notes explaining why you would or would not expect to find such styles of conversational exchange in the text examined in this unit.

Speakers and setting
<S 01>	female (45)
<S 02>	male (19)
<S 03>	male (46)
<S 04>	male (49)
<S 02>	is <S 01> and <S 04>'s son
<S 03>	is <S 04>'s brother

This extract takes place in <S 01>, <S 02> and <S 04>'s house. <S 03> is visiting them.

   - 3 [4 secs]
   - 4 <S 02>   Will it all fit in the one?
   - 5 <S 01>   No you'll have to do two separate ones
   - 6 <S 03>   Right . . . what next?

- 7 [17 secs]
- 8 <S 03>   Foreign body in there
- 9 <S 02>   It's the raisins
- 10 <S 03>   Oh is it oh it's rice with raisins is it?
- 11 <S 02>   No no no it's not supposed to be
- 12 [laughs]   erm
- 13 <S 03>   There must be a raisin for it being in there
- 14 <S 02>   D'you want a biscuit?
- 15 <S 03>   Erm
- 16 <S 02>   Biscuit?
- 17 <S 03>   Er yeah
- 18 [9 secs]
- 19 <S 04>   All right
- 20 <S 03>   Yeah
- 21 [10 secs]
- 22 <S 04>   Didn't know you used boiling water
- 23 <S 02>   Pardon
- 24 <S 04>   Didn't know you used boiling water
- 25 <S 02>   Don't have to but it's erm ... they reckon it's erm quicker
- 26 [5 secs]
- 27 <S 04>   Tony was saying they should have the heating on by about Wed
- 28 <S 02>   Just gonna put the er butter on
- 29 <S 04>   What you making Ian?
- 30 <S 02>   Mm
- 31 <S 04>   What's that?
- 32 <S 02>   Oh er just gonna do some rice
- 33 <S 04>   Mm
- 34 <S 02>   Doing some rice in the micro
- 35 <S 03>   So you put margarine with it
- 36 <S 02>   Pardon yeah little bit don't know why cos otherwise it'll
- 37 <S 03>   Separate it

(R. Carter and M. McCarthy, *Exploring Spoken English*, Cambridge University Press, 1997)

As soon as real speakers in real interactions and in socially and culturally diverse situations are taken into account in models of language, some kind of assessment is required as to how far the features found are universal in the spoken form and to what extent they are particular to that speaker or that context. In this sense, descriptive linguistics meets up rather interestingly with conventional language theories. This is an area that has been under-researched during a phase of rapid improvement in the descriptions of spoken forms and greater emphasis on its importance in the curriculum.

There is, therefore, a great deal of opportunity for fruitful research projects in the area of both descriptive studies of spoken forms and more theoretically informed work on how far one can generalise from these studies.

The above debates lead us to a more practical question for the classroom practitioner, that is, how far one would want actually to incorporate any generalisations about spoken forms into the syllabus as an individual teacher or into course components at an institutional level. In general, the tendency to see the grammatical faculty at such an abstract level has permitted the majority of us to continue to teach via models of grammar that are extremely traditional, and strongly influenced by historically 'high-prestige' standard forms. These forms, as noted by Carter and McCarthy in the quotation given at the start of this section, tend to be closer to the norms of published writing than of casual speech. However, with the growing body of evidence about the grammar of speech, the individual teacher or teacher trainer needs to decide where they stand on the issue of how, and how far, to incorporate descriptive linguistics into their teaching.

The issues of target language are of particular interest in relation to the present section. The questions that are particularly relevant in thinking about the structure and vocabulary of spoken forms are outlined here:

- What dialect form or target accent shall I teach?
- What model of correctness, if any, will I use?
- What model of pragmatic or cultural behaviour will I use?

There is little difficulty in taking real speech data as the material for listening classes, or using actual examples of interaction (for example, in student seminars) as indicative models for raising awareness of pragmatic issues among learners. More contentious, and ideologically charged, issues arise when real instances of the spoken form are taken seriously as grammatical models for the target language.

Would you, for example, teach the following to your students if they were learning English? If you were learning a language, would you want to learn similar expressions in the target language?

1. 'ain't',
2. 'bloomin' thing',
3. 't'window' (instead of 'the window'),
4. 'the man I told you about, his brother's wife's bought my car',
5. 'good job you told me',
6. 'he's a nice man, Harry is'.

Each of the examples given above is more typically found in the spoken form than the written. However, they exemplify different types of features, some of which are traditionally excluded from the standard language-teaching syllabus, for instance forms that are felt to mark uneducated or colloquial speech such as 'ain't'. Equally, informal or archaic expressions such as 'bloomin' thing' while recognised as existing have not normally been felt appropriate for extensive teaching, other than as fairly minor adjuncts to standard grammar and vocabulary or needing to be glossed over in a listening comprehension. Finally forms which cluster together to form the dialects of geographically distinct regions, such as the use of 't'' in place of 'the' in parts of the north of England are again well known, but generally excluded from all but specialist courses.

The final three items in the list are examples of the type of feature described by Carter and McCarthy (1995) 'Grammar and the spoken language' in which the authors suggest a number of forms which are very common in speech but under-described in previous grammatical models. However, the question at this point is whether these forms are the kind that a teacher would want to teach their students and if so in what context. It could be argued that the form of a language that is taught has rarely, if ever, reflected the full range of native speaker forms and registers. There needs to be a balance struck between clearly inadequate models of spoken grammar and the norms of classrooms and published materials.

> **Quote 3.5** Reflecting on research output for teaching
>
> Worthwhile training needs to be informed by mature understanding of research and not by the latest news from the PhD and the research project.
>
> (Davies, 2008: 343)

Overall, at the start of the twenty-first century the field of applied linguistics is in an interesting state of flux over its attitudes to the spoken form and, in particular, spoken grammar. It will take some time for the teaching profession and materials developers to evaluate the multitude of novel ideas about speech that the work of corpus linguists and discourse analysts is throwing up. As I implied above, the fact that a structure is commonly found in the spoken form of a language has never made it automatically a target for language topics in classrooms and materials. Davies (2008) expresses this pithily in Quote 3.5. Here, the time needed to reflect on the output of research in applied and theoretical linguistics and then translate this into the knowledge base for sound pedagogy is highlighted. The rest of the chapter deals with the flow of insights about spoken language into classrooms and the issues surrounding commercial materials developed for teaching speaking.

The 'gap' between research output and the teachers' knowledge base and requirements is particularly evident when cutting-edge research into a dynamic and socially influenced medium such as speech is being carried out, as the applied linguistic community needs time to absorb information and judge the status of the insights before incorporating them into a syllabus. The teaching community in general will in due course need to reach a view on whether structures such as 'he's a nice man, Harry is' or 'good job you told me' (examples of a structural 'tail' and subject + verb ellipsis respectively) have the status of core grammatical features or of less central or simply less widely useful forms such as 'ain't' or 'bloomin' thing'.

In addition to the issues surrounding spoken grammar a significant area where standards and targets of the spoken norm are an issue is the teaching of pronunciation. This is a multi-faceted set of arguments as fluency is often seen as being at odds with accuracy, while at the same time giving the learner plenty of opportunity for unfettered and unselfconscious talk is a key goal of many practitioners. The issue was raised vigorously by Hector Hammerly (1991) in his book *Fluency* and [sic] *Accuracy* (his use of 'sic' indicating an ironic note that at the time the bulk of the readership may have felt there was too much tension between these two to combine them with a co-ordinating conjunction). An indicative extract showing his position is given in Quote 3.6.

Quote 3.6   The problems of the communicative approach in relation to accuracy

With its emphasis on communication, [the communicative approach] stresses early vocabulary development while largely ignoring language structure, whether it be phonological, morphological or syntactic. Most second-language-acquisition-through-classroom-communication/interaction advocates do not seem to care that students mispronounce sounds, use wrong stems or endings, or construct sentences following faulty rules – all of these problems are supposed to disappear, eventually, through communicative classroom interaction. Well, there is no reason why they should, and it is clear that most don't.

(Hammerly, 1991: 9)

Just as explicit grammar teaching has always been carried out, and been very popular with many teachers, despite being unfashionable in current language teaching methodology, the teaching of pronunciation and more broadly 'fluency' skills persisted largely unchanged over at least a thirty-year period.

Quotes 3.7 and 3.8 Social aspects of fluency and pronunciation

It needs to be said at the outset that the aim of pronunciation improvement is not to achieve a perfect imitation of a native accent, but simply to get the learner to pronounce accurately enough to be easily and comfortably comprehensible to other (competent) speakers. 'Perfect' accents are difficult if not impossible for most of us to achieve in a foreign language anyway, and may not even be desirable. Many people – even if subconsciously – feel they wish to maintain a slight mother-tongue accent as an assertion of personal or ethnic identity.

(Ur, 1996: 52)

There is also some evidence that learning background may affect the sort of fluency behavior a learner manifests. Shin (1989) studied two learners of Japanese at similar proficiency levels at a British university. Both were native speakers of English. Subject A had spent only a few months in Japan whereas Subject B had been born in Japan and had lived there until aged 12 years. Subject A had six years of formal study of Japanese, and Subject B only three years, however. To Shin (a native speaker of Japanese), Subject B appeared the more fluent in conversation. Analysis revealed she used more colloquial forms than did Subject A, longer sentences, fewer and more appropriate fillers and fewer repetitions. Although Subject A actually paused less than did Subject B, Subject B's pause positioning seemed more appropriate. Interestingly, Subject B actually made more mistakes than did Subject A, but corrected fewer of them. In particular, she tended to let her grammatical mistakes go quite uncorrected.

(Lennon, 1990: 398)

Approaches to teaching these overt speaking skills generally revolve around awareness-raising activities based on phonemic distinctions and practice focusing on models of correct pronunciation. This approach changed very little for at least thirty years and is still at the heart of teacher training in this field.

The social and cultural aspects of teaching pronunciation are very sensitive to changing attitudes, however. For example, while earlier teacher training manuals spoke unashamedly of the remedial work needed to correct a 'foreign accent' (original scare quotes) the work from the mid-1990s onwards became more circumspect on this topic (see Quotes 3.9 and 3.10, in contrast to Quote 3.11). More recently still, the focus has shifted even further away from accepting the native speaker as the model towards which the learner is aspiring and has been placed more on mutual intelligibility, often between speakers using English as a second or even third language that they find they have in common. In an extreme example of this the Anglophone speaker finds that they are the one who cannot understand the spoken interaction while the lingua franca speakers comprehend one another easily (McCrum, 2006). Clearly in such a case the dominance of the native speaker as a target for spoken language performance will have been reduced and this would, taken to its logical conclusion, affect language-teaching materials.

Concept 3.1   **Common core features and intelligibility**

At the start of the twenty-first century two related strands of research into pronunciation emerged that have clear implications for the classroom. The work of Jennifer Jenkins (2000, 2006) brought insights about certain features of speech being more significant for intelligibility than others, and a debate arose as to whether these should be the focus of the speaking curriculum. This work is closely related to research into English as a lingua franca (see Concept 2.10) which asks what a description of language used solely between non-native speakers of English would be like and whether focusing on the language that emerges between them is preferable to attempting to attain native-speaker norms.

However, while the wider culture of applied linguistics shifts to reflect current mores and beliefs among influential players in the discipline, the basics of pronunciation teaching remain largely untouched and firmly at odds with much of the ideology of modern teaching theory. There can still be seen a strong focus on external models, practice and 'getting it right'. For example, Hewings (2004) begins with a section on awareness-raising but the core of the material is based on approaches and technical knowledge that would be familiar 20 to 30 years before. Equally, in Seidlhofer (2001) the central sections on the 'how' of teaching overlap greatly with earlier approaches despite being embedded in thought-provoking discussions of the issue of the native speaker as a problematic figure. Derwing (2008) notes that, setting aside larger issues such as motivation and amount of exposure to the language, the fundamental factor in teaching pronunciation is perceptual, i.e. whether the learner can distinguish the relevant sounds. This, again, echoes the approaches noted in the quotations from the 1970s and 1990s (Quotes 3.9 and 3.10).

Quotes 3.9 and 3.10 The fundamentals of teaching pronunciation in the final years of the twentieth century

The sounds we make are *phones*. Although the number of phones that can be produced by any individual speaker is practically unlimited, only certain sounds are recognised by the speakers and hearers of the particular language as conveying meaning. The smallest unit of significant or distinctive sound has been called a *phoneme*. A phoneme is actually an abstraction rather than a concrete description of a specific sound. Any particular phoneme comprises a group or class of sounds that are phonetically similar but whose articulations vary according to their position relative to the other sounds which precede or follow them.

(Rivers and Temperley, 1978: 149)

The first thing that needs to be done is to check that the learner can hear and identify the sounds you want to teach. The same goes for intonation, rhythm and stress: can the learner hear the difference between how a competent, or native, speaker of the language says a word, phrase or sentence and how a foreign learner says it?

This can be done by requesting imitation; or seeing if learners can distinguish between minimal pairs (such as ship/sheep, man/men, thick/tick; see Gimson, 1978); or by contrasting acceptable with unacceptable pronunciation through recordings or live demonstration.

(Ur, 1996: 53)

Quote 3.11 Social and contextual aspects in the task of teaching pronunciation

... [P]honetics provides the technical underpinning of pronunciation teaching, and this is what is traditionally given prominence in introductory books and teacher education courses. However, it is probably more helpful to start with considerations of the role of pronunciation in a broader perspective: the 'macro conditions' which in combination eventually lead to specific 'micro conditions' for particular classroom settings. ...

Starting with *pronunciation in individual and social life* [reference to figure not reproduced here], it is easy to see why the notion of 'correct pronunciation' is questionable as a learning target as soon as we realize how inextricably bound up it is with social and individual identity.

(Seidlhofer, 2001: 57–8)

Further debate within teacher education programmes is needed on the teaching of pronunciation in novel ways and in the light of current thinking about individual motivation to acquire native-speaker-like command, common core features and intelligibility. As with the features of grammar that may or may not be incorporated into the pedagogic context, the nature of the target of a pronunciation class relates to issues that are interesting in both theoretical and practical terms. There is some evidence that this process is underway. A guest issue of the influential journal *TESOL Quarterly* – read by many practitioners with an interest in research – addressed these issues and in particular the integration of new thinking about accent and pronunciation in relation to classroom applications and uptake by teachers (*TESOL Quarterly*, 30/3, September 2005).

3.3   The evolution of materials to teach speaking

This section looks at published materials on the spoken form taken from different eras in the evolution of language teaching. It provides a commentary that relates them to some of the broader changes in approaches to language teaching that have been seen. The issue underpinning many of the commentaries is that it is significantly easier to teach speaking as if it were isolated from its users, and the greater the flexibility and authenticity of the materials the harder it can be to manage them in a structured syllabus. In addition to questions of norms of grammar or of targets for pronunciation, real speech brings real people into the classroom and with them complex matters of class, gender, race, religion, politics and other culturally sensitive issues.

3.3.1   The trace of audio-lingual and notional-functional approaches

During the 1970s and into the 1980s a focus on structured practice and de-contextualised tasks was the norm in materials produced to develop speaking skills. In these the long shadow of what had been a dominant paradigm in language teaching, the audio-lingual method, could still be seen. Whereas in the research domain at this time communicative approaches were emerging, and the earlier approach had been largely set aside from the early 1960s, commercial materials still showed features of the older approach. Very few exercises to generate 'free' talk or allow students to negotiate meaning between themselves were evident and pattern practice would take place through a highly structured and constrained set of exercises. In addition, as was the norm in the audio-lingual approach, there would be very little description at the meta-level, that is to say, there would be little or no attempt to explain point of language and the focus was to gain automaticity by filling in gaps and repeating patterns. In some materials however the influence of 'functional' approaches to language teaching – those in which a brief context/scenario and a conversational purpose/ function were related to particular forms which speakers might be expected to produce – also made their way into materials produced for teaching speaking.

An example from the late 1970s combining gap-fill with some attention to functional purpose was *Making Polite Noises* by Roger Hargreaves and Mark Fletcher (1979) in which a selection of structures for language functions are introduced which the student is then required to insert into a taped dialogue (see Quote 3.12).

Quote 3.12 Starting and finishing conversations and showing interest

Sorry to interrupt but   is that a…..?
Excuse me,   didn't we meet in…..?
                                      aren't you…..?
                                      I hear you're a…..

Really? Do they? Is she? Mmmm…..
How are you getting on with the…..?
What was the…..like?
What did you think of the…..?
How interesting, but how…..?
Tell me about the…..

Will you excuse me, I'm
afraid I must go and   see if…..
                                   say hello to…..
                                   get on with…..

It's been very interesting talking to you.
I've enjoyed hearing about…..
I'd better go and…..
See you again soon, I hope.

Dialogue 1
A: Fascinating. I didn't know it could be done like that.
B: Oh yes. And I've got more photos upstairs …
C: Really? But I'm afraid we really must be going now. Thank you for a lovely evening.
D: We've enjoyed it too. We're very glad you could come.

Dialogue 2

A: I've been looking at your brooch. It's very unusual. Where did you get it?
B: I got it in Malaysia.
A: Oh did you? How long were you there? By the way I'm John Gooch ...
B: I'm Sylvia Martin. I was out there for three years actually.
A: Really? That must've been a fascinating experience. How did you like the people ...?

A few minutes later

A: Good lord! How strange! Well, it's been very interesting talking to you Sylvia. I must go and have a word with some people over by the door, so will you excuse me a moment? See you later I hope.

Scenario

You:
A: Yes, it's American. My uncle gave it to me.
You:
A: He used to but he's retired now.
You:
A: Just for a short time – when I was a student.
You:
A: It was. Everything was so different.
You:

Situations

1. You are sitting in a café. A friend arrives with two companions and introduces you. After a short time you have to leave. What do you say?
2. You are in a colleague's office. He wants to tell you about his weekend but you are in rather a hurry. What do you say?
3. A friend has started to build a garage in his garden. Show interest.
4. A friend tells you he went to Saltwood Castle on Saturday. Show interest.
5. Your friend has been talking about Saltwood Castle for the last twenty minutes. How do you get away?

(R. Hargreaves and M. Fletcher, *Making Polite Noises*, Third Impression, 1989)

3.3.2 The early influence of the communicative approach

In contrast to the above, many of the pair-work books which grew out of the drive for communicative materials in the ELT classroom during the 1980s and early 1990s focused less on structural input, and more on scenarios to prompt 'natural' dialogue. Through such interactions the learner would be encouraged to build fluency and from which, in theory, insight about structure would be acquired. For example, *Partners 3* by

Michael Lewis (1982) contains a range of ingenious scenarios and prompts for the more advanced learner (see Quote 3.13). However, it is not that far removed from the earlier materials. In particular, it asks the student to carry out their interactions in something of a void or as if the scenarios being presented were culturally universal or neutral (the British pub and drinking being a culturally loaded set of topics that not all students would appreciate or find appropriate).

Quote 3.13 In the pub

1. You are sitting at a table in a pub having a quiet drink on your own.
   You do not know your partner who is sitting opposite you at the same table. As your partner leaves, your drink, which was half-full, is upset all over everywhere.
   Respond naturally when your partner starts.

2. It is early evening. You have been for a drink with your partner whom you know slightly but not very well. You bought the first round and your partner has bought a round too.
   You are killing time because you are meeting a friend (not your partner) to go to the cinema in half an hour or so, so you would rather like another drink. You think your partner is rather a serious sort of person and are fairly sure that when you offer another drink he will say no. If he does, try to persuade him to have one. Insist if necessary!
   You start.

3. Last night you bought a drink for your partner who popped into the pub while you were having a quiet drink.
   It's now lunch time and a very warm day so you have popped in 'for a quick half'. Your partner is standing at the bar with a drink. Unfortunately, one of the reasons your partner is an acquaintance and not a friend is because you think he is rather mean. You're quite sure you have bought more drinks for him than he has for you.
   You start:
      Oh, hello, did you get there on time last night?

4. You are sitting in a pub talking to some friends. You left your (nearly full) drink on the table behind you.
   Respond naturally when your partner starts.

(M. Lewis, *Partners 3: more demanding pair work practices*, Language Teaching Publications, 1982)

Quote 3.14 Arguments and counter-arguments	
Very often, when we have a plan, someone has an objection or a reservation. We then have to think up a counter-argument to try to persuade them.	**Reservation** Yes, but...
In this dialogue the husband is trying to persuade his wife that they need a cottage in the country.	Yes, but don't forget...

Him: Why don't we buy a cottage in the country – somewhere we could go at weekends and for holidays. **(Plan)**

Her: That's a good idea, but don't you think the children will get bored – can't you hear them – not the cottage AGAIN this summer! **(Reservation)**

That would be great, except...

Him: That's probably true, but I think it would be nice for us, and after all, it won't be long before they'll want to go off with their own friends. **(Counter-argument)**

That's a good idea, but...

Work in pairs with these ideas using the phrases for reservations and counter-arguments.

Counter-arguments

1. A: take up skiing
   B: don't have the time or money
   A: it would be fun, good exercise

   Even so,

   Even if that is so,

2. A: buy a flat
   B: can't afford it
   A: cheaper than paying rent

   That may be so, but...

   That's probably true, but...

3. A: fly to Moscow
   B: cheaper to go by train
   A: we'd lose a week of holiday just travelling, plus all the money on food

   Possibly, but...

4. A: buy a new car – the old one's rusty
   B: we haven't finished paying for the old one
   A: the old one's dangerous

5. A: have a party
   B: the neighbours would object
   A: why not invite the neighbours

6. A: your plan
   B: your reservation
   A: your counter-argument

(E. Keller and S. T. Warner, *Conversation Gambits* (*Real English Conversation Practices*), Language Teaching Publications, 1988)

3.3.3   The influence of discourse analytic approaches

At the mid-point between the first two extracts a popular text at higher levels which also balanced structural items and tasks/scenarios/prompts on each page was Keller and Warner's (1988) *Conversation Gambits* (see Quote 3.14). The influence of 1980s UK discourse analysis can be seen in the categorisation of stretches of conversation (First speaker: PLAN, Second speaker: RESERVATION, First speaker: COUNTER-ARGUMENT). As in the previous example, the cultural norms being tapped into would perhaps be questioned by a later readership (for example, middle-class couple with husband persuading wife to do something and taking rhetorical lead throughout).

3.3.4   Examples of task-based syllabus approaches emerging

Everyday Listening and Speaking by Sarah Cunningham and Peter Moor (1992) was less conversationally oriented but combined some useful language work in a variety of contexts at the intermediate level. The book contrasts with the two previous examples and shows a next stage in the evolution of materials in general in that it integrates structural items being built into the tasks themselves (see Quote 3.15). It also reflected the changing currents of teacher training and the flow of ideas from the academic world to the classroom. In these tasks the active participation of the learner is emphasised, speaking and listening skills are integrated and the student is asked to think about choices and solve problems reflecting moves towards the task-based syllabus and learning by doing.

3.3.5   Task-based learning materials for teaching speaking in the context of English for Academic Purposes

Interestingly, in the fields of ESP and EAP the tendency to isolate speaking processes from broader contextual matters has never been as strong as in general language teaching. For example, in Lynch and Anderson's (1992) *Study Speaking* (see Quote 3.16) or Rignall and Furneaux's (1997) *Speaking* in the English for Academic Study Series, speaking skills are embedded in broader functional areas (such as disagreeing) and in turn presented within appropriate real-world contexts and genres (such as the academic seminar). This highlights the advantage of knowing the specific use to which a learner will put a target language in terms of defining the areas to be introduced into a syllabus. While these appropriacy constraints apply across all skill areas, they are more sensitive in the domain of speech.

Quote 3.15 Everyday listening and speaking

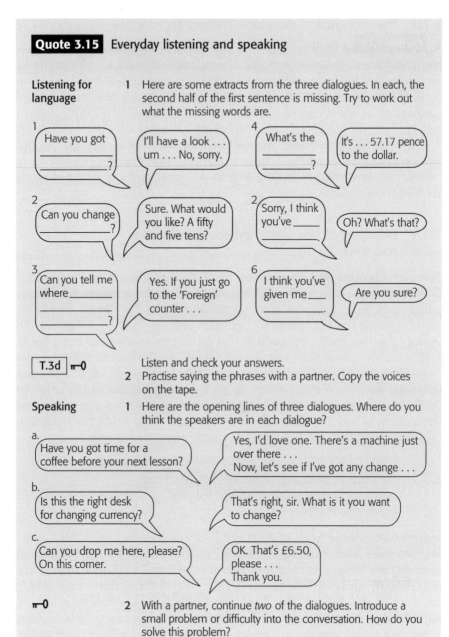

Listening for language

1 Here are some extracts from the three dialogues. In each, the second half of the first sentence is missing. Try to work out what the missing words are.

1
Have you got _____ ?

I'll have a look . . . um . . . No, sorry.

4
What's the _____ ?

It's . . . 57.17 pence to the dollar.

2
Can you change _____ ?

Sure. What would you like? A fifty and five tens?

2
Sorry, I think you've _____ .

Oh? What's that?

3
Can you tell me where _____ ?

Yes. If you just go to the 'Foreign' counter . . .

6
I think you've given me _____ .

Are you sure?

T.3d Listen and check your answers.

2 Practise saying the phrases with a partner. Copy the voices on the tape.

Speaking

1 Here are the opening lines of three dialogues. Where do you think the speakers are in each dialogue?

a.
Have you got time for a coffee before your next lesson?

Yes, I'd love one. There's a machine just over there . . . Now, let's see if I've got any change . . .

b.
Is this the right desk for changing currency?

That's right, sir. What is it you want to change?

c.
Can you drop me here, please? On this corner.

OK. That's £6.50, please . . . Thank you.

2 With a partner, continue *two* of the dialogues. Introduce a small problem or difficulty into the conversation. How do you solve this problem?

(Reproduced by permission of Oxford University Press from *Everyday Listening and Speaking* by Sarah Cunningham and Peter Moor © Oxford University Press, 1992)

Quote 3.16   Seminar skills: questioning

Speakers are expected to allow time at the end of their presentation for questions and discussion. Many people would say that this question-and-answer stage is at least as important as the initial presentation. However, questioning can be a problematic aspect of seminar performance. Often the speaker misunderstands a question (and not only when the questioner is a non-native speaker), because the point is lost in an over-long sentence.

A practical solution is to keep your question short. Don't forget that the presenter may not be sure, when you start to speak, that you are asking a question – you might be wanting to disagree. So you need to make clear:

Example:

a) that it's a question   *'I have a question…*
b) what the topic is   *…about assessment on the course.*
c) what the point is   *What is the overall balance between the examinations and the project work?'*

Discussion point 1
It is sometimes suggested that the speaker should repeat or summarise each question asked from the audience, before beginning to give an answer. Why is this advice given?

Discussion point 2
Questions and answers are not always straightforward. *The speaker* who is asked a question by a listener may understand the question but be unable (or unwilling) to give an answer, in which case, they may *avoid* giving a direct answer. Below are some examples. Can you think of others?

> **Avoiding an answer**
> *(X) is important but it's too complex for us to deal with here.*
> *I think we have to focus on (Y) rather than (X).*
> *It's too early for us to say whether…*
> *We don't have enough evidence to show that…*
> *That's not something I've had time to deal with, but…*

Discussion point 3
The listener may want to say that the answer they have received is inadequate:

> **Following up a question**
> *That's not really what I was asking. My question was about…*
> *Perhaps I didn't make my question clear. In fact what I asked was…*
> *I think you've answered a slightly different question.*
> *I've understood that but what I actually had in mind was…*

These expressions are relatively polite and formal. What words could you omit from each example to make them more direct? What type of words are they?

(T. Lynch and K. Anderson, *Study Speaking*, Cambridge University Press, 1992)

3.4 The current scene in materials to teach speaking

Developments during the latter decades of the twentieth century and more recently continued to reflect the trickle of ideas from the applied linguistics research community. Hand in hand with the greater professionalisation of the ELT community, there has been a tendency for the classroom practitioner to explore corpus- and task-based approaches independently of published materials and/or to engage in their own materials development. However, the small percentage of ELT staff worldwide that has the luxury of time and training in these fields should not be forgotten. The much larger, hard-pressed, often non-native speaker teaching community still requires a range of modern published materials to support the development of speaking skills. However, the needs of such teachers for innovative research informed materials may be being overlooked in modern trends in ELT publishing. There has been some nervousness on the part of the commercial publishers to tackle the issues surrounding teaching spontaneous, richly contextualised speech data. The tendency in the publishing world has been simply to produce a greater variety of coursebooks for different types of learners and levels and retain a strong focus on prompts for discussions, role plays, and tasks to generate interaction (for instance, Gammidge, 2004). Rather than books that draw on research insights about spoken interaction, by far the most prominent development in recent years has been material developed to prepare for the speaking elements of the major international tests of English. A calculation based on web searches suggests that, in terms of materials for speaking/listening, around 50 new titles were produced for the two most widely known tests of English: the International English Language Testing System (IELTS) and the Test of English as a Foreign Language (TOEFL) between 2000 and 2009. This large number was prompted in part by significant changes to the test formats requiring new material to prepare students, but the paucity of commercial teaching material based on, for example, spoken corpora is stark in comparison. In relation to this it is possible to suggest there may be a gap developing between two types of teaching community. The first, larger, is the international community of often non-native speaker teachers who depend on published materials and work in contexts where the use of a textbook is an imperative. The second are those who work in contexts that allow time and training to support the confident teaching of speaking skills by teachers of all backgrounds and languages. In general, the former group will be highly likely to have to teach speaking via standard coursebooks and materials for test preparation such as those shown at the start of the next section.

3.4.1 Two contrasting approaches: teaching to the test and teaching interactive and pragmatic skills

All materials for examination preparation tend to fall into very similar patterns. They introduce the main stages of the test, show typical tasks and model answers, propose hints and strategies for the test-taker, and give plenty of practice materials. They are from a title published to help prepare students for the speaking module of the International English Language Testing System (IELTS) test. Quote 3.17 from Lougheed (2006) shows the typical stages in this process.

Quote 3.17 An examination focused approach

104 SPEAKING MODULE

QUICK STUDY

Overview
There are three parts to the Speaking module, which lasts between 11 and 14 minutes. You will be alone in a room with one examiner who will ask you questions and ask you to talk on certain topics. The interview will be recorded. You will be able to take notes in Part 2 only.

The Speaking modules are the same for both the Academic and the General Training versions of the IELTS. Topics include discussions about you, your family, etc.

Speaking Module

Parts	Time	Tasks
Part 1	4–5 minutes	Introductions Identify self Answer questions
Part 2	3–4 minutes: 1 minute preparation, 1–2 minute speaking, 1 minute follow-up questions	Talk on a topic given on a task card
Part 3	4–5 minutes	Discuss with examiner the issues related to the topic in Part 2

Question Types
There are a variety of questions and prompts the examiner will use to get you to talk during the IELTS Speaking module. You should be familiar with these types.

Part 1 *Wh*-questions
  Yes/No questions

Part 2 Describe and explain
  Wh-questions
  Yes/No questions

Part 3 *Wh*-questions
  Yes/No questions

QUICK STUDY 105

Part 1
PRACTICE A
Write the answer to the examiner's questions for Part 1.

1. What is your name?

2. How do you spell it?

3. Do you have your proof of identification? May I see it?

4. Let's talk about where you live. Can you describe your neighbourhood?

5. What is an advantage of living there?

6. What is a disadvantage of living there?

7. Let's talk about jobs. What kind of job do you have?

8. What is the best thing about your job?

9. Let's talk about free time. What is one activity you enjoy doing in your free time?

10. How did you become interested in this activity?

PRACTICE B
Pretend you are taking the Speaking module. The examiner asked you the questions in Practice A. Now give your answers aloud to the examiner's questions for Part 1.

106 SPEAKING MODULE

Part 2
PRACTICE C
Make notes to answer the questions on the Task Card for Part 2. Try to do this in one minute.

Task Card
   Describe a place that you like to go.

   You should say:
      where the place is
      how you get there
      what it looks like
   and explain why you like the place.

Notes:
   Place   _____

   Location   _____

   Transportation _____

   Appearance   _____

   Why I like it

   _____

   _____

PRACTICE D
Pretend you are taking the Speaking module. The examiner gave you the Task Card in Practice C. Now give your answers out loud to the examiner's questions for Part 2.

PRACTICE E
Write the answers to the examiner's follow-up questions for Part 2.

1. Do you go on your own to this place?
2. Are there similar places you like to go?

PRACTICE F
Pretend you are taking the Speaking module. The examiner asked you the questions in Practice E. Now give your answers out loud to the examiner's questions for Part 2 follow-up.

(Lougheed, 2006: 104–6)

The frame of reference in materials written for test takers is the examination format and rubrics. Any mention of interactive behaviour is linked not to the norms of conversation, but to the best tactic for the candidate in the examination context. For instance, in Kaplan (2009) a useful conversational strategy – buying time by using conversational 'fillers' – is highlighted, but the conversational action is related to the outcome in terms of 'marks for fluency' rather than any wider understanding of pragmatic effects or goals (Quote 3.18). A contrasting approach can be seen in Viney and Viney (1996); see sample material in Quote 3.19.

Quotes 3.18 and 3.19 Examination tactics versus conversational strategies

Strategy 4: You can stall, but not for long.

If you cannot think of an answer to an examiner's question right away, you can say some 'filler' phrases to acknowledge the question and to show the examiner that are [sic] thinking about your answer. However, avoid waiting too long before you speak. This will cause the examiner to give you lower marks for fluency.

Kaplan (2009: 172)

Thinking time

1 Hesitation strategies
Often we want to give ourselves thinking time before we answer a question, especially if we don't understand it! Here are four techniques:

Techniques	Examples	Advantages	Disadvantages
Pretend you haven't heard	*Pardon?* *Sorry?* *Eh?*	Simple – only one word to remember.	Everyone does it.
Repeat the question	*You mean … what is forty-five divided by nine?*	Lots of thinking time.	Can you remember the question?
Use delaying noises	*Well …* *Um …* *Er …*	You can use them several times in the same sentence.	If you use them too often you sound stupid.
Use 'it depends'	*It depends.* *It depends on (the situation).*	You will sound intelligent. (Stroke your chin at the same time.)	You can only use it when there is more than one possible answer.

Don't forget that you can use more than one technique.
Sorry? You want to know what I think about this?
Well... um... it depends, really.
Ask your partner questions. Your partner tries to get thinking time. You can ask:

- mathematical questions *What's five hundred divided by twenty?*
- factual questions *What's the capital of Mongolia?*
- moral questions *Should we kill animals for their fur?*
- personal questions *Do you believe in Father Christmas?*

2 Does this happen to you?
Ask a partner these questions:
- Do you interrupt people to correct their mistakes?
- Do you get angry when other people interrupt you?
- If there is a pause in conversation, do you feel embarrassed?
- Do you say something to fill the pause?
- In a conversation, are you the first person to give an opinion?
- If you get bored by a conversation, do you change the topic, or do you remain quiet?
- Do you like to be the centre of attention (the person everyone is listening to)?
- Do you feel shy in a large group?
- Do you notice when some people in a group are too shy to speak?
- Do you try to include them in the conversation?

(Viney and Viney, 1996: 79)

In this the advantages and disadvantages of using different hesitation forms are weighed up and the conversational impact of them considered. This is followed by tasks to engage the student in reflection on their own conversational style. Of the two approaches, that shown in Quote 3.19 will both motivate and engage the learner in thinking about their own real-world needs in terms of conversation, and will equip them for a wider range of context than a test.

3.5   Bringing the skills together

It is salutary to remember how skilful the competent speaker of any language is, and the multitude of tasks that have to be carried out simultaneously for talk to occur. Quote 3.20 gives a clear reminder of this. Acknowledging the unique complexity of the skill of speaking can help build confidence for teachers and learners in approaches to spoken language. It is not simply a matter of developing accurate mastery of structure and vocabulary combined with effective handling of phonetic detail. The spoken form, unlike the written, calls for the learner to draw on oral/aural, cognitive, processing, pragmatic, inter-personal, cultural and motor skills simultaneously. This dynamic and complex set of achievements comes as naturally to the first language user as the smooth operation of a car to an experienced driver (in contrast to the halting and sometimes humiliating performance of the learner driver). Knowing how to speak is too often presented as a simple translation of linguistic knowledge into the spoken medium. Learners very often have a far higher passive knowledge of the language than the multiply challenging skill of speaking will allow them to deliver under real-time processing pressures. Explaining that the spoken medium brings processing and inter-personal pressures that even first language users will find challenging at times is a good place to begin for any level of learner. Finding the right response to anger in a friend or loved one, defending an idea in an aggressive business meeting or academic seminar, answering an unexpected question in a job interview – none of these are easy in the spoken channel even in a first language under real-time processing constraints.

Quote 3.20 What a good speaker does

Speakers must be able to anticipate and then produce the expected patterns of specific discourse situations. They must also manage discrete elements such as turn-taking, rephrasing, providing feedback or redirecting (Burns and Joyce, 1997)....Other skills and knowledge that instruction might address include the following:

- producing the sounds, stress patterns, rhythmic structure, and intonations of the language;
- using grammar structures accurately;
- assessing characteristics of the target audience, including shared knowledge or shared points of reference, status and power relations of participants, interest levels, or differences in perspectives;
- selecting vocabulary that is understandable and appropriate for the audience, the topic being discussed, and the setting in which the speech act occurs;
- applying strategies to enhance comprehensibility, such as emphasizing key words, rephrasing or checking for listener comprehension;
- using gestures or body language; and
- paying attention to the success of the interaction and adjusting components of speech such as vocabulary, rate of speech, and complexity of grammar structures to maximize listener comprehension and involvement (Brown, 1994).

(Florez, 1999: 2)

Summary

This chapter has looked at the issue of authentic speech, and what model can be used for spoken grammar and for pronunciation. It also addressed the central questions of how far it is possible to teach 'real' speech, the influence of context on speaker choices, and what our expectations are when we teach fluency and pronunciation. Underlying each of these issues is the core question of how much we really know about the spoken form of any target language and how slow the processes are by which research into the spoken form reaches the classroom. The conservative and some-times assessment-driven approach of the larger commercial publishing houses in relation to uptake of innovation in ELT materials for speaking was also discussed.

Further reading

Dat, B. (2003). Materials for developing speaking skills. In B. Tomlinson (ed.), *Developing Materials for Language Teaching*. London: Continuum, pp. 375–393. A good overview article on the issues of materials development for speaking.

Folse, K. S. (2006). *The Art of Teaching Speaking*. Mahwah, NJ: Lawrence Erlbaum. An individual and accessible title that includes case studies and narratives by teachers in different contexts.

Nation, I. S. P. and Newton, J. (2008). *Teaching EFL/ESL Listening and Speaking*. London: Routledge. An interesting volume since it unashamedly draws on very traditional methods (such as drilling and structured dialogues) and sidesteps the issue of 'real' speech and the target or model by giving primary attention to how to foster meaningful interaction in the classroom.

Thornbury, S. and Slade, D. (2006). *Conversation: from description to pedagogy*. New York: Cambridge University Press. More mainstream than either of the two immediately above and drawing on the insights of conversation and discourse analysis.

Usó-Juan, E. and Martínez-Flor, A. (eds) (2006). *Current Trends in the Development and Teaching of the Four Language Skills*. Berlin: Mouton de Gruyter. The sections on speaking are helpful to contextualise approaches to teaching speaking and how materials are used in a variety of contexts.

Chapter 4

Issues in assessing speaking

This chapter will...

- discuss the key issues underlying the assessment of speaking;
- describe and compare the speaking components of internationally recognised tests of spoken English;
- discuss the question of how far oral skills lend themselves to existing test paradigms and whether this is a problem.

4.1 Introduction

> **Quote 4.1** No two listeners hear the same message
>
> The spoken performances of the test takers must be rated in some way. It is almost axiomatic that, because language use is a multicomponential phenomenon, requiring interlocutors to negotiate meanings, no two listeners hear the same message. This aspect of language use is a source of bias in test scores. It leads language test developers to severely limit which features of a performance they require raters to attend to in making their ratings. They hope that, if raters focus attention only on pronunciation, grammar, fluency and comprehensibility, for example, the many other features of the discourse will not influence them. There is mounting evidence that this is a vain hope.
>
> (Douglas, 1997: 22)

The development of the assessment of speaking has gone hand in hand with the emergence of language testing as a recognised sub-field of applied linguistics. Attitudes to oral assessment have been shaped by the changing currents of research paradigms in this field and in linguistics more generally. Early developments in language testing were strongly linked to governmental, colonial, and military requirements for effective language teaching and testing, particularly during the Second World War. This strongly practical focus meant that language assessment practices and theory tended to develop outside the discipline of linguistics and it is only over the last 30 years or so, since the early 1980s, that the somewhat isolated research in assessment has joined up with wider work in the discipline. This tendency has meant that the meta-language of testing can be somewhat off-putting for those not trained in the field and the need for convincingly objective measures can make the process seem very distant from the more humanistic discourse of the classroom. However, given the powerful influence of assessment on teaching it is useful to become familiar with the basic terminology and concepts.

> **Quote 4.2** The difficulty of oral testing
>
> Why have oral tests generally received little attention? Many books have been written about language testing. They follow the changing fashions of language teaching, but they usually make the same basic assumptions about the nature of language testing. Generally, little space is devoted to oral testing compared to testing the other skills. This is partly because of the difficulty of treating oral tests in the same way as other more conventional tests.
>
> (Underhill, 1987: 3)

As is suggested by Quote 4.2 from the late 1980s, the focus on oral assessment *per se* was quite slow to emerge. This was for several reasons, some of which are still influencing the way that oral testing is viewed and carried out. During the 1970s and 1980s a primary concern for those engaged in professional test development echoed the tendency which had gained prominence in the middle decades of the twentieth century in linguistics generally – a strong interest in generalising away from particular instances of discourse to uncover more universal aspects of language. Whereas in linguistic theory this took the form of complex and sometimes arcane accounts of the structure of, for example, universal grammar, in the field of language testing this tendency to generalise/abstract emerged as a strong psychometric orientation in, for example, the work of John Oller (see for instance Oller (1983) for a summary of his thinking as developed during the 1970s). This aimed to distil the complexities of language into 'facets' that could be captured by simple formats such as multiple-choice tests. Psychometric measures and techniques to capture a stable indication of performance across tests and domains remain accepted and influential in current testing circles. Many scholars are, however, challenging the ethical and social effects of tests that are designed for large-scale delivery and at the same time have a powerful effect on life chances and on the priorities of the language classroom (see also Concept 4.5: High stakes testing).

In ways that parallel the influence felt on textbooks and materials development for the skill of speaking (Chapter 3), language testing is influenced to an extent by the interests of the major commercial publishers and the international organisations that research and deliver dominant, high-stakes (see Concept 4.5), and well-known tests of English such as IELTS (International English Language Testing System) and TOEFL (Test of English as a Foreign Language). These tests are hugely influential. They are run by substantial, commercial, international organisations that also provide significant contributions to the research arena in terms of deliverables and monographs on the work underpinning their tests. They fund independent research into their provision through competitive bids and tenders. Less positive, perhaps, is the powerful effect these major high-stakes tests have on what happens in classrooms as teachers 'teach to the test' and the spoken performance that is most highly valued becomes the output that scores highly in the test. Liz Hamp-Lyons's work on 'wash-back' (the effects a test has on the teaching given to candidates) and the culture that this promotes is relevant here. (See Hamp-Lyons (1997) and Hamp-Lyons (2007) for the development of these ideas.) In addition, the ethics of assessment generally and the power relations between test takers and designers, and the influence of testing in society have been questioned (see for instance McNamara (2001), Shohamy (2001), Bachman (2005)).

Within the scholarly community more generally, the debate about oral assessment has gathered pace since the 1990s and in the early years of the twenty-first century has become particularly affected by the growing understanding of the differences between spoken and written language (see in particular Biber *et al.* (2004) for a large-scale project on spoken versus written language in the context of test development research). There has also been a considerable and successful programme of research into how to assess speakers of a variety of backgrounds, cultures and gender (O'Sullivan, 2000; Lumley and O'Sullivan, 2005), and the English as a lingua franca and Critical Discourse Analysis and the World Englishes movements have all played a role (see below for further discussion in relation to models of language in assessment frameworks).

It is against the background factors outlined above about the history and current trends in assessment that any discussion of testing speaking has to take place. As in other fields of applied linguistics, there remains to this day a tension between the early, very practical goals and the later, more professionalised and research-oriented directions of language teaching, research, and testing. Assessment of spoken language asks difficult questions – both practical and ethical – of test developers, and places particular demands on the research community. Considerations to be taken into account in relation to testing speaking are summarised in Concept 4.1. Even the individual classroom practitioner attempting to create a small local speaking test for a particular group of learners will be influenced by similar issues to those outlined in the rest of this chapter once he or she starts to reflect in detail on the questions of what they want their students to achieve, what they regard as stronger or weaker performance, and how to evaluate these criteria consistently and fairly across several speakers.

Concept 4.1   Domains of speaking in relation to assessment

In his 2004 chapter on developing a principled approach to the complexities of teaching and testing speaking, Dan Douglas outlines eight aspects that the learner needs to be aware of in any communicative activities, including testing:

Setting	Tone
Participants	Language
Purpose	Norms of interaction
Topical content	Genre

He argues for far greater and more detailed understanding of the impact of these areas on spoken language than have previously been the case and for the learner to be given a much richer set of contextual information before they try to produce spoken language. For instance in terms of setting he does not completely disallow the idea that in addition to normal written and pictorial prompts other sensory input might be made available to set the scene, such as smells. He sees the impact of the contextual variables above as setting the research agenda for both teaching and testing speaking in future.
(Douglas, 2004: 40–1)

The nature of speech means that the potential for subjectivity, variation in test facets and, due to these two factors, difficulty in maintaining consistency across tests are far higher in the spoken form than the written. As there are so many competing factors which can affect speech production under test conditions – from the health of the candidate to cultural expectations about how a conversation works – test designers have tended to focus on the more quantifiable aspects of language production (for example, number of errors per stretch of speech) and to constrain the test procedure.

A meaningful test of language proficiency rests on how objective, replicable and reliably consistent over time it is for comparative purposes. Speaking challenges all three concepts continuously and it is only by handling it in terms of performance that appears very different from the norms of daily spoken interaction that the examination processes can be carried out. The following sections look at these issues in more detail.

4.2   Why the nature of speaking is a challenge for test designers

4.2.1   Understanding the construct

The first general question asked by any test developer is 'What is the construct that we are aiming to assess?' In lay terms this is simply asking 'What exactly is this a test of?' and our general answer here would be 'Speaking'. However, the diverse nature of speaking makes the definition of the construct challenging. Taken statistically, casual conversation is by far the most prominent genre of speaking. Setting aside formal or prepared public talk such as broadcast material or academic lectures, the vast bulk of spoken discourse is commonplace, situated, informal and as infinitely varied as the participants and their particular concerns at the time of talking. Through such discourse shared understanding of given and new information emerges; relationships, opinions and social identity are formed; and the performative and creative aspects of talk such as jokes, stories and word-play are carried out. However, as the second half of this chapter will show, 'everyday conversation' is clearly not the construct dealt with by the major tests of speaking, and the creative and affective aspects of talk do not appear in the criteria for internationally benchmarked tests of spoken language.

Speaking is also carried out under severe processing constraints in which deleting and editing are impossible and planning difficult. A key skill for the speaker, therefore, is the ability to handle the pressures of speech production well and to maintain flow of ideas and/or self-repair as needed. Unless a stretch of talk can be completely memorised (a skill some test takers try to master for their high-stakes language tests and generally fail) it must be created at the time of utterance by the speaker and will rarely – even when speech acts such as quoting the speech of oneself or others – be identical to what has been uttered before. As the analysis of descriptors and criteria later in this chapter shows, under test conditions the smooth and syntactically complete utterance will be valued more highly than the hesitant self-repair or choppy reformulation. Until oral assessment criteria value skilful handling of self-repair the pressure is on candidates to not produce these natural features in their test performance.

> ### Quote 4.3 The state of knowledge about conversation
>
> ... [O]ne of the central characteristics of naturally occurring conversation ... is that language users are largely unaware of how conversation is typically structured and managed. When asked to articulate conversational practices, native-speaker pronouncements are often at odds with what speakers actually do (Wolfson, 1989). Much of how everyday conversation works is so deceptively familiar that people studying and testing language often overlook fundamental characteristics of conversation.
>
> (Johnson and Tyler, 1998: 27)

In naturally occurring spontaneous speech interlocutors do not focus on the mechanics of their interaction but on the ideas/emotions/information being conveyed. The nature of language testing means that a strong focus tends to be put on the actual samples of language used: their range, variety, complexity, or accuracy in relation to pre-decided criteria. This is a cause of some tension between test criteria and natural oral production. To give an example, many native speakers are extremely hesitant in their speech delivery, particularly when being asked to do something such as form an opinion 'on the hoof'. However, the listener will not attend to the pausing, umming and erring in their interest to hear the answer to their question or the opinion of the speaker. When such discourse is held up for analysis after the event it may appear incoherent and would probably be regarded as dysfluent if produced in a language testing context.

Quote 4.4 shows an example of a university student trying to express an opinion.

> ### Quote 4.4 Articulate or inarticulate?
>
> The plan was always ... [=*pause*]. The plan was never to let go but to er assimilate em the Africans into er sort of wider France [inaudible] or whatever was to er assimilate the Africans into a larger France, never to sort of ... like Britain. The plan was, I mean they saw an end to the road, they never said they would hold on to it.
>
> (Carter and McCarthy, 1997: 137)

This (male) student had already given a presentation on the topic of 'Does France need Africa as much as Africa needs France?' in a politics seminar and had therefore had time to think about the central concepts and opinions he held. However, set against oral proficiency criteria which value the ability to produce a smooth, literate, polished utterance this native speaker of English would not fare particularly well.

Whether carried out via an external observer/rater, an interactive examiner, or self-assessment test, performance is held up against a set of beliefs about 'better' or 'worse' or 'more effective' or 'weaker' language use. Crucial in this area therefore is the state of knowledge (and beliefs or preconceptions) about speech and how this relates to a fundamental question in assessing speaking and defining the construct: what is authentic speech like in a variety of contexts and what is regarded as good or appropriate speech in these contexts? As noted above, spontaneous interactive speech will be full of hesitations, false starts and grammatical inaccuracies, have a limited vocabulary, tend towards repetition and be structured around short thought units or quasi-clauses based on the constraints of breath and of spoken language processing. However, it would take a considerable change in preconceptions about language proficiency for, for example, single word answers to be regarded as 'good'. The notion of range, structural complexity and quantity equating to valuable output is deeply embedded in the thinking of language test developers and much attention is given to, for example, 'designing tasks that elicit spoken language of the type and quantity that will allow meaningful inferences to be drawn from scores to the learners' ability on the construct the test is designed to measure' (Fulcher, 2003). See also Quote 4.5. While it is not unreasonable to want the candidate to speak as fully as possible to allow the measurement of their performance, there are contexts in which simple, single word, or fragmented utterances are not only more natural but better. The sophisticated interactive skill of 'listenership' or showing readiness to take up the opportunity to speak is often realised via monosyllabic utterances, for example.

Quote 4.5 Preconceptions about speech

Conversation with friends calls for common, simple, familiar vocabulary. When students in my third year undergraduate/junior level 'Introduction to Language Studies' course at the University of Washington first listen in depth to an excerpt of dinner table conversation involving four native speaker adults, their first impressions often include descriptions of the native speakers as uneducated, based, in part, on their simple, unremarkable vocabulary usage.

This impression also applies to native speaker fluency. For novice conversation analyses, the amount of repair, hesitation, and lack of smoothness in normal native speaker conversation comes as something of a shock. Traditional definitions of fluency – reflected in rating scales designed to assess non-native speaker speech such as the Test of Spoken English – include phrases such as 'smoothness of speech', 'effortlessness', and 'speech exhibiting automaticity'... Typical native speaker speech in conversation is often lacking in these qualities.

(Riggenbach, 1998: 63–64)

So far, we have looked at the construct (i.e. the model towards which assessment is oriented) in terms of the norms of spoken interaction and speech processing features. However, a further strand of debate relates to the norms of speech in a different sense: whose language represents the standards for assessment?

Quote 4.6 **Testing criteria and changing attitudes to spoken language**

It's worth recalling that English language proficiency tests once looked and sounded very different from the way they are today; they reflected a standard usage known as 'Queen's English' and a manner of speaking known as 'Received Pronunciation' (RP). As the case of ELTS/IELTS shows, there is good reason to assume that over time other English varieties will take their place alongside the traditional NS Englishes in international as well as local tests. Over the next 10 or 20 years, emerging Englishes – including EIL – may well grow in status and take on a role as pedagogic and assessment models for English learners.

(Taylor, 2006: 59)

Quote 4.6 from Taylor (2006) is from a rebuttal of a paper suggesting that the major test developers will be unable to cope with the growth of English as a dominant lingua franca (Jenkins, 2006). It introduces us to a further key question relating to what the model or target is, or should be, in relation to assessing speaking. If a language exists mainly in the world in the form of a spoken variant or set of variants very different from those of native speakers, why is the norm of most assessment still taken to be the output of a much smaller community of native speakers? The answers given are generally twofold: first, as suggested by Taylor above, the test paradigms do shift, slowly, to recognise change in the use of language in the world with an inevitable time lag allowing for carefully thought-through change to occur. The second, more theoretical, answer is that the spoken form has never been as homogeneous as the written and test designers have to create a model that, to their mind, reflects their understanding of the construct. However, there is a third position that could be pursued in future research in this area. This asks the extent to which the norms of native speakers are actually the basis of any of the major tests currently available and suggests on the basis of authentic data and test criteria they are not, and never have been. Indeed, as I have been arguing in this chapter the construct is precisely not authentic spoken interaction between speakers, native or otherwise. Clearly as the lingua franca debates continue, it will be important to tease out aspects of the construct that have always been under-represented in test design (for instance ability to handle dysfluency or repair) and allow society in general to continue to influence what it regards as the norms of educated speech in a variety of contexts. Exciting work will be needed to bridge the gaps between our emerging state of knowledge of the norms of speech – in both senses used here – and what it is realistically possible to assess fairly and consistently.

4.2.2   Formats and interactions

A further influential aspect of oral assessment is the way in which candidate and examiner interact. Concept 4.2 summarises the main formats that are generally used in assessing speaking.

Concept 4.2   **Test formats and task types**

Speaking examinations take many different forms. These vary from non-interactive tasks responding to a pre-recorded, written or visual prompt (as for instance in the internet-based TOEFL speaking test) to one-to-one interactive talk between examiner and candidate (as in the IELTS speaking test) to two-party (or more) discussions between candidates rated by a non-participating examiner. The University of Cambridge ESOL general English certificate examinations (often referred to as 'main suite' examinations) have several different task types in one speaking test in which two examiners and two candidates participate in a variety of interactions.

The examiner and candidate participating in oral discourse under test conditions are in an atypical relationship in terms of everyday speaking, in several ways. A key skill in spoken language production involves understanding listener needs and adapting speech in the light of this. For instance, speakers using the same geographical dialect and from a similar social background will use distinctive forms and lexical items with people they feel close to in terms of social identity. The same speakers may, in different circumstances, monitor and adjust their way of speaking if, for example, they are speaking to someone of their own generation but from a different location or language background. They may adjust their talk again if they speak to someone much older than themselves who speaks their local dialect. A fine-grained and well-judged adjustment of talk is the mark of a proficient speaker and cannot be evaluated without reference to the recipient (see also Quotes 4.7 to 4.10). Some test formats allow interaction between two or more test takers. There is clearly no benefit to them to accommodate to one another to the point where the examiner does not understand them. However, the nature of informal talk is that it is often difficult for the 'outsider' to understand. Under examination conditions, inevitably, speakers are speaking for the examiner, not for their interlocutor.

Quotes 4.7 and 4.8 Speakers adjust to speakers

Because oral communication involves the negotiation of meaning between two or more persons, it is always related to the context in which it occurs. Speaking means negotiating intended meanings and adjusting one's speech to produce the desired effect on the listener.

(O'Malley and Valdez Pierce, 1996: 59)

Based on this instance, it is evident to us that a group oral discussion task of this kind has the potential to provide opportunities for students to demonstrate not only their linguistic competence, but also their interactional abilities to relate to each other in spoken interaction, for example, to initiate, expand, or close a topic, provided authentic conditions for communication are established, in particular topic engagement.

(Gan *et al.*, 2009: 17)

Whether a candidate is asked to interact with an examiner or with another student, the interactive nature of speech and the level of personal involvement which even formal speaking will lead to mean that it is extremely hard to eliminate the effects of one speaker on another. This is in part because good oral communication is founded on one speaker actually having an effect on another, and on the reactions and responses that take place between interlocutors. Quote 4.7 captures the problem of assessing interactive talk and Quote 4.8 suggests that work in conversation analysis may be providing a way forward.

Quote 4.9 The issue of test conditions and interactivity

It is important to recognize that a test imposes certain constraints on the character of the interactions that are created in the assessment and thus on the validity of generalizations from performances on the test to performance in ordinary interactions outside the test. Success in spoken interaction is determined by (a) the nature of the tasks that the interaction requires and the roles in that interaction; (b) the conditions under which the participants are required to perform; and (c) the resources the individual brings to the interaction.

(Butler *et al.*, 2000: 2)

Quote 4.10 Fulcher on the issues of pairing test takers

First is the issue of who is paired with whom. Should the two test takers be familiar with each other, or does it matter if they are strangers?

- Does it matter if their first language is not the same?
- Should they be at roughly the same stage of learning the second language, or can they be at different stages?
- If the age, race, social class or profession of the two test takers is different, would it make a difference to how they would interact?
- What is the effect of personality differences between the test takers?
- Should test takers be paired if one is extrovert and the other introvert, for example?

Secondly, in the paired format there is an interlocutor and an 'observer' whose only task is to rate the two test takers.

- What is the impact of this role on the test takers?
- The interlocutor also rates the two candidates, although he or she also participates in the interaction. Does this enhance the validity of the rating process?
- How do the raters assign grades to each of the test takers separately when, given whatever differences there may be in all the candidate variables listed above, one may be supporting another, one may not be providing the other with an opportunity to show how well he can 'negotiate' or take turns?

Thirdly, what is the role of the interlocutor in cases where the two test takers are incapable (as a pair) of undertaking the task?

- How much should the interlocutor intervene?
- What is the effect on discourse and scores if 'significant intervention' is required, or if one (probably the stronger) test taker gets more talking time than the other? ...

Fourthly, in a 15-minute interview with four tasks that have to be explained by the interlocutor, is the speaking time for each of the test takers enough to elicit a ratable sample of speech?

Fifthly, does the test format result in a reduction or increase in test-taking anxiety, depending once again on the various combinations of 'pair types' that are possible?

(Fulcher, 2003: 187–8)

The more constrained the response types and interactive context the more neutral and objective the test process would appear to be and therefore the lower the effects of participant on participant and examiner on candidate. An extreme version of this is the physical separation of the candidate and the examiner and the use of a recorded sample of speech as the basis of the test. The advantage of this approach is that the aural and visual stimuli remain rigorously the same for all test takers and, given the impersonality of the test procedure, differences due to inter-personal factors will be minimised. Thus, the comparability of candidate responses is higher than in interactions that are more natural. However, the question we return to here is whether the response to such inauthentic stimuli can be regarded as 'authentic speech'. This approach would not claim to be capturing interactive facets such as those in Riggenbach's outline of discourse competence (see Quote 4.11).

Quote 4.11   A breakdown of discourse competence

Some of the skills that display a learner's discourse and strategic competence in conversation are listed below. These skills, micro both in the sense of relative length and functional scale, are necessary elements in coherent, fluid turn-taking (discourse competence) and in successful negotiation of meaning in the case of potential communication breakdown (strategic competence).

Conversation micro skills

the ability to claim turns of talk

the ability to maintain turns of talk, once claimed

the ability to yield turns of talk

the ability to backchannel

the ability to self-repair

the ability to ensure comprehension on the part of the listener (e.g. comprehension checks such as Does that make sense? Are you with me?
Get it?)

the ability to initiate repair when there is a potential breakdown (e.g. clarification requests)

the ability to employ compensatory strategies (e.g. avoidance of structures
or vocabulary beyond the learner's proficiency, word coinage, circumlocution, and even shifting topics or asking questions that stimulate the other
interlocutor to share the responsibility for maintaining the conversation
flow).

(Riggenbach, 1998: 57)

The counter-argument to criticisms of highly constrained oral test conditions is that a correlation exists between test performance and genuine
speaking skills. That is to say, although there is an almost inevitable
mismatch between the test criteria and conditions and naturally occurring
speech (see Quote 4.12) the test may still give an accurate indication of
speaking ability. A number of TOEFL research papers have been produced
which suggest this to be the case. For instance Sarwark *et al.* (1995) found
that the oral performance in a class of teaching assistants correlated well
with their performance in the SPEAK test (an easily administered test that
can be given at an institution via a 'kit' of tapes and answer key and does
not require trained examiners on site). These questions of oral performance
in and outside constrained test conditions remain a productive area for
further research (see Section 4.2.4).

Quote 4.12 **A summary of the problem of natural spoken discourse
under test conditions**

Speaking is . . . the most difficult language skill to assess reliably. A person's
speaking ability is usually judged during a face to face interaction, in real time,
between an interlocutor and a candidate. The assessor has to make instanta-
neous judgments about a range of aspects of what is being said as it is being
said. This means that the assessment might depend not only upon what
particular features of speech (e.g. pronunciation, accuracy, fluency) the interlocutor pays attention to at any time, but upon a host of other factors such as
the language level, gender and status of the interlocutor, his or her familiarity
to the candidate, and the personal characteristics of the interlocutor and the
candidate.

(Series editors' preface to Luoma, 2004: ix–x)

4.2.3   Genres and skills

Concept 4.3   Field-specific tests and/or assessing genres of speaking

Field-specific oral tests relate to testing speech in specific contexts and, in a sense, are tests of speech genres. Some professional contexts require very specific oral language use (for example, air traffic control; doctor–patient encounters) and tests can be constructed which are designed to assess the test taker's ability to communicate in relation to typical language of these target genres. The term 'field-specific' is an example of the particular terminology that assessment research has developed and this is a well-established concept in the literature of assessment – more so, it could be said, than more general work on speech genres.

Field-specific testing is often regarded as superior to general proficiency testing as it is possible to examine the use, context and variety of language (for example subject specialist or technical vocabulary) more clearly and in some depth when designing the test.

A wider issue is that of genres of speaking, a concept that has been less tied to the development of oral testing in general. This is possibly because the term 'speech genre' is somewhat under-defined and emerges in several distinct domains in language theory. It is associated with the work of Mikhail Bakhtin (1986) on utterance, dialogue and texts, with the work of Michael Halliday on register and genre, and in corpus studies where the potential for large corpora has allowed some analysis of language variation and spoken genres.

A further issue in oral assessment relates to the question of what speech genres, if any, are being tested, and of 'field-specific' or specific purpose tests versus general tests. Both these issues are discussed in greater detail in Dan Douglas's book *Assessing Languages for Specific Purposes* (Douglas, 2000). In the case of speech genres, there is some evidence from the field of corpus linguistics to suggest that the language choices made by speakers are strongly influenced by the genre of talk in which they are engaged. For example, the densely informative (and therefore noun-phrase packed) monologue of a seminar presentation versus the less densely structured conversational content which takes place during 'language-in-action' or service encounters. Webber (2005) constructed a corpus of medical conference presentations and noted the surprising prevalence of interactive features in what might have been predicted to be a formal monologue genre. Using such insights within a field-specific test of medical oral discourse in a range of genres is one way for speaking assessment to provide a more fine-grained and relevant set of criteria (for example the Occupational English Test (OET) developed in Australia for health professionals) than are generally available in the generic tests of speaking.

However, much more work is needed if the oral test designer is to be able to construct test conditions in which realistic speech genres can be produced; and if test criteria are to be matched more closely to real speech data. In addition, the extensive retraining of raters would also be essential. As noted above, in terms of a general test of informal spoken English, it takes a change of mindset to realise that hesitancy, short clauses (or even single word turns), ellipsis, repetitions, self-repair and simple or inexplicit vocabulary may be the essence of excellent speech production in certain conversational genres. In contrast, long turns, explicit phrasing and densely structured talk may be found in a spoken genre such as narrative. This is why the issue of speech genres, context and purpose of talk needs to be taken into account in relation to a full discussion of 'authentic' oral testing (see also Quote 4.13).

Quote 4.13 The role and influence of test methods

While it is generally recognized that [specification of the task or test domain] involves the specification of the ability domain, what is often ignored is that examining content relevance also requires the specification of the test method facets.

(Bachman, 1990: 244)

Another issue in the testing of oral skills is the degree to which it is possible to isolate speech from other skills in test design. This is known as the distinction between integrated versus discrete skills testing. The question arises in all language testing, for example, the degree to which reading ability influences performance in a written test; however, the matter is particularly critical in relation to the testing of oral/aural skills.

Quote 4.14 and 4.15 The issue of integrated or discrete testing of speaking skills

At present, however, it seems to me that listening and speaking are theoretically and practically very difficult to separate. I recommend that serious consideration be given to integrating them, both methodologically and psychometrically. That is, I believe we should consider an oral/aural skills test, where the test taker uses his or her communicative language ability to produce and comprehend meanings in a variety of tasks and receives a single score reflecting the performance.

(Douglas, 1997: 25–26)

In terms of tasks, different types of tasks are associated with different types of input stimuli (e.g. a lecture, a reading passage, a stand-alone prompt) in the new speaking assessment. Thus, one intriguing research issue is whether examinees' performance on one task would be very similar to their performance on other tasks designed to measure a common construct of interest (i.e. speaking proficiency). Potentially, each of these task types might be tapping a somewhat distinct aspect of speaking and – if the speaking scores are based on a set of these heterogeneous task types – the reliability of the composite scores would be negatively impacted (or the impact of other skills may be confounded with speaking scores). In that respect, it is very important to examine the generalizability of speaking scores across tasks and task types in evaluating and validating a new speaking measure.

(Lee, 2006: 132)

The two extracts shown as Quotes 4.13 and 4.14 are separated by nearly ten years. They give a sense of the continued difficulties, both practical and theoretical, of teasing out the influence of one skill on another in language test design. This has led many to conclude that an individual test for each skill is desirable. However, a more challenging view in terms of the testing of oral-aural communication is that it is only our present, very 'literate', conceptualisation of language that brings us to the position where we consider it feasible to test discrete language skills in any meaningful sense (see also Hughes (2004)). The presence of the individually produced written text, such as the exam essay, which persists through time as a discrete object for analysis by assessors, encourages us to believe that all aspects of language can be tested in this assessment-friendly way. It would be refreshing and radical (and possibly fruitful) to regard the testing of fixed, decontextualised 'product' as not the best model for all four language skills. Furthermore, it is increasingly clear that dynamic and inter-personal skills such as speaking and listening need to be assessed by criteria that incorporate and score interactive and prosodic competencies, in detail. Such criteria would not be constrained and defined by the norms of the written mode and would reflect essential aspects of the spoken mode. There is considerable room for a research agenda that addresses these ideas and for further scholarly work relating field-specific testing to genres, language output and tasks.

4.2.4 Linking performance within the test to performance outside the test

Knowledgeable designers, deliverers and users of tests of speaking and their scores would agree that there is no single test that can claim to be

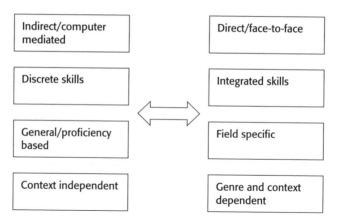

Figure 4.1   End points of a continuum of oral test types

comprehensive and wholly predictive of speaking ability in a range of contexts beyond a test score achieved on a particular day. The desire for objective, neutral, decontextualised and acultural testing is somewhat at odds with the nature of the spoken form when its distinctive properties are taken fully into consideration. At its most extreme, this view would imply that direct testing of speaking is not possible. There is, however, a huge amount of very valuable assessment of speaking that is undertaken together with considerable efforts by the creators of the major international tests to explain the usefulness and validity of their particular approach and to remain as convincing as possible in terms of ability accurately to test the construct 'speaking'.

Figure 4.1 attempts to summarise some of the various 'cultures' of test types by presenting them as a continuum with contrasting features at either end and on which different forms of assessment could be positioned. For instance, although they are not mutually exclusive, face-to-face tests will tend to favour and make possible the more 'holistic' approaches of integrated skills testing and conversely an online test will tend to promote the more atomised approach to skills assessment.

Concept 4.4   **Direct and indirect testing**

The terms 'direct' and 'indirect' are used in two ways in relation to assessment. One use relates to oral test formats and simply indicates whether there is a present interlocutor ('direct' speaking tests) or not ('indirect'). The second use is also of interest in relation to the discussion of the complexities of spoken assessment, but should not be confused with it. Within testing and assessment theory a direct test is one that claims a strong relationship between candidate performance under test conditions and the aspect being tested. In contrast, an indirect test will take the performance as indicative of, but not the same as, the type of language being tested. This is a very fundamental question in debates about test design and evaluation. It questions the correlation between language produced in the test and the extent to which you can extrapolate from it. In particular those who incline towards paradigms in which performance is tested indirectly (in the sense relating to theory rather than implementation) will be happy to argue that candidate performance in a one-to-one, asymmetric, formal and non-spontaneous context will provide enough evidence of speaking ability to infer communicative level in very different contexts.

4.3   A comparison of contrasting test paradigms for oral assessment in three high-stakes tests

Concept 4.5   High-stakes testing

'High-stakes testing' is a term used to describe any test that has a major influence on the life of the test taker. While it could be argued that any test has an effect on the person taking it, significant barriers are placed before those who fail some tests, and are raised for those who pass them. Examples of these kinds of tests outside language learning would be passing a certificate to practise law or medicine or at an earlier stage a test in a school context that permits a student to progress to higher examinations, or limits their subsequent subject choices in some way.

By their nature, these tests draw a line between groups of people and the opportunities and constraints of each group are defined by the outcome of the test. This is what makes them 'high stakes'. Some language tests are particularly significant in the lives of those who take them. Since 2004, the United Kingdom has had tests of English as a Second or Other Language (ESOL) for foreign nationals who want to settle in the country. The university systems in all Anglophone countries, and a growing number where English is the medium of instruction for higher education, require evidence of English language ability for entry to a desired programme of study. Both these are examples of high-stakes testing in the realm of language learning. When the stakes are high the pressure on the assessment system is also significant. A small, local test provided in a class by a teacher to show relative progress of students may have little impact on their lives, but passing or failing one of these high-stakes tests will potentially change life chances considerably. This means that providers of such tests are somewhat conservative and cautious in their development. Their clients – whether individual or organisational – are very demanding. The conservative tendency in high-stakes testing has particular effects in relation to testing speaking – a form which is by its nature dynamic, inter-personal, context dependent, and fast changing.

The final sections of the chapter examine three contrasting tests of speaking to see what they reveal about the attitudes to the spoken form that underpin them and where they lie in relation to the testing chltures presented in Figure 4.1. It is interesting to note that it is in the arena of large-scale, high-stakes testing that the tensions between the norms of everyday talk and the needs of test developers are most evident. As Quote 4.16 suggests, there may be challenges to the underlying paradigms of these large-scale tests. Testing informed by the ethos of a 'culture of learning' that, as Hamp-Lyons suggests, would require attention to 'the individual, the changing, the changeable' (2007: 487) resonates with much that, I have been arguing, defines the spoken form.

Quote 4.16 Cultures of testing versus cultures of learning

The contexts and needs of classrooms and teachers are not the same as those of large scale testing. The large scale needs to discriminate, to separate, to categorize and label. It seeks the general, the common, the group identifier, the scaleable, the replicable, the predictable, the consistent and the characteristic. The teacher, the classroom, seeks the special, the individual, the changing, the changeable, the surprising, the subtle, the textured, and the unique. Neither is better but they are different. We have only started to realize the extent of the difference in recent years.

(Hamp-Lyons, 2007: 487)

4.3.1 Internet-based Teaching English as a Foreign Language (TOEFL) speaking test

Figure 4.2 shows the underlying relationships of the various aspects of speaking as conceived by the test development community in the highly influential Educational Testing Service ('ETS' see *www.ets.org*). This is the organisation that researches, develops and delivers the widely used and influential TOEFL test. At the time of writing the test was accepted by over 7,300 institutions and organisations worldwide as a recognised benchmark for English proficiency and is used in 'high stakes' testing such as university entrance and immigration.

On the continuum of testing paradigms outlined in Figure 4.1, this test is firmly situated close to the left-hand end. The rhetoric surrounding it is allied to 'hard' science ('complexity', 'accuracy', 'precision'), objective measures that attempt to remove the individual and context from the picture (the test taker is not an element included in the overview), and an atomisation of the skill of speaking into discrete levels and aspects that can

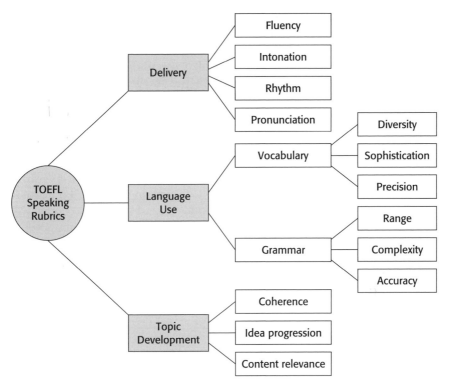

Figure 4.2   Categories underlying the speaking construct (from Xi *et al.*, 2008: 29)

be measured. Both the diagram itself and the descriptive language used to accompany it present a clear and stable framework on which to build the assessment of test takers' performances. Each level of the skill is regarded as built up of sub-components and facets and although the diagram itself does not represent the aspects hierarchically it is clear that they are regarded as 'nested', with 'Topic Development' being conceptualised as a higher order skill that builds on 'Language Use' which is in turn broken down into the specifics of 'Delivery'. This diagrammatic representation of the construct in terms of unique and clearly defined areas is itself closely connected to the ethos of the ETS test development approach in general.

The format and the rating process in the speaking element of the 'iBT/ New Generation TOEFL' (hereafter 'TOEFL' or 'TOEFL speaking') are deliberately impersonal. This is in order to sidestep a number of the issues concerning bias that can affect face-to-face assessments of speaking. Six tasks in TOEFL are designed to test different aspects of speaking. Two ('independent') call on the candidate to express an opinion on a familiar topic and four others ('integrated') ask the candidate to speak in response to written or spoken material that provides input. The rubrics for the independent and integrated tasks are based on the same underlying facets although the detail of the criteria differs slightly. Due to the nature of the test format, all responses are in recorded monologue. In essence, the difference between the independent and the integrated tasks relates to the source of the material, the topic being generated from students' own experience in the case of the independent tasks; and from external prompts and visual stimuli in the integrated tasks. There is also a strong connection between ability to perform the task and the ability of the candidate to process and synthesise the written and heard material.

The performance of the candidate in the six different speaking tasks is captured as audio files and sent, separately, for scoring by the ETS team of trained raters via an online scoring network. At least three scorers rate the same candidate (i.e. the different tasks are not all sent to the same scorer) and some tasks are rated by two scorers to check reliability. The TOEFL speaking scoring consists of four levels and each level is broken down into the facets represented in Figure 4.1 (Delivery, Language Use and Topic Development). These scores of between zero (no response or off topic) and four in each of the six tasks are then averaged and translated into a single score of between 0 and 30. The descriptive criteria for the highest and lowest scores are shown in Table 4.1. Overall, the key assumption underpinning the test is that the highly impersonal test delivery minimises rater bias and that the ability to perform in these contexts can be extrapolated to other, more interactive and informal, domains. In all six tasks the essential criteria for the four levels regard 'high' scoring performance as smooth, error free and coherent and 'low' scoring performance as lacking in content, hesitant, repetitive, and containing basic ideas. As has been noted earlier in this chapter, care is needed when categorising these features as in the native speaker they are consistent with many forms of casual talk or talk when attempting to form and express an opinion under pressure, and further discussion of this point can be found later in this chapter.

In sharp contrast to the somewhat 'dehumanised' ethos of the approach to testing speaking that underpins the test, the TOEFL developers and ETS have an extremely user-friendly interface with their public. The chatty, communicative style and detailed tactical advice (see for instance Quote 4.17) gives the test taker a strong sense of systematic progress towards achieving the test result they need, and that individual, isolated efforts will bring results. Since test performance is judged by scorers within the same frames of reference, this is good advice in terms of test outcomes. In addition, given the massive pressure on the English language teaching and testing community brought about by the continued growth of the use of the language in international business, commerce and scholarship, having a means for individuals to practise by themselves and take tests that are well researched and rigorously benchmarked is a benefit for all

Table 4.1   **Based on iBT/Next Generation TOEFL Test ETS Independent Speaking Rubrics (ETS 2008).**

Score	General description	Delivery	Language Use	Topic Development
4 (Descriptions of highest level performance)	The response fulfils the demands of the task, with at most minor lapses in completeness. It is highly intelligible and exhibits sustained, coherent discourse.	Generally well-paced flow (fluid expression). Speech is clear. It may include minor lapses, or minor difficulties with pronunciation or intonation patterns, which do not affect overall intelligibility.	The response demonstrates effective use of grammar and vocabulary. It exhibits a fairly high degree of automaticity with good control of basic and complex structures (as appropriate). Some minor (or systematic) errors are noticeable but do not obscure meaning.	Response is sustained and sufficient to the task. It is generally well developed and coherent; relationships between ideas are clear (or clear progression of ideas).
1 (Descriptions of lowest levels of achievement above 'no attempt' or 'response unrelated to the topic' which gain 0)	The response is very limited in content and/or coherence or is only minimally connected to the task, or speech is largely unintelligible.	Consistent pronunciation, stress, and intonation difficulties cause considerable listener effort; delivery is choppy, fragmented or telegraphic; frequent pauses and hesitations.	Range and control of grammar and vocabulary severely limit (or prevent) expression of ideas and connections among ideas. Some low-level responses may rely heavily on practised or formulaic expressions.	Limited relevant content is expressed. The response generally lacks substance beyond expression of very basic ideas. Speaker may be unable to sustain speech to complete the task and may rely heavily on repetition of the prompt.

concerned. Less easy to predict is the ability of the test taker to translate these scores that reflect largely non-dialogic skills into a more dynamic and unpredictable context such as a seminar or fast-flowing conversation.

Quote 4.17   The TOEFL® iBT: improving your speaking skills

Advice for Speaking

Skill: Speaking about Familiar Topics

Performance Level: Fair

Score Range: 18–25

Look for opportunities to speak to native speakers of English. Interaction with others will help improve your speaking ability.

Find a speaking partner. Set aside time each week to practice speaking to each other in English.

If you can't find a native English speaker, find a friend who wants to practice speaking English and promise to speak only English for a certain period of time.

Practice speaking for a limited time on different topics without a lot of preparation. Time your responses to questions.

Make a list of some general speaking topics –

people/persons you admire
places you enjoy visiting
things you enjoy doing

Think of a specific example for each topic (a parent, the market, reading books) and talk about each for one minute.

Select one of the topics above and write down 3 verbs and 3 adjectives relevant to the topic. Try to use the words as you speak.

Concentrate on speaking clearly with good pronunciation and intonation. Speak with confidence and open your mouth more widely than you normally do.

It is difficult to understand you if you speak word by word. Try to speak in 'thought groups.'

Take a reading passage and mark the thought groups first. Then read it aloud paying close attention to these groups of words and ideas.

Get a book on tape or get a transcript from a news report, interview, or play.

Listen to the performance and mark the pauses, stress, and intonation on the transcript.

Then read the transcript and try to imitate the pauses, stress, and intonation patterns.

Use books that come with audio recordings to study pronunciation, stress, and intonation in English.

(ETS, 2009)

4.3.2 The IELTS speaking test

In contrast to the iBT TOEFL speaking test, the IELTS speaking test is conducted with a face-to-face interlocutor/examiner. It is a test with a stronger focus on holistic communicative skills than on the hierarchy of separate language facets underlying the TOEFL test. Each test lasts 10 to 15 minutes and is recorded. A three-stage interview takes place beginning with general and familiar topics for around 4 minutes. A card with a prompt is presented to the candidate in the second stage of the test and they are asked to prepare what they are going to say (around 1 minute) and then speak in monologue for 2 minutes about the given topic. A transition takes place to part 3 in which a dialogue at a more abstract level is developed between the examiner and the candidate out of the material in part 2.

In 2001, the revised version of the IELTS speaking test (described above) was launched on the basis of work begun around 1998. Some changes were made to the format but more significantly in terms of analysis of the approach to the underlying construct, whereas the previous version scored candidates on a single set of criteria the new version analysed performance in terms of four distinct areas: Fluency and coherence; Lexical resource; Grammatical range and accuracy, Pronunciation. The full (public versions) of the descriptors are available at the IELTS website and a search on a major internet search engine with the keywords 'IELTS speaking band descriptors' will take the reader to current versions of these for a given year. An overview of the test criteria is given in Quote 4.18, and Table 4.2 provides the top and bottom analytic descriptors of the rating scale: 2 and 9 (0 being used if a candidate fails to attend the interview and the score of 1 being used for 'no communication possible' or 'no ratable language').

What is noticeable in both these influential tests is that despite the greater focus on interactive skills in the IELTS speaking test and the apparently stronger focus on proficiency in the more depersonalised TOEFL speaking there are large areas of agreement over what are perceived as positive and negative aspects of the construct 'speaking'. Tables 4.3 and 4.4 summarise these features. The combined criteria from these two major international tests of speaking allow us to consider the way in which a test and tasks are designed together, and the attitude to 'good speaking' that the scoring system reveals. There is a clear set of assumptions revealed by the criteria in relation to what is being tested (the construct as defined by the developer), what is thought to be appropriate material to base a test result on (the output of the candidate in a task designed by the developer) and the categories of positive and negative features that will ultimately be used by each examiner in a standardised test (the descriptors designed to discriminate between levels). The major international tests of speaking

Table 4.2 Top and bottom criteria for the IELTS speaking test (IELTS 2009)

Band	Fluency and coherence	Lexical resource	Grammatical range and accuracy	Pronunciation
9	• Speaks fluently with only rare repetition or self-correction; any hesitation is content-related rather than to find words or grammar • Speaks coherently with fully appropriate cohesive features • Develops topics fully and appropriately	• Uses vocabulary with full flexibility and precision in all topics • Uses idiomatic language naturally and accurately	• Uses a full range of structures naturally and appropriately • Produces consistently accurate structures apart from 'slips' characteristic of native speaker speech	• Uses a full range of pronunciation features with precision and subtlety • Sustains flexible use of features throughout • Is effortless to understand
3	• Speaks with long pauses • Has limited ability to link simple sentences • Gives only simple responses and is frequently unable to convey basic message	• Uses simple vocabulary to convey personal information • Has insufficient vocabulary for less familiar topics	• Attempts basic sentence forms but with limited success, or relies on apparently memorised utterances • Makes numerous errors except in memorised expressions	• Shows some of the features of band 2 and some, but not all, of the positive features of band 4 • [for example: 'attempts to control features but lapses are frequent']
2 (1 = 'no communication possible'/'no ratable language', 0 = 'does not attend')	• Pauses lengthily before most words • Little communication possible	• Only produces isolated words or memorised utterances	• Cannot produce basic sentence forms	• Speech is often unintelligible

Quote 4.18 Marking and assessment

Fluency and Coherence
This criterion refers to the ability to talk with normal levels of continuity, rate and effort and to link ideas and language together to form coherent, connected speech. The key indicators of fluency are speech rate and speech continuity. The key indicators of coherence are logical sequencing of sentences, clear marking of stages in a discussion, narration or argument, and the use of cohesive devices (e.g. connectors, pronouns and conjunctions) within and between sentences.

Lexical Resource
This criterion refers to the range of vocabulary the candidate can use and the precision with which meanings and attitudes can be expressed. The key indicators are the variety of words used, the adequacy and appropriacy of the words used and the ability to circumlocute (get round a vocabulary gap by using other words) with or without noticeable hesitation.

Grammatical Range and Accuracy
This criterion refers to the range and the accurate and appropriate use of the candidate's grammatical resource. The key indicators of grammatical range are the length and complexity of the spoken sentences, the appropriate use of subordinate clauses, and the range of sentence structures, especially to move elements around for information focus. The key indicators of grammatical accuracy are the number of grammatical errors in a given amount of speech and the communicative effect of error.

Pronunciation
This criterion refers to the ability to produce comprehensible speech to fulfil the Speaking test requirements. The key indicators will be the amount of strain caused to the listener, the amount of the speech which is unintelligible and the noticeability of L1 influence.

(IELTS, 2007: 12)

tasks are, therefore, generally designed to allow the candidate to perform at an imagined 'peak' that represents the highest level of achievement in the test, and be given an opportunity to produce language with the features that are highly thought of in the test framework. It is notable that, as Tables 4.3 and 4.4 show, high-value performance will generally mean a full, coherent, lexically dense 'long turn'. Aspects of normal spoken conversational discourse such as simplicity, hesitation, self-correction, incompleteness, and using pre-packaged, sometimes repetitive 'chunks' of language are regarded, conversely (again see Tables 4.3 and 4.4), as undesirable; while fluency, precision, accuracy, control, range and completeness are valued highly. As noted above, the ability to produce discourse that is free of

Table 4.3   Summary of perceived negative features in oral discourse represented in iBT Speaking and IELTS speaking (tick represents mention of feature in descriptors covering weaker performance)

FEATURE	IELTS	TOEFL
Repetition	✓	✓
Hesitation	✓	✓
Unintelligible	✓	✓
Pauses (long)	✓	
Pauses (frequent)		✓
Self-correction	✓	
'Finding words'	✓	
'Slips'	✓	
Lapses (in completeness)		✓
Lapses (pronunciation)		✓
Difficulties (pronunciation)		✓
Isolated words	✓	
Choppy		✓
Fragmented		✓
Telegraphic		✓
Memorised	✓	
Practised		✓
Formulaic		✓
Limited (content)		✓
Limited (grammar and vocabulary)		✓
Basic (sentence forms)	✓	
Basic (ideas)		✓
Insufficient (vocabulary)	✓	
Simple (linking)	✓	
Simple (sentences)	✓	
Simple (responses)	✓	
Simple (vocabulary)	✓	
Personal (information)	✓	

the former and distinguished by the latter is not easy for anyone. It is not the norm for native speaker speech in a spontaneous interactive setting.

A research topic of relevance here could be to investigate what, exactly, examiners perceive as self-correcting moments in the candidate's performance and compare these with moments in the candidate's discourse elsewhere or with native speaker performance in this area. It may show that an apparently negative feature is quite the reverse in spontaneous talk and is in fact a neutral or positive feature. A language learner who can handle this in a target language while maintaining the flow of ideas without allowing it to 'get in the way' is to be seen as a high achiever. Similar reconsideration

Table 4.4   Summary of perceived positive features in oral discourse represented in iBT Speaking and IELTS speaking (tick represents mention of feature in descriptors covering stronger performance)

FEATURE	IELTS	TOEFL
Fluent	✓	✓
Effortless to understand	✓	
Intelligible	✓	✓
Fluid		✓
Well paced		✓
Clear (production)		✓
Automatic		✓
Coherent	✓	✓
Cohesive (devices/features)	✓	
Full (topic)	✓	
Full (range of structures)	✓	
Full (range of pronunciation features)	✓	
Complete		✓
Relevant (content)		✓
Precise (vocabulary)	✓	
Idiomatic	✓	
Accurate (vocabulary and idiom)	✓	
Accurate (structures)	✓	
Controlled (structures)		✓
Sustained/consistent	✓	✓

of aspects of normal talk such as discourse that has low lexical range or is repetitious would be fruitful, as in many contexts a listener-friendly speaker will be at their most effective when keeping the language clear, simple and repeating the message.

4.3.3   UK Border Agency Knowledge of Language and Life assessments

In 2005, the UK government began applying new criteria to foreign nationals seeking to settle in the country. This took the form of a Knowledge of Language and Life in the UK test (KOL test) one function of which, as the name suggests, is to provide evidence of some competence in English language. Applicants need to show that they have reached Entry Level 3 in the UK National Qualifications Framework (equivalent to Common European Framework B1). One of the ways that applicants wishing to settle in Britain can show this level of competence is by taking and passing the KOL test. This test is a hybrid between an assessment of knowledge and of language. The criteria for the assessment are not designed directly for the KOL test but are taken from/link to the UK national literacy curriculum that includes this level. The criteria from this are summarised in Quote 4.19.

Quote 4.19

Sc/E3.1: speak clearly to be heard and understood using appropriate clarity, speed and phrasing

    a) use stress, intonation and pronunciation to be understood and to make meaning clear
    b) articulate the sounds of English to make meaning clear

Sc/E3.2: use formal language and register when appropriate

    a) use formal language and register when appropriate

Sc/E3.3: make requests and ask questions to obtain information in familiar and unfamiliar contexts

    a) make requests
    b) ask questions to obtain personal or factual information
    c) ask for directions, instructions or explanation
    d) ask for descriptions of people, places and things

Sc/E3.4: express clearly statements of fact and give short explanations, accounts and descriptions

    a) express clearly statements of fact
    b) give personal information
    c) give an account/narrate events in the past
    d) give an explanation
    e) give directions and instructions
    f) give a short description and make comparisons

(DIUS, 2009, from *http://www.dcsf.gov.uk/curriculum_esol/tree/speaking/ speaktocommunicate/e3/*, reproduced under the terms of the Click-Use Licence)

The KOL test consists of 24 multiple choice format questions based on general knowledge of British life and culture. Taking and passing it assumes language knowledge at Entry Level 3. Those who do not reach this level can continue to retake the KOL test until they pass, or can opt to take an 'ESOL with citizenship materials' qualification through an approved body. To meet the immigration criteria they need to progress by one level from the level they come into the programme at, for example achieve Entry Level 2 if they were at Entry Level 1 when they joined the programme. Only a small number of accreditation bodies provide qualifications that meet the ESOL programme criteria for the alternative to KOL testing, one of these being Cambridge ESOL 'Skills for Life' examinations. Immigration-related testing will tend to focus on the communicative and functional aspects of spoken language and the assessment criteria of these ESOL examinations, like all those in the Cambridge ESOL suite, are built around the Common European Framework of Reference (CEFR) for language assessment.

Our final test therefore contrasts with both the IELTS speaking and the iBT speaking in the format of delivery and provides an example of multi-candidate format. The ESOL 'Skills for Life' tests also contrast with the two major tests already described in not only this higher focus on interaction but on the benchmarking to the CEFR's 'Can do' statements and incorporating a strand of criteria assessing interactive ability. Quote 4.20 provides the overview of the first three levels in terms of what the candidate is expected to achieve. The final level of these three equates to the E3 minimum speaking ability required by the UK Border and Immigration service for citizenship mentioned above.

Quote 4.20 First three levels of speaking and listening, Cambridge ESOL Skills For Life

Speaking test assessment focus
Entry 1
Assessment focus:

  listen and respond to spoken language, including simple narratives, statements, questions and single-step instructions
  speak to communicate basic information, feelings and opinions on familiar topics
  engage in discussion with another person in a familiar situation about familiar topics.

Information on Pass criteria
Functions may include (among others):

  describing
  giving opinions
  giving personal information
  stating (dis)likes and preferences
  commenting
  asking for information or descriptions
  (dis)agreeing
  explaining/giving reasons/justifying

exchanging opinions
deciding
suggesting
selecting.

Entry 2
Assessment focus:

listen and respond to spoken language, including straightforward information, short narratives, explanations and instructions

speak to communicate information, feelings and opinions on familiar topics

engage in discussion with one or more people in a familiar situation, to establish shared understanding about familiar topics.

Information on Pass criteria
In addition to those at Entry 1, functions may include (among others):

comparing
prioritising
planning
persuading.

Entry 3
Assessment focus:

listen and respond to spoken language, including straightforward information and narratives, and follow straightforward explanations and instructions, both face-to-face and on the telephone

speak to communicate information, feelings and opinions on familiar topics, using appropriate formality, both face-to-face and on the telephone

engage in discussion with one or more people in a familiar situation, making relevant points and responding to what others say to reach a shared understanding about familiar topics.

Information on Pass criteria
In addition to those at Entry 1, functions may include (among others):

comparing/making comparative questions
showing contrast/cause/reason/purpose
prioritising
planning
persuading
narrating
asking about past or future events
expressing future certainty/possibility.

(Cambridge ESOL, 2009a)

The format of the ESOL Skills for Life tests of speaking and listening is markedly different from either of the tests described so far. Candidates are assessed in pairs, an interlocutor (member of staff in the testing centre, often a college) and an external assessor provided by the Cambridge team are present and participate in a range of tasks and types of interaction, including both monologue and dialogue. At levels E1–E3, the assessor does not participate but at all levels has the task of scoring the participants on the spot. The nature of the assessment criteria for passing relate to this more holistic and interactive approach based on 'can do' statements. The Cambridge ESOL assessors are trained on sample material at the different levels of the CEF framework (with criteria which are applied across all the Cambridge ESOL/Main Suite tests rather than just the 'Skills for Life' tests which are being discussed here) and then relate these to the performance of the participants. An overview of the E3 level required for immigration purposes is given in Quote 4.21.

Quote 4.21   Overview of CEF level B1/Cambridge ESOL E3

Relates comprehensibly the main points he/she wants to make.
Can keep going comprehensibly, even though pausing for grammatical and lexical planning and repair may be very evident. Can link discrete, simple elements into a connected sequence to give straightforward descriptions on a variety of familiar subjects within his/her field of interest. Reasonably accurate use of main repertoire associated with more predictable situations.

(Cambridge ESOL, 2009b:11)

The up-to-date criteria can be found by means of an internet search ('Cambridge ESOL assessor training' for example) and those current at the time of writing in Cambridge ESOL (2009b: 12). The full criteria include 'interaction' as well as topics more familiar from the previous tests described, 'range', 'accuracy', 'fluency' and 'coherence'. The inclusion of this test of speaking is intended to highlight the fact that no test should be seen outside its context and consideration always needs to be given to the links between purpose, ethos, test design, delivery and marking. In this test, for instance, there are the multi-party tasks and therefore it is appropriate to include interaction in the scoring system. In contrast, the iBT speaking is largely based on monologue and, in that scoring system, the interactive criteria would be superfluous. More slippery is the notion of what the construct 'speaking' is in this close dovetailing of the overall design of a test and the features that are drawn on in scoring the test.

The assessment of language for immigration purposes is an interesting example of what happens when a test of speaking is being used in a very high-stakes context but one that is hard to specify without controversy. The sensitive politics surrounding language requirements and citizenship are brought home by the fact that an applicant to live in the United Kingdom can opt to take the KOL test in Welsh or Gaelic, but the accepted alternative to passing KOL is an ESOL ((*English* as Second or Other Language) with citizenship course. This means that two very different assessment types, one testing reading and cultural knowledge through multiple choice in a minority language, the other testing English language mainly through listening and speaking, are regarded as on a par for immigration purposes. Furthermore, a speaker of one of the languages spoken by a large ethnic minority in the multi-cultural Britain of the twenty-first century may find this offer of a Celtic medium test puzzling. At the time of writing, the lowest estimates of Urdu speakers living as residents in the UK range from 400,000, whereas those for Gaelic were put at just under 60,000 in the 2001 census.

Other countries have more unflinchingly consistent language requirements. Australia, for instance, states that evidence is needed for all four language skills and that the language of the nation is English. Canada requires listening and speaking from all applicants and has requirements that can be met in either English or French. Germany caused huge controversy when it started to apply language and cultural knowledge tests to prospective immigrants in 2005.

The discursive practices in spoken language testing for such high-stakes assessments highlight, and clearly link back to, current concerns about the ethical and social responsibilities of the academic and professional language testing community.

Summary

A number of questions surrounding oral assessment have been raised in this chapter, including three central ones:

- What can we learn about attitudes to speaking from analysing how the assessment community define the construct, and how they go about the practicalities of testing it?
- Are the criteria for assessing speaking more aligned to the norms of writing than of speaking?
- If we had a better understanding of 'good', 'effective' or 'appropriate' speaking in different contexts, could we move towards oral test criteria which are more closely aligned to the micro-skills and structures which create speaking ability?

Similar to the issues raised in Chapter 3 surrounding materials development, the inclusion of real people and real speech contexts, and the dynamic, personal orientation of key aspects of speaking, raise crucial issues for assessment. There is a considerable tension between the dynamic, transient and inter-personal nature of speech and the underlying principles of professional language testing. These questions are interesting starting points for research projects into speaking proficiency. Such research, together with further work on the correlations between test performance and communicative ability outside test conditions, would form a basis for answering the bigger question which is how far it is realistically possible to assess speaking from a perspective other than 'language proficiency'.

Note

The situation reported here, regarding the assessment of language for immigration purposes, changed somewhat in April 2010. The level requirement and test formats remained unchanged, however. For up-to-date information see *www.ukba.homeoffice.gov.uk/settlement*.

Further reading

Bachman, L. and Palmer, A. S. (1996). *Language Assessment in Practice: designing and developing useful language tests*. Oxford: Oxford University Press. A good initial title linking practice and theory.

Butler, F. A., Eignor, D., Jones, S., McNamara, T. and Suomi, B. K. (2000). TOEFL 2000 speaking framework: a working paper. *TOEFL Monograph Series* 20. Princeton, NJ: Educational Testing Service. Further detailed information about the iBT/TOEFL speaking test and the thinking behind it.

Fulcher, G. (2003). *Testing Second Language Speaking*. Harlow: Pearson Education.

Luoma, S. (2004). *Assessing Speaking*. Cambridge: Cambridge University Press. Both Fulcher (2003) and Luoma (2004) are accessible titles dealing with some of the key theoretical issues for assessing speaking, together with practical examples of a wide variety of test formats.

Shohamy, E. (2001). *The Power of Tests: a critical perspective on the uses of language tests*. London: Longman. A readable introduction to the issue of the social consequences of language testing.

Taylor, L. and Falvey, P. (2007). *IELTS Collected Papers: research in speaking and writing assessment*. Cambridge: Cambridge University Press. An example of a research monograph sponsored by Cambridge ESOL.

Chapter 5

Approaches to researching speech

This chapter will . . .

- Introduce qualitative, quantitative and theory-driven approaches to researching speaking;

- consider the effects of researcher stance and research approaches described in a variety of projects;

- present summaries of case studies into various aspects of research that are relevant to broadening our understanding of speech.

5.1 Introduction

Approaches to researching speaking are very eclectic. This reflects the fact that the spoken form touches many aspects of life and spoken language data are seen as relevant to a variety of research domains and research questions. These can range from the qualitative, for example, analysing role-plays using conversation analytical techniques to understand business negotiation in inter-cultural contexts, to the highly quantitative, for instance, a statistical analysis in an experimental setting of how listeners perceive accent. The reasons for choosing one approach over another are perhaps best understood by beginning from the relationship between research topics, data, and the conclusions that can be drawn from these. As noted elsewhere in this book, there is a complex relationship between spoken language and theories of language. Our view of language is strongly shaped by the means we have to collect, describe and then analyse it and this is particularly the case in researching speaking. This chapter examines both quantitative and qualitative approaches to research questions in the domain of speech and discusses the role of speech data in relation to the methods used in each.

The studies described here are presented in terms of three broad (often in reality overlapping) categories. Two – quantitative and qualitative approaches – are clearly oriented towards data, and the third covers work that would not be described by either of these terms and can be thought of as primarily theory- or ideas-led. These terms relate to the overall methodological framework or approach being used for the research and are closely linked to the underlying philosophy of the researcher. They are not by any means mutually exclusive categories but it is helpful to understand that research into speaking, as with any of the language skills, is not carried out from within a single or neutral perspective. The epistemological standpoint of the researcher significantly affects what they consider important and the way in which they approach their investigations.

Concept 5.1   **The influence of epistemological standpoint**

Epistemology is a branch of philosophy that studies knowledge. Terms such as 'epistemological standpoint/perspective/stance' are derived from this discipline for more day-to-day use in academic life. Here, they are used in a looser sense to mean 'where the researcher is coming from'. Obvious examples of differences in epistemology would be between a religious and a non-religious person in relation to accounts of creation, or between someone living before the discovery of the shape of the Earth and the majority of people today. One's standpoint affects beliefs about a topic and what is regarded as valid evidence or proof of what is true. In terms of research this also relates to how you proceed with your investigation. If you believe in the gathering, comparison and analysis of 'hard facts' you will be drawn towards quantitative approaches. If on the other hand you are more convinced by the importance of relationships between people, ideas, and contexts you may be less convinced by the quantitative way of working and want to approach a research topic through detailed, qualitative work. Both approaches are used to investigate speaking.

A small number of academics in applied linguistics engage in work that is neither quantitative nor qualitative but, rather, an attempt to work with ideas in order to consider the theoretical underpinning to a topic. These studies are quite rare, but can be highly influential. The work of Harvey Sacks for example, although he died very young, remains key to any literature review on the topic of conversation analysis. This is because his work involved setting out a theoretical framework (especially with Gail Jefferson and Emmanuel Schegloff) that was coherent, applicable, and convincing.

The overall approach and standpoint of the researcher will shape what they regard as a relevant question and coherent outcome. The scholarly community reads an article or evaluates findings with a certain understanding that the terms of reference are clear both to them and to the researcher. What would be unacceptable in a statistical survey (for example extrapolating from a single individual to all speakers) is perfectly acceptable in a research project that does not orient towards that framework. It is important for the novice researcher approaching an investigation into spoken discourse and carrying out initial literature reviews and searches to be aware of the influential relationship between the assumptions of the researcher and the framework(s) available for research. There is not one best way to investigate a topic; rather a multitude of ways. The approach used needs to have internal consistency and show awareness of any discrepancies between what is regarded as the standard research procedures and assumptions and what is being carried out.

In addition to these groupings (quantitative, qualitative, theory/ideas driven) which apply to all research methods, the approach used affects how speech data are regarded in the process of research. For instance, a researcher might gather speech data to test an idea, model or hypothesis; or they might use spoken examples to challenge pre-existing conclusions; or the investigation may be primarily concerned to put forward a new theoretical model and is merely using speech data to exemplify this. In broad terms these differences between the role of speech in the research process map on to the more quantitatively oriented approach (testing a hypothesis), the qualitative methods that have been gaining some ground since the 1980s (beginning from data to possibly challenge pre-existing models (or the idea of a 'model' itself)), and the rather small number of researchers who engage in trying to construct a theory.

5.2   Quantitative and qualitative approaches towards researching speaking

Quantitative approaches are very prevalent in researching speaking. They have been used to carry out research into the form at all levels, from the way a very specific acoustic feature affects clear speech (Maniwa *et al.*, 2009), to how a medical discourse community shows trust (Kvarnström and Cedersund, 2006). The apparent preponderance of quantitative methods does not mean that there is a necessary affinity between the spoken form and quantitative approaches and, in fact, the situation may simply reflect the balance between the approaches generally found in the discipline of applied linguistics. Research by Benson *et al.* (2009) among others suggests that overall around 20 per cent or less of research in applied linguistics is carried out by qualitative means. Therefore, the likelihood is that spoken language research, like other areas of language, will be carried out in the dominant, quantitative paradigm. Quantitative approaches provide a powerful and a well-tested framework for an investigation by moving from pre-existing questions/hypotheses to the appropriate methods to investigate these – for instance looking at the frequency of a feature in natural data or designing a laboratory-based experiment to elicit speech data and then analyse this. Very often, whatever the method of data gathering, the findings are analysed by means of statistics and these give the researcher the basis for generalising from particular results to something beyond the data in question. *Not* finding what you predicted in this approach is almost as interesting as finding evidence for what you imagined would be the case, and this is part of the strength of the approach.

Quantitative approaches tend to analyse data in terms of pre-existing categories and the researcher then seeks to investigate the nature of these items in the data. For something as dynamic and socially grounded as spoken discourse, this use of pre-determined categories can be unhelpful. The strength of the qualitative paradigm is that it works from the 'inside' of instances of talk towards patterns and regularities and is able to uncover aspects that the investigator may not have imagined existed.

A widely used method among the qualitative approaches to researching speaking is conversation analysis (CA) (see Concept 1.6). This method puts high value on the careful analysis of examples of real (i.e. non-elicited) talk to understand how speakers create meaning and organise their discourse as social action. The CA analyst is interested also in what linguistic resources (syntax, prosody, gaze, laughter, silence, and so on) speakers use to 'do talk' and how these are different in specific varieties of language and discourse contexts. The 'pure' CA approach, therefore, is unique in that it seeks to understand the nature of speech primarily from observation of non-elicited data and through this process gain insights about broader patterns and meaningful regularities appearing in the interaction.

Two contrasting studies dealing with the same linguistic phenomenon can show the differences between quantitative and qualitative approaches to researching speaking. Watanabe *et al.* (2008) and Mushin and Gardner (2009) both deal with the topic of pausing or silence in conversational interaction. The former follows a classic quantitative approach using prediction based on previous work (evidence from corpora that filled pauses precede complex utterances); a hypothesis (that listeners interpret a filled pause as a precursor of a complex utterance of some kind), an experiment designed to test the hypothesis (participants asked to listen to a description of a shape with and without a filled pause preceding it and press a button when they have matched description to shape) and analysis of the time taken to make the match in the different conditions by means of statistics (two-way ANOVA). Their findings supported the idea that a filled pause appears to 'prime' a listener to expect a complex description. Interestingly, when proficient and less proficient language users were compared, the effect was not significant, suggesting a link between proficiency level in the language and understanding the predictive link between the pause and the ensuing material.

Mushin and Gardner (2009) were also interested in understanding more about conversational pauses but in sharp contrast to Watanabe *et al.* (2008) used a conversation analytical approach to probe the topic. In something of a return to CA's ethnographic roots, they investigated Australian Aboriginal talk and began from assumptions found in cross-cultural studies that silence is used differently in Aboriginal and in white Australian talk. Rather than transforming this into a formal research question and hypotheses as the quantitatively oriented academics might, they use it as a jumping-off point for a series of rhetorical questions. These provide the link between previous findings and the current study and explain to the reader what interests them and motivates the study. See Quote 5.1.

Quote 5.1 Using rhetorical questions to show research focus

Such characterisations [that Aboriginal talk tends towards more silence] are presented as evidence of the considerable differences in interactional styles between Australian Aboriginal people and mainstream white Australians. Yet we still have little understanding of how Aboriginal conversation is organised outside of cross-cultural settings. What does it mean to be 'comfortable' with longer silences? What constitutes 'quite lengthy silences'? Are comfortable lengthy silences a feature of an Australian Aboriginal conversation style (i.e. a cultural feature), or are they a reflection of more general interactional features (i.e. a consequence of the local interactional context)?

(Mushin and Gardner, 2009: 2034)

Their analysis was based on extensive samples of speakers of the Garrwa language (four audio recordings and one video recording, the latter lasting for approximately two hours). What is important to note is that while the authors use a quantitative feature (length of pauses) the dominant paradigm is a qualitative, CA, one. They are principally interested in how the speakers orient towards one another and in what emerges as salient for these speakers. In their attempt to understand more about the role of silence in this speech community what concerns them is not, primarily, the length of the silence (although this can be measured and is one useful source of data) but seeing how the speakers handle turns and respond, or do not respond, to one another in a variety of speech contexts. Quote 5.2 gives an example of this type of analysis.

Quote 5.2 An example of a CA interpretation of interactive behaviour

For an Anglo-Australian, the acknowledging response...seems to occur so late as to lack relevance, yet here it is treated as unproblematic. The falling terminal intonation contour suggests perhaps that this Mh hm is proffered as a sequence closing device, rather than as a continuer....This is supported by Daphne's overt termination of the sequence in the very next turn with barriwa, a form which is conventionally used to finish a sequence. This extract is thus a nice example of the ordinariness of long silences in this interaction.

(Mushin and Gardner, 2009: 2047)

The key phrase in Quote 5.2 indicating the qualitative ethos of the paper is 'is treated as'. Unlike the quantitative tendency to map pre-existing constructs to the data and use them to test a hypothesis, the CA tradition assumes that linguistic resources are handled and shaped by participants in the process of communication. Further, they would argue that any analysis must give primacy to the apparent importance of different features as they emerge at the time of interaction.

The distinction between the orientation of a researcher towards quantitative work or otherwise is not, in real-life research, as clear-cut as this introductory outline has been suggesting. The examples chosen here have been selected to give a clear taste of work that falls mainly into one camp or the other in relation to investigating some aspect of speech or of using spoken data to investigate a broader question in linguistics. In addition, the field of applied linguistics appears to be becoming more interdisciplinary as the twenty-first century progresses and some of the boundaries between what have been opposing disciplines are becoming more blurred. For instance, among the second language acquisition (SLA) community there is a growing acknowledgment of the potential benefits of borrowing from disciplines that study actual instances of the spoken form and the situated practices of interaction. Mori (2007) provides a thoughtful overview of the relationships between SLA and CA, for example. The emerging field of interactional linguistics also draws on the detailed analysis of the spoken form, and the boundaries between this and CA are particularly permeable.

5.3 Theory-driven, positional, or ideas-based approaches to researching speaking

All research is about theory and ideas, however in some work the questioning of the theory or the discussion of a possible alternative theory is the *primary* focus of the study. These studies are interesting because they can question how an aspect of speaking is conceptualised and researched and, if they lead to challenging debate about their strengths and weaknesses among other scholars, they are extremely influential. Liberman (1998) 'When theories of speech meet the real world' is an example of what is known as a 'position paper'. This means that the research text in question (they are generally journal articles) encapsulates an academic's stance on a broad topic and they generally deal with an issue that is open to debate. These can be difficult to write as there is a need to understand the ideas being criticised, summarise the relevant arguments and present a coherent alternative to them.

The idea under attack in Liberman (1998) is that the stream of speech is made up of individual segments of sound that are in turn decoded by the brain into comprehensible discourse. The whole article revolves around a single underlying question: why is it so much easier to learn to speak than it is to learn to write? The more subtle point that Liberman is making is the following: if there really is a rough parity between arbitrary symbols that make up writing systems and arbitrary sounds which make up speech, why is speech not as cognitively challenging as writing? Quote 5.3 summarises the question.

Quote 5.3   Liberman's main research question

What did evolution do for speech that gave it such a biological advantage over writing/reading? A theory of speech – or more broadly, language – can avoid that question, as most do, but it cannot avoid implying an answer; and if that answer does not sit comfortably with the priority of speech, then the scientists should consider that they have got hold of the wrong theory.

(Liberman, 1998: 112)

Theoretical research questions very often begin life as 'what if . . . ?' thoughts, and in a 'position paper' these can, and are often intended to, present fundamental challenges to existing paradigms. It should be noted, however, that even the most robust theoretical thinkers are selective in what they present as 'given' and what is challenged. Liberman, for example, does not question his own fundamental assumption that speaking really *is* easier than writing. Nor does he address the issue of the extent and quality of the differences in the two learning processes that are involved. It could be argued, for instance, that it takes several years practising for ten or more hours a day for the child to become a fluent, grammatically standard (within the norms of their own social or family group) speaker.

Nonetheless, by framing a question which sums up his position so completely (the 'why is speaking easier than writing?' question), Liberman is able to develop a coherent line of thought which contrasts the inadequacies of conventional theory and generative phonology in the first half of the paper against the satisfactory nature of his less generally accepted stance presented in the second half (see Research summary).

Research summary: The structure of Liberman's elaboration of his research question regarding the biological advantage of speech over writing

Conventional theories of speech sounds suggest that they are not intrinsically any different from any other sounds in the world, but are the vehicles of meaningful segments of sound roughly equating to visual segments in a writing system.

If there is no biological basis for speech sounds 'how is it that people who cannot spell a single word – lacking even the awareness that words can be spelled – nevertheless find, each time they speak, that producing perfectly spelled phonetic structures is dead easy?'

Conventional theories also suggest that speech perception is a two-stage process in which the primary sounds are translated into phonetic elements by the brain. '. . . [T]he two processes are exactly parallel, requiring the same kind of cognitive step to endow their ordinary auditory and visual percepts with phonetic significance. Why, then, should the one be so much easier and more natural than the other?'

If ease of perception of discrete elements is the key to language, then the oral/aural channel is in fact *less* suitable than the visual/motoric.

We are asked to conclude that language as it evolved merely appropriated sounds to put them to the use of the language system. Existing theory has difficulty answering his initial question: what exactly was it that evolved?

In the rest of the paper Liberman proposes a 'phonetic module' which deals directly with the sounds of speech and which requires no intervening processing or translation of these into any other form. These 'articulatory gestures of the vocal tract' are, he argues, the product of an evolutionary process rather than being standard sounds appropriated for the use of language. In discussions of Liberman's work his position has often been referred to by an acronym 'SiS' (speech is special). A powerfully influential theory frequently has a very elegant basic idea such as this which assists with its understanding and acceptance by people in a range of contexts, whether or not they agree with it.

Liberman's discussion here also shows the way a questioning technique can be used as the basis of both a critical evaluation of a theory, and a framework for presenting that evaluation. By taking a step back from the data a theoretical approach can ask questions at a very universal or general level (some might argue too general and abstract) and provide a clear framework for others to use or to challenge. His work was widely cited, was contentious as soon as it was published, and yet has proved to cast a very long shadow. In the first decade of the twenty-first century debate about the 'Motor theory' of speech remains ongoing and sometimes heated (for example, Fowler (2008)). Liberman's work has also influenced, and is still cited as a key source in, the scholarly 'landscape' in the emerging studies of speech processing using magnetic resonance imaging (Lotto *et al.*, 2008). Outside speech processing, his ideas are regarded as relevant (and often still controversial) in fields as diverse as the study of dyslexia (Uppstad and Tønnessen, 2007, see also Quote 5.4) and the evolution of language (Fitch *et al.*, 2005).

Quote 5.4 The lasting resonance of a theory-driven paper

As a consequence, we have a situation where the phoneme is both rejected and accepted, which naturally only enhances the confusions. The inductive character of theory-building is especially clearly seen in the writings of Alvin and Isabel Liberman (Liberman, 1997, 1999; Liberman *et al.*, 1989), where dogmatic arguments are deployed against features of theoretical positions which are not at all compatible with the authors' own position. While this kind of controversy is of course not unusual in science, the proportion of arguments belonging to the dogmatic category is alarming. These arguments are clearly not sufficient to prove A. M. Liberman's claim about the relationship between spoken and written language. In our view, dogmatic positions should be avoided in order to maintain high standards of empirical science. This can be done by studying behaviour in written and spoken language, without a priori assumptions of causal relationships.

(Uppstad and Tønnessen, 2007: 163)

5.4   Examples of contrasting approaches in researching speaking

This section provides summaries of different approaches to researching speaking, ranging from more examples of 'position' papers, to qualitative work, to technically oriented papers reporting experimental findings. The papers are organised so that the more quantitative papers are grouped together later in the section and the more theory-oriented or qualitative work is presented earlier. The intention is for the reader to gain a sense of the richly diverse approaches that have been taken to the investigation of speech.

5.4.1   How methods and research questions are woven into a position paper: a study of first language acquisition and prosody

A different way of constructing a position paper from our earlier example can be seen in Speer and Ito (2009) 'Prosody in First Language Acquisition – Acquiring Intonation as a Tool to Organise Information in Conversation'. Rather than an adversarial style, the authors present a comprehensive survey of approaches to researching first language acquisition with a particular focus on prosody.

The authors combine the review of previous work with a discussion of the implications of the various approaches. In particular, this article aims to convince the reader that an aspect of spoken language development has been under-researched, to map out the potential for research to fill this gap, and to explain the major problems with previous methods which this new research programme would need to consider if it were undertaken (see also Quote 5.5). The topic the authors are interested in is the relationship between prosody and the development of a very young child's comprehension of the presentation of information and subsequent handling of similar prosodic resources to signal focus on different information as they learn to speak. They suggest that two aspects of prosody could be a source of information 'packaging' and focus drawn on by listeners: grouping of words into 'chunks' or phrases, and intonational prominence. They discuss through a wide-ranging literature review the state of knowledge and the methods used in previous studies in the area and by doing this make the case for the centrality of these questions for the comprehension and production of spoken syntax and for language development in general. As much of the work is with infants of less than 12 months, the methodological challenges are fascinating and provide insights into the relationship between research methods design and wider theoretical issues, especially the care needed in reaching conclusions about the implications of findings made via a particular experimental method.

Quote 5.5   Presenting a position and showing relevance

Recent research on children's acquisition of prosody, or the rhythm and melody in language, demonstrates that young children use prosody in their comprehension and production of utterances to a greater extent than was previously documented. Spoken language, structured by prosodic form, is the primary input on which the mental representations and processes that comprise language use are built. Understanding how children acquire prosody and develop the mapping between prosody and other aspects of language is crucial to any effort to model the role of prosody in the processing system. We focus on two aspects of prosody that have been shown to play a primary role in its use as an organizational device in human languages, prosodic phrasal grouping, and intonational prominence.

(Speer and Ito, 2009: 90)

Comprehension of speech in very young infants has been measured by a variety of standard methods. These include correlations between attention to language phenomena and head-turning in the very young infant; actions carried out in response to visual or oral prompts, or analysis of actual utterances in children as they become able to produce them. However, experiments carried out by these means have to be designed extremely carefully in relation to the research question. This is due to the potential influence of the restricted cognitive development of the child, the difficulty of the task in relation to a child's state of development, and the need to interpret linguistic phenomena often through paralinguistic evidence such as gaze and gesture.

Concept 5.2   **Methodological challenges in investigating the very young infant's understanding of speech**

Evidence for a child's language development begins from a very early age, four months or possibly earlier, as the infant becomes able to show attention and share this with others. The challenge for the applied linguist is how to uncover what is happening in this process and a number of creative research design methods have been used to investigate this. These range from an artificial nipple with an electronic sensor to assumed correlations between gaze or gesture and underlying linguistic functions or structures. In the case of the former method the speed and strength of sucking are linked to renewed interest in the child in the sounds they are hearing and therefore can be used to test what linguistic features are noticed by the child – for instance attention paid to phrases in mother tongue versus non-mother tongue, or phrases pronounced with and without standard intonation boundaries for the mother tongue. Özçalışkan and Goldin-Meadow (2005) provide a particularly convincing account of the relationship between the progress of child language development and the links to gesture. Electro-encephalography and event-related potential ('ERP') methods have also been used, allowing researchers to investigate brain activity in young children in relation to spoken and visual input (for example, Tan and Molfese (2009)). These methods use electrodes placed on the scalp of the child and analyse the correlations between input (for example, video scenes that match or do not match a simple spoken description) and the levels of activity in the brain in response to these events.

Speer and Ito (2009) report a series of studies on the relationship between the development of syntactic and prosodic processing in infants from the late 1980s to the time of writing and note the inconclusive nature of some of these when fine-grained investigations of the relationship are undertaken. They support the idea that the relationship between the processing demands of the tasks and the nature of the child's cognitive development will play a key part and results will be skewed or contradictory if this is not taken into account. For example, they note the difference between studies that have simply indicated a child's preference for phrases that fall into syntactic groups over those that do not and the evidence that would be needed to show the child's ability to understand syntactic relationships. A child, they imply, may hear that appropriate groups of words are being said and what the boundaries are between these, and yet this may not translate into a precise understanding of the relationships between these groupings and the underlying syntax, nor would it be clear from previous work at what age both the comprehension of syntactic information via prosody was evident nor, similarly, how and when the child develops mastery of prosodic–syntactic relations in their own speech. Such issues are at the heart of their position paper and they build on the idea through a summary and critique of work that has attempted to deal with similar questions. They note that the testing of hypotheses regarding syntactic awareness in relation to prosodic cues has generally been carried out by asking children between the ages of around 3 to 7 years to respond to syntactically ambiguous sentences by means of an action. For instance, Snedeker and Trueswell's (2001, 2004) toy-moving experiments in which children heard the sentence 'Tap the frog with the flower' presented in two ways: [Tap] [the frog with the flower] and [Tap the frog] [with the flower] and differentiated by prosody. They go on to give a balanced summary of other similar experiments but point out that task complexity and the experimental setting may undermine the ability to reach firm conclusions about the level of the child's understanding. Different results (better correlation between syntactic cues and actions) were found, they noted, when the child was given the prompt first without the visual excitement of the toys and instruments to manipulate which may have led them to be distracted from the language element under scrutiny (Meroni and Crain, 2003). Speer and Ito suggest that the areas they are promoting for further research (child's understanding of phrasing and information focus in relation to prosody) are critical to developing our understanding of the acquisition of language more generally. They conclude that the programme of research they have been exploring in the rest of the article is well worthwhile, nevertheless: 'As experimental techniques continue to be refined over time, we may continue to find evidence for children's surprisingly sophisticated use of intonation at younger and younger ages' (Speer and Ito, 2009: 106).

Overall, this paper provides a carefully structured case for further research and unites theoretically interesting questions with the practical issues of how to probe them. The methodological challenges of investigating the spoken form are magnified in the context of child language experiments and understanding the implications of these is a good starting point for researchers aiming to deal with this transitory and context-embedded mode.

5.4.2   A position paper on qualitative principles: clause, grammar and interaction

In their paper 'The Clause as the locus of grammar and interaction' (2005), Sandra Thompson and Elizabeth Couper-Kuhlen present a case for the clause as a fundamental linguistic feature towards which speakers orient in interaction. Quote 5.6 provides a summary of their position and approach.

They use the term 'format' to discuss the 'patterns or templates' that speakers use to create their utterances and interact with one another and build a discussion and argument around the significance of this as an important topic for the field of interactional linguistics. The significance of this work may be difficult for those unfamiliar with CA or with interactional linguistics to fully appreciate, but the article provides a tightly argued case building on key types of speaker behaviour – how speakers start a turn, co-construct a turn with others, or add an incremental phrase or utterance to an apparently completed turn (providing a 'turn-unit extension'). The paper is strengthened by its use of cross-linguistic comparisons – Japanese and English – to help make the case that the nature of the clause in a given language constrains and affects the way speakers handle these three types of conversational action. They argue that whereas in English the verb phrase allows relatively early projection of the rest of an utterance (a subject leading to a verb and then the expected additional

---

Quote 5.6 Making the case for a new conceptualisation of spoken clauses

This article draws on work at the interface of grammar and interaction to argue that the clause is a locus of interaction, in the sense that it is one of the most frequent grammatical formats which speakers orient to in projecting what actions are being done by others' utterances and in acting on these projections. Yet the way in which the clause affords grammatical projectability varies significantly from language to language. In fact, it depends on the nature of the clausal grammatical formats which are available as resources in a language: in some languages these allow early projection of the turn unit (as in English), in others they do not (as in Japanese). We focus here on these two languages and show that their variable grammatical projectability has repercussions on the way in which three interactional phenomena – next-turn onset, co-construction, and turn-unit extension – are realized in the respective speech communities. In each case the practices used are precisely the ones which the clausal grammatical formats in the given language promote. The evidence thus suggests that clauses are interactionally warranted, if variably built, formats for social action.

(Thompson and Couper-Kuhlen, 2005: 807)

---

words and phrases linked back to this, for example, direct objects or obligatory phrasal elements), in Japanese the construction remains far more open and clausal elements are less frequently made explicit. Despite this, they argue, speakers in both languages show clear sensitivity to clause boundaries, whether or not elements are fully expressed, in terms of how they handle incoming turns, co-construction, and increments.

Whereas Speer and Ito (2009) are interested in the relationship between experimental methods and what can be concluded about spoken language development, Thompson and Couper-Kuhlen (2005) are working in a very different paradigm. Their methods, those of conversation analysis, are a given and they build their argument – extremely convincingly – based on the internal logic of this approach. Quote 5.7 shows a typical example of how conversational evidence is interpreted and then related to the central topic of the article.

The point to note is that the CA approach does not simply assume that a given linguistic resource/feature equates to a particular interactive function, rather it develops a tentative interpretation of the events in context based on the local context ('. . . exquisitely "well-placed" in the sense that . . .'), and on previous work in the field ('. . . none of the characteristic speech perturbations found to accompany violative incomes are present here' (French and Local, 1983; Schegloff, 1987). A further point to note is

> **Quote 5.7** A typical CA analysis
>
> Ford *et al.* (2002) point out that English increments [words or phrases tagged on after a possible completion point by a speaker] typically involve adverbial constituents. We note that all of these elements – although they can in principle be placed within the clause – are more typically positioned at its edges. This reflects the fact that they are external to the clausal format. And they are frequently overlapped by an incoming next speaker. Here is an example from our data collection:
>
> | (4) | Carsales 5 (Ono and Thompson 1995: 87) |
> |---|---|
> | 1 | G: .. (H) the only thing you can do is be the best you can. |
> | 2 | .. [right]? |
> | 3 | D: [but definitely]. |
>
> In this example, G comes to a point of possible completion at the end of his clause in line 1. It is just at this point that D concurs with *but definitely*, but inadvertently, D's turn unit overlaps with the tag *right* (as shown by the brackets), which G has just appended at the same time to his possibly complete clause in line 1. Yet D's turn is exquisitely 'well-placed' in the sense that it comes just at the end of a clausal format with prosody suggesting completion of a turn. This is reflected in the fact that none of the characteristic speech perturbations found to accompany violative incomes are present here (French and Local 1983, Schegloff 1987).
>
> (Thompson and Couper-Kuhlen, 2005: 820)

that, in keeping with the qualitative paradigm, a multiplicity of pieces of evidence are gathered to make the case for a particular interpretation, rather than a single dominant or authoritative piece of evidence being promoted. In this example it is both the prosodic features of the completing turn (indicating closure), the syntactic features of the turn, the timing of the increment, and the lack of features normally associated with a problematic interruption in the incoming turn that are put together by the authors to infer that the speakers are orienting towards the clause format and positioning turns and increments in relation to something that has salience for both of them. A further significant point related to the lack of a one-to-one relationship between linguistic features and their interpretation out of context is the case made by the authors that the nature of the grammatical formats differs from language to language and significantly affects how speakers handle turn, increment and collaboration. Although the authors do not mention it, the implications for second language teaching and learning are clear and further work on this area would be of great interest.

5.4.3 A qualitative 'privileged insider' approach

An unusual but effective approach to gaining understanding of speech genres is taken by Janne Morton in her paper 'Genre and disciplinary competence: A case study of contextualization in an academic speech genre' (2009). Spoken genres are an under-researched topic and the article is interesting therefore not only in its own right but also as it provides a distinctive method of evaluating them. Two main strands of work on spoken genres have been evident in applied linguistics: one more ethnographically focused and the other more linguistically focused, often with a link to corpus studies and the analysis of the features of language that correlate to particular genres (for instance, Biber, 2006). Morton (2009) is in the former tradition and takes as a given that the student architectural presentation is a distinct genre, and that it is one of the means by which the novice becomes accepted into the professional community. Showing an understanding of the genre and handling information in an appropriate rhetorical framework is as important, if not more important, than the content of the presentation. By performing the spoken genre the students align themselves to their discipline with greater or less success and become socialised into it (see Quote 5.8).

Quote 5.8 Introducing the idea of socialisation into a profession

The process of disciplinary socialisation has been linked to a gradual mastery of a discipline's genres. This article takes a view of genre, as indexing a wide range of often implicit understandings about knowledge creation and use within a discipline, and as fully rhetorical. Within such a framework, novice and near-expert examples of one academic assessment genre – the student architecture presentation – are compared. The face-to-face nature of the academic presentation directs attention to the interpersonal dimension involved in the speaker persuading the audience of the value of their design. The analysis thus focused on identifying the rhetorical strategies that successful students used to accomplish this interpersonal dimension in a manner valued by disciplinary experts. From our data, it seemed that the contextualisation practices that students drew upon to facilitate intended interpretations of their design distinguished successful from less successful presentations. These practices were found to include a narrative style, metaphorical images, and dynamic grammar. Such practices served to animate students' design artefacts and to help take the audience beyond the design artefacts into the world of the students' designs that the artefacts represented.

(Morton, 2009: 1)

In terms of methods, Morton compared presentations in two groups: first and fourth year students and categorised them as successful or not according to an insider perspective – that of their lecturer – without any additional comments, criteria or analysis from the researcher. This approach is in line with an emerging strand of work on assessment in which 'indigenous' criteria (rather than those imposed by an outsider's perspective) are highly valued (see Yu (2007) for a useful summary of literature and a research project investigating this idea). From this then flowed the detailed analysis of three presentations selected as typifying three levels of socialisation towards being a fully fledged architect: (least successful) 'The "Janitor's Tour"'; (more successful) 'Novice emerging architect'; and (most successful) 'Playful near-expert'. The analysis of rhetorical features, linguistic and non-linguistic devices incorporated (images, models, gesture and so on) and cross comparisons between the presentations led the researcher to conclude what aspects of each may be correlated to 'success'. While all students managed to handle and incorporate linguistic and non-linguistic elements into something which could be recognised as the architecture presentation it was, Morton suggests, the capacity to draw on certain 'contextualisation practices' distinguished the successful from the less successful presentations. These included handling embedded narratives and storytelling, shifting narrative voice and stance, humour, and the overall ability to contextualise the designs being presented within a rhetorical narrative. Whereas the novice presenter used images in simple 'technical' manner, the near-expert would use them in a more associative and metaphorical way, for example bringing historical and artistic references into the presentation. Noteworthy also in the successful presentations was what Morton describes as 'dynamic grammar' including active verbs of motion to describe the often static blocks of the architectural structures (for instance, a building being described as 'stretching' or 'folding'). Finally, in terms of what is valued by those judging architecture presentations there appeared to be a requirement for the student to project a sense of an architectural 'self'. This self needed to be involved closely with the ideas being presented rather than to simply describe the work as something objective and distanced from the presenter (an approach which may, in contrast, be highly valued in a different discipline, such as engineering (Darling, 2005).

This in-depth look at three presentations based on insider perspectives provides a good example of the strengths of the qualitative approach. The links between spoken discourse, context of delivery, the handling of linguistic and non-linguistic features, and socialisation practices in a professional community are probed in a multi-faceted analysis that a less 'open' approach would find difficult to achieve.

5.4.4   An experimental and control group approach with pre- and post-testing to investigate fluency improvement

In contrast to the preceding examples, this paper presents work firmly in the quantitative paradigm. Blake's (2009) paper 'Potential of text-based internet chats for improving oral fluency in a second language' asks whether exposure to online chat-room discourse would increase the oral ability of students in offline settings. The topic is clearly of great interest to anyone working on second language oral development as the details of cross-modal effects on language proficiency have rarely been considered. In addition, the paper links ideas about theories of language processing (Levelt's (1989) model of articulation) to pedagogic environments. It also provides a clear example of a very frequently used approach to reaching a conclusion about a research question in a pedagogic setting. This is to establish a hypothesis or hypotheses relating to your research question, decide on a teaching intervention to test this, and then carry out a programme of instruction with testing of the students on the feature(s) before and after the intervention. See also Quote 5.9.

Quote 5.9 Introducing an experimental method

Although a number of studies have reported on the positive effects of Internet chats in the second language classroom, to the best of my knowledge no studies to date have examined the effect of text-based chats on oral fluency development. This exploratory study addressed the above question by examining the oral fluency development of 34 English as a second language learners who participated in the same 6-week course but in separate instructional environments: a text-based Internet chat environment, a traditional face-to-face environment, and a control environment that involved no student inter-action. The study found that the gain scores of participants in the text-based Internet chat environment were significantly higher on the phonation time ratio and mean length of run measures than the gain scores of participants in the face-to-face and control environments (prior to Bonferroni adjustment). Gain scores on the three other measures were not significant. The author discusses these findings in relationship to Levelt's (1989) model of language production and argues that text-based Internet chat environments can be a useful way of building oral fluency by facilitating the automatization of lexical and grammatical knowledge at the formulator level.

(Blake, 2009: 227)

Generally this approach is strengthened and made more methodologically robust by using a control group (given standard instruction), and an experimental group (given different instruction involving the factor under investigation). In this way the results of the pre- and post-test can be interpreted in relation to the effects of the differences in instruction between the control and the experimental group. These interpretations are generally based on statistical analyses which allow the researcher to comment on the level of significance of the results in ways that are meaningful to other researchers. Blake (2009) is a model of this approach. He uses three groups to probe the effects of the medium of instruction on fluency development. This is because he wishes to tease out the differences between a simple online environment with no 'real-time' interaction between students, a face-to-face traditional classroom environment, and an online chat-room context (more technically a context of synchronous computer mediated communication 'SCMC' as opposed to asynchronous interactions online such as bulletin boards or discussion forums). The control group in his experiment was therefore a group who studied online, carried out the listening and vocabulary exercises which formed the syllabus for all groups, but simply received emailed feedback from the tutor rather than experiencing immediate feedback and interaction with other students. The two experimental groups differed in that one participated entirely online with a tutor participating simultaneously with them and the other entirely in a face-to-face environment with classmates and teacher together. The obvious need to select participants at a similar level, and to take into account gender, first language, syllabus content and who was providing the instruction were all carefully planned for in the experiment. The fascinating result that Blake reported was that the group using chat-room as the medium of instruction showed the greatest gains in terms of oral fluency in the post-test. He suggests that whereas the face-to-face environment may seem the most likely one to support the development of oral skills, the dynamics of a class actually lead to very few students having the chance to speak and the norms of turn-taking mean that a learner will assume that when someone else is speaking they will not be called on to speak. In contrast to this, a discussion carried out via instant messaging allows all participants to be actively putting forward their ideas simultaneously. In line with the paradigm he is using, Blake also has a thoughtful section on the limitations of his findings, some questioning of his definition of fluency, and the need for more researchers to investigate the kinds of questions he asked in this project. All in all, the article provides both a model for the novice researcher and a starting point for further work.

5.4.5   Using a single-factor within-participant group experimental design to investigate oral performance

The second example of a quantitative approach to investigating speaking looks at speaker interaction. It asks what effects different kinds of listener response have in terms of 'backchannels' (short, often non-verbal responses

---

Quote 5.10   Introducing different experimental conditions

This article reports on an experimental study that investigated the effect of different conditions of listener backchannels on the fluency of L2 speakers. Participants were 14 non-advanced Japanese learners of English who each performed three oral tasks in three different backchannel conditions: (1) verbal/nonverbal (V/NV), (2) nonverbal-only (NV), and (3) no backchannels (NB). Verbal backchannels included 'mm-hm' and 'uh-huh' while the nonverbal backchannels involved head nodding. Fluency was assessed via five temporal measures. As hypothesized, the results showed that the 14 Japanese participants were, on average, most fluent in the V/NV condition, less fluent in the NV condition and least fluent in the NB condition. The differences obtained in fluency between the V/NV and NB conditions were found to be significant. These results lend support to the 'backchannel output hypothesis' which suggests that backchannels may facilitate the fluency of non-advanced learners of English during oral tasks depending on the nature of backchannel use in their L1 and sociocultural environments.

(Wolf, 2008: 279)

---

by a listener to acknowledge understanding or encourage continuation) on oral production. In the article 'The effects of backchannels on fluency in L2 oral task production' (2008) James Wolf uses a classic research question plus experimental approach to test a hypothesis and reach quantifiable results. The framework he uses is based on the statistical method he will adopt for the analysis. He describes it as a 'single-factor' (i.e. the independent feature being investigated, in this case backchannel) 'within-participant' approach (i.e. the variable is tested on a single group of subjects with similar language background and levels of proficiency). See also Quote 5.10. This means that a researcher takes a single main feature they want to investigate and sees it in action under slightly varied conditions in relation to the same subjects. The differences in output from the subjects can then be interpreted in light of the varied conditions. A multi-factor/factorial approach would look at two (or more) independent features (for instance, backchannel and syllable rate) and a between-group approach would have two clearly defined categories of subjects (for example, Japanese L1 versus Mandarin L1 speakers). The approach is therefore embedded in the quantitative paradigm as its success depends on the ability to clearly delimit and categorise features and groups, to demarcate the conditions you wish to apply to subjects, and to have some reliable and objective form of measurement of the output from the participants.

Wolf's fundamental question is how English backchannel cues might influence Japanese EFL learners' fluency during oral tasks (Wolf, 2008:

281). More specifically he is intrigued by the differences between Japanese and English in terms of typical use of backchannel and hypothesises that for the intermediate EFL student this will have a significant effect on oral fluency. He argues that, whereas there is some evidence that advanced EFL students adopt the backchannel behaviour of the target language, the lower proficiency students will be influenced by what the norms are in their first language. He also assumes that the Japanese learners will show a preference for a combination of verbal and non-verbal backchannel signals (head nod plus short utterance which previous literature suggests is typical for the Japanese context) and will be more fluent under these conditions than when a non-verbal gesture is made or no backchannel is forthcoming. He designs an experiment in which 14 intermediate Japanese speakers tell a narrative from pictures in these three conditions – with the researcher either giving a combination of verbal and non-verbal signals, head nods without verbalisation, or no backchannels. The design is exemplary in that factors such as the effect of the different story type and the repetition of the story task are all factored into the methods.

Wolf (2008) found that his hypotheses were generally supported, with the highest levels of oral fluency being found in the condition when the narrative was told in combination of both verbal and non-verbal backchannel cues. The differences between the other two conditions were less marked but the lowest scores for fluency were found in the condition of zero feedback through backchannel signalling.

A weakness of the paper is the leap to a conclusion that what is being uncovered is a fine-grained relationship between L1 backchannel expectations and L2 behaviour. The evidence presented could equally support the hypothesis that the intermediate learner is encouraged and made less anxious by the quality/quantity of feedback from an interlocutor, not the nature of it in relation to L1 expectations. Nevertheless, the paper provides a carefully thought through experimental approach with findings that can clearly be ascribed to the three conditions under which the learner is producing the oral narratives. As such it provides an interesting starting point for further work on cross-linguistic comparisons of interaction and has clear implications for other domains, for instance oral assessment where speaker to speaker effects may alter performance.

5.4.6   Using a video corpus approach to allow a multi-modal analysis

The final example of how research into speaking has been carried out deals with the emerging field of multi-modal analyses. This field attempts to understand the spoken mode via one or more forms of traditional linguistic analysis (here, for example, number of words, types of turn, and length of utterances) carried out via video-taped interactions that allow speech, gesture, gaze and contextual references to be looked at in combination (see

Quote 5.11 Explaining a multi-modal approach to a research question

Speakers monitor their own speech and, when they discover problems, make repairs. In the proposal examined here, speakers also monitor addressees for understanding and, when necessary, alter their utterances in progress. Addressees cooperate by displaying and signaling their understanding in progress. Pairs of participants were videotaped as a director instructed a builder in assembling 10 Lego models. In one group, directors could see the builders' workspace; in a second, they could not; in a third, they gave instructions by audiotape. Two partners were much slower when directors could not see the builders' workspace, and they made many more errors when the instructions were audiotaped. When their workspace was visible, builders communicated with directors by exhibiting, poising, pointing at, placing, and orienting blocks, and by eye gaze, head nods, and head shakes, all timed with precision. Directors often responded by altering their utterances midcourse, also timed with precision.

(Clark and Krych, 2004: 62)

also Quote 5.11). Clark and Krych (2004) present a quantitatively oriented research project in which they develop a radical view of spoken language. They argue that theoretical frameworks that do not take into account the effects on speakers of the availability of visual signals provide a fundamentally incomplete picture of the mode. Their conclusion can be seen in Quote 5.12.

Quote 5.12 The case for a multi-modal view of language

[Speakers] rely not only on each other's vocal signals, but on each other's gestural signals such as exhibiting, poising, pointing at, and placing physical objects, nodding and shaking heads, and directing eye gaze, and on other mutually visible events. They use the signals to create projective pairs by which they ground what they are currently saying. Dialogues are the artful orchestration of these actions. Models of language use that are limited to only part of this process are necessarily incomplete and, for many purposes, incorrect.

(Clark and Krych, 2004: 79)

They work towards this conclusion through a meticulous study of a small corpus of videotapes of dyads (pairs of speakers) attempting to carry out a simple task together. The aim is to put together ten 'Lego' models correctly and as quickly as possible. In the task, one of the pair is the director and the other the builder. The director can see the prototypes of the models; the builder cannot and relies on the director to guide them in building the models from loose bricks. To investigate the relationship between spoken interactions, gesture and shared visual 'workspace' the authors created two different conditions under which the tasks were carried out. They termed these 'interactive' and 'non-interactive'. In the former both the director and builder could interact verbally and in half the pairs could see the builder's workspace as well as interact verbally (a sub-condition was set up in which faces could be seen or not seen, but the researchers noted that this made no significant difference and they do not report on it further). These were labelled as 'interactive-workspace-hidden' and 'interactive-workspace-visible'. In the non-interactive condition, the director recorded the instructions and was told that the builder would make the model a week later. The builder was then given the task of creating the models from the recorded instructions and was allowed to play the instructions as often as they liked and to rewind and repeat sections of the instructions.

Clark and Krych measured a range of aspects of the task performance including: the average time taken to complete a model under the different conditions; the number of words per task and per turn used by director versus builder in the three conditions; time spent checking that actions had been carried out correctly; percentage of errors made; number of deictic expressions (*here, there, this, these, that, those, like this, like these, like those*), action and gesture types (for example, show a block to the director, position a block tentatively). To show the relationships between speech and actions they create 'action graphs' (see Figure 5.1).

Their results suggested that there were significant differences on all measures between the interactive and the non-interactive conditions and between the interactive conditions where the workspace was visible to both participants and where it was not. For instance, hiding the workspace from the director doubled the average length of time taken to create the model and significantly increased the number of words used by both the director and the builder to carry out the task. The non-interactive conditions (builder responding to instructions on a recording) increased the task time further and hugely increased the errors in the final models (by eight times in final model structures and by fourteen times in terms of misuse of individual blocks (e.g. wrong colour)). At the level of detailed analysis of gesture, efficiency and verbal behaviour, the authors note the increases in deictic references when the workspace is visible. They ascribe the increased efficiency in the interactive-workspace-visible conditions to the delicate interplay between gesture, action, and verbal input, for instance

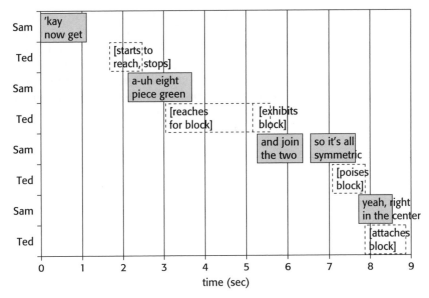

Figure 5.1   Action graph showing gesture timings in relation to spoken directions (from Clark and Krych, 2004: 72)

the builder being able to 'poise' a block in a location to seek assurance that it is both the correct block and correct placement. It is this interplay that the authors see as key in terms of the theoretical stance they are promoting and they provide compelling evidence for the need to see spoken discourse in terms of fundamentally bilateral processes: 'Our findings have general implications for models of speaking. Perhaps the most basic is that speakers and listeners do not use the same processes in dialogue – the primary site for language – as they do when they are alone' (Clark and Krych, 2004: 76).

5.5   New directions

This section ends the chapter with a brief overview of current trends in applied linguistics that will have particular significance for researching speaking. It is an exciting time for those interested in the spoken mode, as major trends appear to be emerging that have reshaped and will continue to reshape the research landscape. The first of these is the breaking down of some of the barriers between different 'camps' in the discipline, the acceptance of a less adversarial, more eclectic, approach to language theory and respect for inter-disciplinarity. As noted, this trend can be seen in the field itself as linkages are made between areas that have traditionally not had much dialogue, for instance conversation analysis and second language acquisition or assessment of second language speaking and critical linguistics. It can also be seen in cross-disciplinary work where the interface between applied linguistic insights into talk is transferred into work in fields as diverse as business studies or health sciences. The approach shown in Burns and Moore (2008) towards gaining a better understanding of accountancy discourse described in Chapter 7 provides an example of this.

A second major trend is that of the effect of the World Englishes (WE), and English as a lingua franca (ELF) movements. In both, the notion of whose spoken English is the norm and the political, pedagogic, and policy-related issues that flow from seeing English as not, primarily, owned by those who speak it as a first language are creating a source of interesting debate. As noted in earlier chapters, the impact of these debates on issues of assessment and language pedagogy will take considerable time to filter through to syllabuses, published materials, classrooms and examination boards. It is a trend with which everyone who teaches or researches speaking will need to engage at some level. Work in the new sub-discipline of 'variational pragmatics' is starting to provide both theoretical underpinning and the stability to allow some of the insights to reach the classroom (Barron, 2005). The research article described in Chapter 7 reporting work by Cheng and Tsui (2009) provides a further indication of work in this area. Work at the interface between corpus linguistics and ELF also appears to be becoming particularly strongly established, and major sources of data showing the norms of interaction between non-native speakers are now available for scholars and teachers to examine and begin to ask what the 'core' of this language is like and whether they wish to teach it (Prodromou, 2008). Two projects in Chapter 7 exemplify this: Lam (forthcoming) which contrasts corpus data and materials for the classroom against the backdrop of Hong Kong English, and Hincks (2010) which looks at the issue of the effects of using English as a lingua franca on the content and speech rate in student presentations.

Finally, the consolidation of technological advances over a twenty-year period and the incorporation of entirely new technologies have had, and will continue to have, a major effect on our understanding of the spoken mode and how to research it. At its most basic level, technology has allowed the development of large corpora of speech and at its more sophisticated one, it has permitted multi-modal work combining speech, transcriptions, digital audio and video material for the researcher to probe. This brings a wealth of data for the researcher and will probably be particularly effective in helping us gain insights about spoken grammar: '. . . it seems reasonable to assume that these are just the early days of "conversational grammar" and that what little we already know about it may well appear as just the humble beginnings in the decades to come' (Rühlemann, 2006: 406). Interactional linguistics has not yet emerged as a discipline that taps into these large corpora but with the increasing capacity to combine audio files with transcriptions it would be fascinating to see this happen. There would be great strength to an approach that could take account of an emergent and collaborative structure and seek parallels in other contexts and languages very speedily.

Two further technological advances may have significant impact on our understanding of spoken language. The first of these is the adoption of brain scanning techniques to the analysis of language processing. This has tended to be mainly at the level of semantic processing but will soon develop into other linguistic domains. The 'hard' evidence that fMRI scanning provides has the potential to answer some of the major theoretical questions in terms of speech production in due course (see p. 38). Straube *et al.* (2010) describes in some detail how this work is carried out and a summary of the article and ideas for further work are given in Chapter 7. The second major development is that of the World Wide Web in the twenty-first century. A search on the term 'conversation' in a popular website on which users can display video brings the user a 'corpus' of many million more words than have ever been designed by a linguist. In addition, the ethical position of many who are developing the next generation of the web means that the open sharing of data will be the norm and protocols to allow different sets of data to talk to one another and to be analysed by different groups will be developed. This combination of direct access to data and continued technical advances in accessing and analysing speech data may well drive our understanding of the norms of speech in future.

Further reading

Boxer, D. and Cohen, A. D. (2004). *Studying Speaking to Inform Second Language Learning*. Clevedon: Multilingual Matters.

Dörnyei, Z. (2007). *Research Methods in Applied Linguistics: quantitative, qualitative, and mixed methodologies*. Oxford: Oxford University Press.

Hughes, R. (2010). Researching speaking. In B. Paltridge and A. Phakiti (eds), *Continuum Companion to Research Methods in Applied Linguistics*. London: Continuum.

||| Researching speaking

Chapter 6

Spoken language and the classroom

This chapter will ...

- discuss some theories of language development that have strongly influenced classroom practice;
- revise some key features of speech and relate these to the treatment of the spoken form in the language classroom;
- outline some of the issues at the interface between language teaching methodology and research into the spoken mode.

6.1 Introduction

As Quotes 6.1 and 6.2 imply, speaking has for a long time played a special role in language education and applied linguistic theory beyond what might be simply regarded as 'teaching speaking'. This fact has affected how speaking is regarded in the classroom and in teacher training. An aim of the current chapter is to highlight and explain these links.

Quotes 6.1 and 6.2 The importance given to speech in language pedagogy

It is evident that our strongest and most direct associations ought to be with the spoken language, for in speaking we must have all our associations between ideas and words in perfect working order: we have no time to pick and choose our words and constructions, as when we are writing. ...

> If, then, we first get a thorough knowledge of the spoken form of the foreign language, and then proceed to learn its literary form, we shall be in exactly the same position as regards relative strength of associations as the natives themselves: we shall think in the spoken language, because our associations are directly with it.
>
> (Sweet, 1900: 52–3)

> For the teacher, understanding classroom communication, being able to 'shape' learner contributions and making strategic decisions in the moment-by-moment unfolding of a lesson are regarded as being crucial to developing SLA in the formal, L2 classroom context.
>
> (Walsh, 2006: 133)

6.2 The status of speaking in classrooms

Historically, there are several reasons for the special status of spoken interaction in applied linguistics and language pedagogy. These perspectives have a strong influence on what is regarded as good classroom practice whether the explicit name of the component in the syllabus is speaking or not. Spoken interaction is seen as an important, if not key, aspect of the language learning process and has been for over a hundred years. The spoken form is variously conceived of as:

- the primary mode in which 'natural uptake' can occur (as in 'The Natural Method' or 'The Oral Approach' prevalent in the early years of the last century until the early 1960s),
- a powerful tool for developing automatic and fluent output, together with consolidation of grammatical patterns (as in 'The Direct Method' or 'The Audio-lingual Approach'),
- the ideal medium for the exploration of language and one that allows a focus on communication to take precedence over form (a fundamental aspect of 'The Communicative Approach' and later developments such as 'Task Based Language Teaching').

In terms of approaches, methods or techniques (to use Anthony's (1963) often used and still useful categorisation to distinguish different levels of teaching methodology) the spoken form has for a long time retained a very significant status in the language classroom.

However, the status and handling of the mode have not remained static and, in particular, the decade of the 1970s marked a significant transition.

The language learner in a 1950s and 1960s classroom, whether in the UK or the United States or contexts influenced by these major Anglophone communities, would have had a very high chance of being exposed to the spoken form. Indeed the influence of early British applied linguists such as Henry Sweet remained powerful throughout the first half of the century and, as Quote 6.1 suggests, led to a strong emphasis on the oral mode. What emerged as 'The Natural Method' relied on introducing language items systematically and almost entirely through speech, and then on the very accurate (in phonetic terms) oral practice of explicitly taught language rules and features. In the United States, ethnographic approaches which depended on close and careful scrutiny of the oral form were also influential and these were superseded by what eventually became known as 'The Audio-lingual Method'. This again relied heavily on oral input, exposure to native-speaker models, and repetitive oral work ('drilling') which could be carried out with very little reference to meaning or context. The role of speech in the language classroom during these post-Second World War to late 1960s years was rather similar to a Petri dish in an experiment. It was the 'medium' or container of carefully selected (in the better programmes) linguistic items that would flourish in this sheltered environment and then become automatic and natural for the learner who had absorbed and internalised them through extensive practice. The focus was not primarily on communication but on structure and accurate production.

There was, however, a gradual acknowledgment from the late 1960s onwards that language rules and explicit focus on input and practice could only take the learner so far. Quote 6.3 gives an example of an early statement of the issues.

Quote 6.3 Widdowson on the role of communication in language teaching

The difficulty is that the ability to compose sentences is not the only ability we need to communicate. Communication only takes place when we make use of sentences to perform a variety of different acts of an essentially social nature. Thus we do not communicate by composing sentences, but by using sentences to make statements of different kinds, to describe, to record, to classify and so on, or to ask questions, make requests, give orders. Knowing what is involved in putting sentences together correctly is only one part of what we mean by knowing a language, and it has very little value on its own: it has to be supplemented by a knowledge of what sentences count as in their normal use as a means of communicating. And I do not think that the recommended approach makes adequate provision for the teaching of this kind of knowledge.

(Widdowson, 1972: 16)

The acknowledgment of the limitations of 'putting sentences together correctly' came about at the same time as a changing ethos in educational circles in liberal Western thinking. These repositioned 'The Teacher' and 'The Student' and made the idea of an authoritative model presented by a native speaker less attractive. Several simultaneous factors therefore combined to mean that the learner in a 1980s classroom would be asked to carry out a very different set of tasks from his or her counterpart of the post-war era. This language learner would, in classrooms influenced by Western academic applied linguistic thinking, be far less likely to be asked to carry out structured oral practice of a language feature and much more likely to be involved in a student-led task involving negotiation and discussion with peers, carried out in the medium of speech and with little explicit focus on rules and 'getting it right'. In this early 'communicative' classroom the spoken mode was, and still is, vitally important but it was no longer merely the receptacle or tool of instruction, rather it was coming to be seen as the actual medium through which the learner's state of linguistic knowledge is shaped and altered. To understand this change it is necessary to go back to another highly influential set of trends and discussions in linguistics and applied linguistics that took place from the mid-1960s, and which continues to be relevant today. In particular, there was a strand of debate from that period onwards about how to incorporate the dominant Chomskyan paradigm of the time into the language-teaching arena: how could language practitioners approach second language teaching in ways that reflected his insights about first language development?

One answer was based on the premise that there is no real difference between the two acquisition processes. These ideas were not new but were most extensively explored as a method or approach for the ELT classroom by Stephen Krashen (Krashen, 1981 through Krashen, 2008) in what came to be called 'The Natural Approach' (not to be confused with the early twentieth-century 'Natural Method' which emerged as part of the reaction to 'Grammar-Translation' methods). Like the Communicative Language Teaching movement this theory suggested that a second language is best acquired not by a learner being presented with grammatical information and rules by a teacher but by active engagement in meaningful communication (the 'learning–acquisition' distinction), and by the student needing to comprehend discourse which is slightly beyond that which they can express themselves (Krashen's 'input hypothesis'). See also Quote 6.4 and Concept 6.1.

The idea underpinning Krashen's theory was that in the process of exposure to the target language just beyond a student's current capacity and in the engagement of meaningful and enjoyable communication in it, something akin to a child's acquisition of language would occur. This was an exciting idea offering to bridge the gap between classrooms and the current language theories that dealt with language as an idealised system

Quote 6.4 Krashen on the role of spoken interaction in language acquisition

Language *acquisition* [original emphasis] is very similar to the process children use in acquiring first and second languages. It requires meaningful interaction in the target language – natural communication – in which speakers are concerned not with the form of their utterances but with the messages they are conveying and understanding.

(Krashen, 1981:1)

The input hypothesis runs counter to our usual pedagogical approach in second and foreign language teaching. ... [O]ur assumption has been that we first learn structures, then practice using them in communication, and this is how fluency develops. The input hypothesis says the opposite. It says we acquire by 'going for meaning' first, and as a result, we acquire structure!

(Krashen, 1982: 21)

difficult to relate to the realities of the language-teaching classroom. The reason it was well received, therefore, was that it gave a theoretically convincing answer to the language practitioner who had faced the issue of how to relate the specifics of language 'performance' in their classrooms to underlying development of L2 'competence'. Krashen's model appeared to provide the solution: the process will happen as naturally as L1 acquisition, if you provide the right conditions. Because spoken interaction was the primary channel for child language development, this perspective placed great emphasis on the spoken mode in second language learning theory and was one of the major drivers of change to what was regarded as good practice in the language teaching classroom by the late 1980s.

Rather quickly, however, Krashen's theory became the subject of heated debate concerning how to apply and how to verify it (for example, White, 1987), together with the growing sense in the field that L2 acquisition differs from L1 in a variety of ways (see for instance, Ellis, 1986). The significant impact that the ideas had means that Krashen's ideas are retained in the standard English language teacher training syllabus and the focus on interaction rather than explicit instruction that they promoted provides part of the explanation for the strong focus on speaking in language acquisition that remains to this day. As noted, the change of emphasis from explicit tuition and drilling to looking at language in use was also shared by the Communicative Language Teaching movement that began to be highly influential from the early 1970s.

Concept 6.1   **Learning versus acquisition and input hypothesis in the 'Natural Approach'**

During the early 1980s Stephen Krashen developed his influential theory of second language development in what came to be referred to as the 'Natural Approach'. This has been challenged on several fronts, but some of the central ideas helped to shape second language acquisition theory (SLA) and remain influential to this day. Two of his ideas – the distinction between learning and acquisition and the input hypothesis – are relevant to how spoken interaction is handled in the language classroom today.

In this framework consciously learning a language was at best a secondary process and the real focus of interest was acquisition. The L2 student, Krashen posited, like the child learning a first language, engaged with language at a deeper level than superficial grammatical knowledge and by exposure to it tapped into the underlying 'hard wiring' of the brain (i.e. the system which would be called 'competence' in Chomskyan theory). The strongest version of this theory suggested that one simply could not 'learn' a language and that too much emphasis on learning versus finding the right conditions for acquisition was harmful to L2 development.

In discussing the question of what the conditions for acquisition might be, the second key concept became relevant: the input hypothesis. This was presented in a formula 'i+1' (Krashen, 1982, 20–1) in which 'i' represents the current state of knowledge of a language and '1' equates to the next stage of its acquisition. The ideal conditions for acquisition were, Krashen suggested, those in which stimulating and motivating input at the level just beyond 'i' were presented to the student, leading them to naturally engage with it and thus reshape their state of knowledge towards '1'. This very neat statement, although soon challenged as unverifiable (McLaughlin, 1987), provided a paradigm or framework for SLA which remains highly influential.

6.3 The role of spoken interaction in Communicative Language Teaching classrooms

The Communicative Language Teaching (CLT) approach that has dominated English language teaching from the 1980s if not earlier and the Natural Approach that retains a strong influence on teacher training were developed around the idea of meaningful interaction and the focus on communication rather than linguistic facts. Both therefore valued, and were interested in encouraging students to engage in, copious amounts of spoken language in the classroom.

The handling of classroom talk has therefore become something of a marker of ability to promote good language learning environments. It is also used as a measure of the level of learner versus teacher centredness of a class, with a correlation being between low levels of teacher talking time (TTT) and higher levels of student engagement and autonomy. The focus on the importance of speaking and its links to a dominant philosophy in the teaching of English has markedly affected the nature of classroom management and also influenced how particular instances of spoken interaction are valued. At the global level teacher training in the communicative method explicitly discouraged too much teacher input and one of several 'alternative' approaches was 'The Silent Way' (Gattegno, 1976). This, as its name suggests, promoted the reduction of teacher talk to an absolute minimum. The popularity of small group and pair work that emerged as teachers began to make constructs such as the communicatively oriented 'notional-functional' syllabus real during the 1980s was also linked to the high value placed on students' spoken interaction in the classroom.

Considerable attention is still paid to how to handle classroom dynamics effectively to promote greatest output from the student and position the teacher as a facilitator of exploratory and autonomous learning through negotiation rather than a dominant voice of authority on what is correct. This philosophy has continued to shape what is regarded as good practice in the classroom over the last 30 to 40 years. The more recent emergence of, for example, task-based learning and focus-on-form has been a refinement rather than a sea change in the primary status given to the role of spoken interaction and its management in the ELT classroom. The emphasis has shifted more recently from a concern about the relative 'air time' of the teacher versus the student towards gaining a better understanding of how spoken interaction between teacher and student or student and student can influence language learning (see for example Quote 6.2 with which the chapter opened).

CLT has itself become more refined and diverse over the years but the basic assumption that language is best approached as action and interaction rather than a set of rules has remained the bedrock of English language teacher training. An example of how classroom management of interaction is seen as influencing language acquisition is in the role of feedback and error correction by a teacher. In the Focus-on-Form movement, for instance, the handling of immediate feedback by drawing attention to an item just said by a student is part of the approach. It is felt to enhance the process of becoming more aware of a correct form and promote accurate spoken output by the student (see Quote 6.5 for an example of this process in action).

Another influential development in CLT that places great emphasis on the spoken mode has been the Task-Based Language Teaching (TBLT)

Quote 6.5 Example of didactic focus-on-form

In Example 3, the student leaves out the definite article 'the'. The teacher has no difficulty in understanding him but focuses attention on the error by correcting the utterance. The focus-on-form episode that results from this type of error treatment constitutes a kind of pedagogic 'time-out' from meaning-focussed communication and for this reason can be considered 'didactic'. It involves a 'negotiation of form' rather than a 'negotiation of meaning'. It is possible that students do not notice the target of such negotiation as no meaning is at stake. There is no evidence in Example 3 that the student has paid attention to the teacher's feedback. Ellis *et al.* (1999) found that didactic focus-on-form was far more common than conversational [focus-on-form] in communicative ESL lessons involving adult learners.

Example 3: Didactic focus-on-form
  S: I was in pub
  (2.0)
  S: I was in pub
  T: in the pub?
  S: yeah and I was drinking beer

(Ellis *et al.*, 2002: 434–5)

movement (see Concept 6.2). This approach is not without controversy – in particular the role of explicit versus implicit focus on linguistic items – but the ideas underlying it chimed particularly clearly with the prevailing ethos of CLT and have meant that the task-based approach remains a current topic for scholarly debate and classroom applications.

Concept 6.2 **Task-based language teaching – TBLT**

This is an approach to language learning based on insights first outlined in the late 1980s by Prabhu (1987) and which has remained a central topic in syllabus design and debate about language learning generally. Reporting on his work in India, Prabhu suggested that learners who were mainly focused on a real world task made as good if not better progress than language learners given explicitly language focused instruction. This led to a variety of attempts to implement 'task-based learning' more widely and to relate them to the language classroom more generally. This was done by designing tasks that promoted the use of authentic language and required active engagement by the student in their completion, generally with a high level of spoken inter-action being required. A typical pattern for a lesson would be to provide an introduction to the task in the form of a 'warm-up' discussion to focus the attention of the students on the topic in question and help to generate some of the language required, a phase introducing the task and checking that students have fully understood the task and their roles (depending on the stance of the teacher to explicit linguistic input this phase may include focus on particular language items needed to complete the task, or not), a phase in which the students carry out the task with the teacher taking the role of facilitator and interlocutor, and a phase of rounding up and reflection on the task and the language used. One of the aspects that teachers found refreshing was that the typical pattern of structured input and very constrained practice of particular items was abandoned. In the task-based classroom students are placed in a role of greater independence and, in a carefully constructed task, the idea is that they will generate language before getting further feedback and clarification of it both from other students and from the teacher.

A useful overview of how these ideas developed can be found in Bygate *et al.* (2001) *Researching Pedagogic Tasks: second language learning, teaching, and testing* and Samuda and Bygate (2008) *Tasks in Second Language Learning*. A more practically oriented title with ideas on how to implement TBLT in detail is Willis and Willis (2007). On the theoretical side, Peter Skehan has developed TBLT thinking in relation to task-design and the balance between cognitive demands, focus on language, and maintaining some level of authenticity in the task. Skehan (2007) gives a balanced summary of the state of thinking on TBLT, including an account of why it remains controversial.

A very extensive investigation of how to transfer TBLT theory into the classroom was carried out in Belgium and reported in van den Branden (2006). Quote 6.6 shows the importance of the spoken mode in this approach and gives a sense of the relationship that develops between teacher and student as the approach is implemented.

Quote 6.6 The role of teacher–student spoken interaction in the task-based classroom

In task-based language teaching (TBLT), the teacher can be regarded in many ways as the learners' most privileged interlocutor. Although the teacher's role in TBLT differs from the role teachers assume in more 'linguistic', structure-oriented approaches, it is equally crucial. . . . In a nutshell we will argue and illustrate that there are two core actions that we believe the teacher should take in order for tasks to elicit rich learner activity and to enhance the chances that this activity turns into actual learning. These are:

a) motivating the learner to invest intensive mental energy in task completion;

b) interactionally supporting task performance in such a way as to trigger processes such as the negotiation of meaning and content, the comprehension of rich input, the production of output and focus on form, which are believed to be central to (second) language learning.

Van Avermaet *et al.* (2007: 175)

The trends in language teaching theory outlined above have meant that it is almost commonplace to say that it is better for students to talk in the classroom than teachers, and that there is a strong link between talk in the classroom and language acquisition processes. This in turn affects how the spoken mode is handled in the classroom. However, its dominant role in some theories may, paradoxically, not be a good thing for teaching spoken language, *per se*. Promoting student talk and providing tasks that allow 'meaningful interaction' may not promote fluent, accurate, and stylistically diverse talk. The apparent focus on the spoken mode in the classroom may mask significant issues for understanding the nature of speech and how best to teach and assess this skill in its own right. Quote 6.7 also captures something of this tension.

Quote 6.7 Interaction, important but under-researched?

Despite this enthusiasm for 'interactivity' as a defining notion in language teaching, a model of 'Language as Interaction' has not been described in the same level of detail as those models that have been developed for structural and functional views of language theory.

(Richards and Rodgers, 2001: 22)

The rest of this chapter provides a brief overview of some of the implications of the nature of speech for the classroom. It looks at some of the needs that practitioners may have in relation to handling spoken discourse in the speaking class as opposed to a class in which speaking is treated as the medium for language acquisition more generally.

6.4   Drawing on classroom practice for research and *vice versa*

Activities based around speaking need to be managed and fostered through careful planning and direction by the teacher, and through a choice of suitable tasks to stimulate speech. Where there are groups of students from different language backgrounds co-operating to carry out a task there is rich potential for the reflective practitioner to draw on existing research, or to carry out their own classroom-based project in this area. There are also, however, factors that need to be taken into account, some of which have been under-researched in relation to the language classroom.

When we consider the complex nature of speech interaction, it is perhaps unsurprising that even the most advanced students still feel most at a loss when they are trying to take part in spontaneous, informal conversation in a new language. While the communicative classroom gives abundant opportunity for the student to interact, it is fruitful to raise awareness of the fundamentals of spoken discourse in order to give students a better understanding of how very different speaking is from the stringing together of grammatically correct (or incorrect) sentences. Language awareness activities based around the norms of spontaneous interaction in the target language can provide both an increased understanding of the problems, pitfalls and skills needed for successful communication with native speakers, and provide the learner with a meta-language to ask further questions about the difficulties they are encountering.

Three basic aspects of spontaneous speech that language learners need to be aware of and which language teachers may find helpful to reflect on with their students are:

- speaking is fundamentally an interactive process and is defined by interactivity;
- speaking happens under real-time processing constraints;
- speaking is more fundamentally linked to the individual who produces it than the written form is.

These are the elements that stem directly from the way speech is produced and distinguish it from standard written forms. I will discuss each of them further in the following three sub-sections and outline the implications for the language learner.

6.4.1   The higher interactive potential of the spoken form than the written

There is a far greater potential for interactivity in the spoken mode than the written. Even online 'chat' that takes place in writing cannot match the interplay of speakers in face-to-face or mediated (telephone or online) oral interactions. This leads to features such as not only interruptions, corrections and overlaps, but also the potential for speaker co-operation as two or more people seek to speak and understand one another in real time. A written text and classroom tasks that are based on written mode are therefore generally more predictable and easy to manage than tasks involving large amounts of 'free' speaking. As the earlier sections have suggested, generation of peer-to-peer talk is a commonly seen goal in the current language classroom. There may be several underlying issues to consider.

In the context of group task completion learners need to become aware of the potentially different mechanics of interaction in their own language and the target language (see Concept 6.3 for some examples). The practitioner may also find that learning more from the literature on conversational norms in the cultures of his or her students can explain the dynamics of what they see happening between students in their classroom. A classroom-based research project on the impact of different cultural expectations in spoken communication when completing a particular task would be valuable.

Concept 6.3   **The non-transferability of conversational patterns across cultures**

A fundamental issue for the language teacher is the extent to which the norms of a target language's interactions mirror those of the learners' mother tongue. Nelson, Mahmood and Nichols (1996), for example, investigated the different ways in which Syrians and Americans respond to compliments. Although there were a number of similarities (for instance mitigating the compliment), there were also some significant differences. Americans were more likely than Syrians simply to say 'thank you'. Syrians were more likely to produce a long or a formulaic response (for instance offering the object of the compliment to the giver of the compliment). Where there is a combination of similarities and differences in the ways that cultures handle conversational functions there can be particular difficulties for the teacher of spoken forms.

These issues of intercultural expectations and their impact on communication extend beyond the language classroom and are particularly relevant for teaching staff involved with language training in professional settings. For example, Meeuwesen et al. (2007) examined doctor–patient discourse between Dutch doctors and patients from different ethnic and linguistic backgrounds. They discovered that the Dutch patients were much more capable of signalling a lack of understanding to the doctor than those from other backgrounds. Therefore intercultural communication awareness raising and training for L1 and L2 users may be vital in a range of settings other than 'simple' language acquisition. Interestingly, more work has currently been carried out in professional settings on these issues than on their impact in Language for Specific Purposes classrooms. A consistent programme of applied research to consider the implications for language teaching would clearly be beneficial.

6.4.2   The production of speech happens under real-time processing constraints

While the written form can generally be edited, rewritten and 'polished', speech – even speech that is prepared in advance – is delivered to the listener with no possibility for the recall of a word or erasure of a grammatical error. The exception is, of course, spoken discourse that is pre-recorded, and can be retaped if necessary. However, the greater part of speech, that is, conversational data, is created spontaneously in real time. This means that speakers tend to use simpler vocabulary, use a higher frequency of coordinated clauses, and use many fixed, filler expressions, such as 'you know', 'you see', to buy processing time. Learners need to realise that simple, even repetitive vocabulary is not unacceptable in speech, or rather that they should not spend so long making lexical choices that they lose the chance to speak. Equally, they need to gain a repertoire of natural time-buying devices to help them plan and process their discourse more easily.

Concept 6.4   **Speech processing and language demands**

Recognising what is said in any language is a remarkable feat. Recognising what is said in an unfamiliar language is a more difficult task but one that shares the basic processing system with L1 comprehension. Rather than presenting the learner with a binary of L1 (in which they are expert) versus L2 (in which they are currently in deficit) it is preferable to consider the demands of speech processing generally. Current thinking on how this process happens neurologically may help the learner understand the challenge they are facing and the strategies that they need to adopt to help them participate in spoken interaction. Interlocutors are constantly analysing spoken input and matching this against their linguistic expectations. Consensus in neurolinguistics is that '. . . candidate words are identified immediately, considered in parallel, and compete in some way' (McMurray *et al.*, 2009: 3). The acoustic clues in this process are, naturally, crucial as the stream of speech unfolds and is interpreted. In considering the capacity for successful spoken interaction in the L2 classroom it is worth bearing in mind that the student in a multi-lingual group performing a task is processing not only the competing lexical items that are normal for L1 speech processing, but also mapping a diverse set of realisations of phonemes from a variety of L1 background speakers and dealing with these against a perhaps partial understanding of the target language syntax. These processing demands are in addition to the potential cultural and pragmatic differences already mentioned. It may, therefore, be fruitful for the practitioner to address the L1 differences and levels of mutual intelligibility at an early stage in planning communicative tasks.

6.4.3   A strong, perceptible link exists between the deliverer of the discourse and the discourse itself

Spoken discourse reaches the world directly from the human vocal tract. As such it is a less mediated form than the written, which is transferred onto (or with technological advances such as computers and personal communication devices into) another medium before it is read. Something of this is reflected in the greater evidence of personal involvement shown by the spoken form, for example high frequency of personal pronouns, especially first and second, and verbs showing stance to the topic such as 'think', 'feel', 'believe' and so on.

Concept 6.5   **Stereotype effects on speech perception**

Perception of speech is strongly affected by preconceptions about the person who is producing the speech. Unlike the written mode, where, to a far greater extent, the content of the discourse can be disconnected from the author, the message carried by the stream of speech is processed in real time as output from a particular person and is interpreted by an interlocutor not only as speech sounds but also as the production of this specific individual. This means that whatever preconceptions the listener carries with them about the race, age, gender and personality of the speaker can have a powerful effect on how the spoken discourse is understood. To investigate these issues researchers have created a method known as the 'matched-guise' approach. In this listeners are played an extract of talk and are told a fact about the speaker, often their nationality. The results suggest that the perception of sounds and attitudes to the presumed fact about the speaker correlate and influence what is heard to the point that perception and input are clearly at odds. For example, Hu and Lindemann (2009) conducted an experiment on attitudes to Cantonese accented English. All the examples played to the subjects were spoken by American speakers of English but half the time the subjects were told that they were Cantonese speakers of English. When this was the case, listeners were more likely to perceive one of the features associated with the accent – missed final consonants. These 'hidden' factors that influence what a listener hears provide a fascinating insight into how strong the connections are between perception and attitude to the individual speaking. Gaining a greater understanding of stereotype effects can help promote good classroom dynamics, can indicate to the learner that the spoken mode is fundamentally dependent on interpretation, and is of clear relevance in the assessment of speaking.

An awareness of the effects of the interactive, spontaneous and personally oriented nature of speech can, therefore, be of great benefit to learners, both in terms of confidence in production and also to help to improve global listening skills. If, however, speech is taught without greater regard for some of the basic features that shape the process of listening and speaking then learners will constantly be striving, and failing, to speak in the complete, grammatically standard, and impersonal discourse that is quite untypical of naturally occurring speech.

Summary

The chapter has outlined some of the reasons for the emphasis on the spoken mode in language acquisition theories and the influence this has had on classroom practice. Some instances of the use of spoken interaction to promote language acquisition were given. It was suggested that there are possible tensions between the importance given to spoken interaction for general language uptake, and the particular needs of teaching speaking as a skill in its own right. The chapter ended with a review of the issues involved in the teaching of speaking *per se* due to its interactive and context dependent nature.

Further reading

Kumaravadivelu, B. (2006). *Understanding Language Teaching: from method to post-method*. London: Routledge. A more unusual but still full overview of the development of language teaching methods and approaches.

Richards, J. C. and Rodgers, S. T. (2001). *Approaches and Methods in Language Teaching*, 2nd edn. Cambridge: Cambridge University Press. A comprehensive and 'standard' text on the history of classroom practices in language teaching.

Chapter 7

Research project ideas and frameworks

This chapter will . . .

- introduce a cross-section of research projects which have been carried out on spoken discourse;
- describe related projects which could be carried out in similar areas;
- discuss the research approaches and frameworks for these projects.

7.1 Introduction

The projects selected here for summary show different approaches to moving from investigations into the spoken mode towards generalisations that can be used either in wider descriptions of spoken discourse, or applied in the language classroom. Articles have been selected to show a diverse range of approaches to researching speaking and include qualitative, quantitative, corpus informed, conversation analytic, ethnographic, phonetic, pragmatic, and modern brain scanning techniques. In the commentary, key skills and features for the novice researcher are also highlighted, such as the benefits of a null hypothesis, explaining limitations, and the potential criticism of an approach or findings.

In each case, some further topics for research are included which could grow naturally from the findings described, and ideas for reader projects are outlined.

7.2 A project on spoken language found in textbooks versus a corpus

> **Quote 7.1** From Lam (2010) 'Discourse particles in corpus data and textbooks: the case of *well*'
>
> Discourse particles are ubiquitous in spoken discourse. Yet despite their pervasiveness very few studies attempt to look at their use in the pedagogical setting.... the present study compares the use of discourse particles by expert users of English in Hong Kong with their descriptions and presentations in textbooks designed for learners of English in the same community. Specifically, it investigates the similarities and differences in the use of the discourse particle *well* between the two datasets in terms of its frequency of occurrence, its positional preference and its discourse function.
>
> (Lam, 2010: 1)

7.2.1 Commentary and ideas for further work

This study of the use of 'well' (as a discourse marker/particle) as presented in textbooks and as found in authentic speech is interesting because it covers many areas that are relevant to current debates in applied linguistics and aims to provide an analysis that integrates insights about spoken language, research and pedagogy.

Lam (2010) compared a corpus of speech with a range of textbooks supporting the development of oral skills for high intermediate English learners in secondary schools in Hong Kong. She was interested in particular in how a well-researched linguistic item that is typical of speech (the discourse particle 'well') was presented in the textbooks both in terms of frequency and function/context, and in what the implications of any differences might be for the classroom. She found significant differences in terms of both the frequency and nature of the particle in the two sources and between genres. Lam focused on both less interactive and more interactive contexts in the two sources. For example, sample 'made up' presentations from the textbooks were compared with prepared business presentations from the corpus and sample discussions created for the former were contrasted with interviews and meetings in the latter. Overall, she discovered that textbook discussions strongly over-emphasised the use of 'well' in comparison to overall use in the corpus (over 80 instances per 10,000 words in the textbook discussion genre versus around 20–30 in the corresponding number of words in the corpus). In contrast, the sample material for presentations greatly under-represented the particle – by up to five times – leading, Lam suggests, to a false impression of the use of the word being formed in the minds of the learner. She then goes on to give a detailed analysis of the functions of 'well' in the different sources, concluding 'textbook writers seem to pay excessive attention to *well* in responses while ignoring other important discourse functions such as framing which are also highly common in naturally-occurring spoken examples' (Lam, 2010: 16–17).

At the most general level, the work is a useful starting point for the new researcher with an interest in the classroom because it asks several questions about the contrasts between speech that can be heard outside the classroom and the material presented to learners in the medium of published textbooks. Lam comments, 'One might . . . quite reasonably, query whether such textbooks are so detached from reality that they have ultimately lost their pedagogical value' (Lam, 2010: 18). The novice researcher interested in continuing this debate might be moved to ask the extent to which they agree with this statement, and what further work they might carry out to reach their own conclusions. One underlying question is the precise meaning of 'pedagogical value' as the discrepancies between the bulk of published material and the complexities of spontaneous talk have been discussed elsewhere in this book. Yet people learn to speak the language. A natural next step would be to write some sample materials that are closer to the norms Lam has pointed to and try these with an experimental and a control group. A simpler variant of this would be to use the same published materials with two groups and provide additional awareness raising input with the experimental group.

From a different perspective, the article also deals with the issue of what the best model or target for the learner should be – 'native speaker' or high achieving 'non-native speaker'. The corpus of speech and the textbooks Lam analyses are not internationally focused but rather both are defined by a local setting: that of the high achieving Cantonese speaker of English living and working in Hong Kong (the majority of the corpus data participants) and the learner with a similar language background aspiring to this level of achievement. The article deals with this more at the stage of setting out the methodology than in the discussion, and the local versus more general models would be an interesting area for further work. If the reader works in a different language acquisition setting where there is a source of English as a lingua franca and data and published materials tailored for the local market are available, a replication study could be carried out. Alternatively, a different discourse feature could be analysed using the same approach and the same corpus and textbooks. A more theoretical paper could also be written on the pros and cons of a local model as a basis for materials, and some consideration given to the constraints imposed by the publishing world on what is made available in a variety of contexts. The questions to ask here are:

- Are there, and should there be, differences in principle between materials produced in a context where English is a strong second language alongside the mother tongue (such as Hong Kong) and materials produced for the learner where it is not (such as rural China)?
- Are there always benefits in seeking to reproduce the exact frequencies found in corpus data in classroom materials?

7.2.2   Potential reader project: extension to classroom talk

Lam (2010) suggested that an important use of 'well' in her authentic data was the function of framing:

> The framing use of *well* to insert a point of division or transition for easy comprehension is one of the most frequently occurring functions in the corpus data. In these examples, *well* acts as a boundary marker in discourse to signal transitions in topic and discourse stage. At times, it plays a role similar to punctuation marks in the written language in dividing words into clauses and sentences. In Example 6, the speaker uses *well* together with a meta-linguistic comment *let's talk a little bit about conflict* to indicate a topic change:

> (6)
> . . . but yet at the same time not violate our group harmony (.) yea it can be done (.) it can be done okay well let's talk a little bit about conflict why is conflict management so important . . .
> (HKCSE, B123)

> Apart from segmenting texts, *well* could be used as a link to introduce explanations and additional information to the preceding discourse.
> (Lam, 2010: 11)

She notes that this use is helpful to the listener in extended speech as it marks transition points or slight divergence from the expected flow of ideas (such as giving some additional information or a self-correction). In the data she has analysed, it would seem that students are being presented with a model that over-represents a different function – simple response at the start of a turn, particularly when disagreeing with someone. A possible research question is 'how do students actually use "well" in their own discourse?' A related question is what relationship, if any, there is between this and the input they have received from materials in their speaking classes.

Stage 1: Preliminary decisions

A first stage would be to decide the discourse type to be the main focus in relation to the categories found in Lam (2010) – these were presentations or discussions. A further decision would relate to whether the goal is a small-scale classroom-based project or an investigation that is aimed at a peer-reviewed journal or similar. These factors would affect the amount of data required, and the criteria against which the findings would be judged.

Stage 2: Data gathering

There are two possible approaches to gathering data for this project. The first is to design a task in which students will be asked to carry out one or other of these genres of talk. This has the advantage of being under the control of the researcher and decisions about the topic, length of task and instructions given to the students can all be carefully tailored to the project. Alternatively, in the context of practitioner-led research a speaking class that is already available could be used as a source of data as such classes often contain both individual presentations and discussions. In the latter case, the researcher would get permission to record sessions of the appropriate type as they occur to create the data set for analysis.

Stage 3: Preliminary analysis

Record as many student presentations or discussions as appropriate. As noted above, this will be different depending on the overall aim of the research. If this is intended as a small 'action research' project a data set involving around 4–5 students would be enough. If the project is to be published, a more substantial number of examples would be required for statistically useful findings. In this case, the researcher will also need to think through issues such as the gender and first language of subjects and try to ensure that the classroom context and task are well matched. In either approach, the larger the data set the more that can be said in relation to the findings.

In terms of how to find and analyse the frequencies, contexts and functions of 'well' the approach will also be influenced by the nature of the overall approach. For a small-scale project, simply listening to the recordings/watching the videos and noting the instances of 'well' being used would be adequate. For a large-scale project, the data should be transcribed more fully and a searchable corpus could be created from the electronic transcripts and the audio recordings. This would automate the process of finding instances of 'well' and would allow concordances of the context to be pulled out easily for further analysis.

In addition, data regarding the input in the speaking materials would also need to be gathered so that a comparison could be made between what the students have been exposed to in relation to the discourse particle and their subsequent use in a task providing free practice.

Stage 4: Results and discussion of findings

Even in a small sample, something very significant may be seen. For example, the investigator may find that the students only use the term 'well' for the function that they have been taught (perhaps 'introducing disagreement' a function that Lam suggested was never actually seen in her authentic data). This would lend some credibility to the argument that students' pragmatic behaviour may be affected negatively by the inappropriate model being found in a textbook. Alternatively, the students may not use the particle when they might be expected to, or they may use it for functions that they have not explicitly been taught. In either of these cases, there would be support for a counter-argument to Lam in terms of the significance of the effects of input from teaching materials on student behaviour. That is to say, although the model does not match authentic material students are not directly transferring the uses and contexts to their own speech anyway, and therefore the impact is less than might be assumed.

7.3 A project on the effects of speech rate in the context of English as lingua franca presentations

> **Quote 7.2** From Hincks (2010) 'Speaking rate and information content in English lingua franca oral presentations'
>
> This paper quantifies differences in speaking rates in a first and second language, and examines the effects of slower rates on the speakers' abilities to convey information. The participants were 14 fluent (CEF B2/C1) English L2 speakers who held the same oral presentation twice, once in English and once in their native Swedish. The temporal variables of mean length of runs and speaking rate in syllables per second were calculated for each language. Speaking rate was found to be 23% slower when using English. The slower rate of speech was found to significantly reduce the information content of the presentations when speaking time was held constant. Implications for teaching as European universities adopt English as a medium of instruction are discussed.
>
> (Hincks, 2010: 4)

7.3.1 Commentary and ideas for further work

The growth of English as a medium of instruction internationally means that work such as reported in Hincks (2010) will have increasing usefulness and relevance. This paper is interesting in that it analysed the same speakers (Swedish mother tongue with a good level of fluency in English as L2) doing a speaking task – a presentation – in their L1 and their L2. Very often conclusions are drawn about L2 speaking without reference to the characteristics of the speaker in their first language. One of Hincks' findings was that speech rate transferred from L1 to L2 and when a speaker was slower than average in Swedish this would also be the case in English. She comments on the importance of bearing in mind L1 speaker norms in reaching conclusions about L2 performance. Hincks developed a system to analyse difference in terms of both speech rate and, more significantly, 'points of difference' or PODs. The latter were, for example, the number of information items that could be included under time constraints in the presentation in each language. She concludes:

> The least fluent English speaker, S1, was so hampered by his L2 that his L1 presentation included three times the PODs when time was normalized. However, the gap between the two languages was also apparent for more fluent speakers, such as S13 and S10. These two participants were exceptionally knowledgeable about their topics (one was a salesperson and one went on to do a PhD related to the subject of his presentations), raising the worrisome concern that the more one knows about a topic, the bigger the differences that appear when one is required to talk about it in an L2. (Hincks, 2010: 16)

In addition, she points to more subtle contrasts between the presentations in the two languages; for instance, although a speaker can communicate a definition literally the stylistically engaging use of resources such as metaphor was missing in the L2 context. This was not counted as a POD but noted in the discussion as a noteworthy difference and one that adds to the overall conclusion she makes that students working in the English medium may not be able to reach their fullest potential.

This work could be taken further in several different ways. Hincks herself suggests some of these. They include the links between comprehension ability of a mixed audience of L1 and L2 and speaking speed in lectures, the development of an electronic monitor for speakers to international audiences to show when their syllable per second rate becomes too high for comfortable comprehension, and the question of the amount of content that an L2 lecturer can include in a given amount of time compared to an L1 user. Her findings suggest that around 25 per cent more time might be expected to be taken by the L2 speaker in similar contexts, for example. At a more theoretical level, the work also raises interesting areas for further work and debate. For example, her article includes a reference to the fact that speakers in conversation adapt their speech rate to their interlocutor if they are speaking to someone who has a different first language and needs this slower pace. Speakers in monologue rarely do this. However, as Hincks herself noted, not all L1 speakers behave in the same way conversationally. It would be intriguing to gain a better understanding of the conditions under which a speaker adjusts speech rate and whether there are other conversational contexts or speaker types who do/do not do this.

7.3.2 Potential reader project: extension by replication and additional qualitative phase

The work reported by Hincks (2010) is in the quantitative tradition. It would be interesting to do two things to follow up on these findings. First would be to replicate the study with a different language or with several languages and second would be to add a reflective phase to the study where the speakers are interviewed about the experience of presenting in each language.

Stage 1: Preliminary questions

If the research is being undertaken in a classroom with a monolingual setting and the researcher has good competence in both the local language and English, it will be relatively simple to replicate the study. If the investigator is not familiar with the language of the students then they will need to employ an assistant to help with the analysis. Factors such as the level of the students and the amount of input and practice before the presentations were gathered should also be matched as closely as possible to the Hincks study.

A particular decision will be how central the subsequent interview data will become in this project. It could be handled as a very simple feedback session or a more elaborate semi-structured interview. In the latter instance, the interview could be designed around some of the key findings in Hincks (2010) such as being able to convey less in the time available, or having to use literal versus metaphoric language to get a point across.

Stage 2: Quantitative data collection

The data collection section in Hincks (2010) should be adapted to the circumstances of the current research and the context of the investigator. In the original study, students were asked to choose a topic for themselves on a semi-technical theme and speak for 10 minutes in English. This was part of their programme. They were then invited to repeat the presentation at a later date for research purposes, for a small fee, in their first language. Where the current study deviates from the approach in the original article significantly, a comment should be added to any methods section. This allows the reader of the eventual research report to understand the points of exact similarity and difference between the new study and the original. The presentations would then be recorded and transcribed using the method described in Hincks (2010: 9).

Stage 3: Qualitative data collection

Having decided on the general approach of the reflective interview in the preliminary phase, the material from the students would be gathered after the second presentation in the mother tongue had been completed. Small focus groups of students could be arranged to discuss the experience of presenting in the two languages and recordings made of them. Alternatively, you may wish to conduct a full one-to-one interview with all subjects, basing this around the core topics you are interested in.

Stage 4: Analysis, results, discussion

The kinds of questions that the researcher will expect to be able to answer by the end of the replication of the study are as follows. Do the students in the new study find that they are also unable to deliver the same amount of content in the two languages? Are the differences as marked as those discovered between the advanced English learners and the Swedish native speakers? Do they show differences in speaking rate when syllables per second in the two languages are compared? Are there any significant differences in the findings in comparison to Hincks? Is there evidence of a more literal style in the lingua franca versus the mother tongue? How do the students feel about speaking in the two languages? How do you explain the difference, if so? What do their reflections suggest to you in terms of helping them in future?

7.4 An exploration of inter-cultural expectations in conversation

Quote 7.3 From Cheng and Tsui (2009) 'Ahh ((laugh)) Well there is no comparison between the two I think: how do Hong Kong Chinese and native speakers of English disagree with each other?'

[C]ontrary to the stereotypic accounts of Chinese culture, HKC [Hong Kong Chinese] are not at all shy to disagree with their NSE [Native Speakers of English] interlocutors. Neither are HKC less likely, if not more likely, to disagree in order to present their different, or alternative, views. However, when they disagree, they are more inclined to address the face-want of both themselves and the addressees by using redressive language and mitigating devices. Qualitative analysis of sequences of disagreements in a conversational excerpt has shown the varying efforts HKC and NSE speakers make to align themselves with the interlocutor to manage interpersonal relationships and negotiate common ground.

(Cheng and Tsui, 2009: 2365)

7.4.1   Commentary and ideas for further work

This article presents work on intercultural pragmatics. The authors are particularly interested in probing the conversational behaviour of native and Chinese users of English when they find that they disagree with each other and need to re-establish some kind of consensus. Through their analysis they reach wider conclusions about conversational behaviour and relate them to previous preconceptions and conclusions about Western versus Asian behaviour and values. The project is thus presented via a 'classical' research paper structure including a review of previous work, hypotheses, data against which hypotheses are compared, and a revision and conclusion in light of the starting point of the article. The project is interesting in that it combines quantitative analysis – for example proportions of disagreements with and without redressive language (efforts at 'softening' the level of disagreement) – with conversation analytic tools. In the first sections of the article, three main hypotheses are set up about what conversational behaviour the researchers think they may see on the basis of earlier work on language users from Anglophone cultures (called here native speakers of English, NSE) versus their interlocutors who are Hong Kong Chinese (HKC). Quote 7.4 provides the broad hypotheses that the researchers were interested in.

Quote 7.4   Hypotheses developed by Cheng and Tsui (2009)

1. HKC will disagree with NSE less frequently than NSE will disagree with HKC.
2. HKC will use bald-on-record strategies in their disagreements less frequently than NSE will use bald-on-record strategies in their disagreements.
3. HKC will use redressive language in their disagreements more frequently than NSE will use redressive language in their disagreements.

(Cheng and Tsui, 2009: 2368).

After collecting and statistically analysing 13 hours of conversation between NSE and HKC speakers the researchers concluded that the first hypothesis was not supported in their data but that the other two were supported. HKC speakers were less blunt in their expression of disagreement (using fewer than half the frequency of 'bald-on-record' strategies shown by NSEs) and used more softening language. Whereas nearly 90 per cent of the instances of disagreement were surrounded by redressive language in the turns of HKC speakers, just over 70 per cent of similar conversational moments were 'softened' in this way by NSEs. The finding that HKC speakers did *not* avoid conversational conflict is a particularly clear instance of why a 'null hypothesis' (one that does not find evidence to support it) can lead to a very valuable research result. While earlier work might have suggested that the orientation towards harmony, face saving, and consensus would dominate the conversational input of the HKC the findings showed that these speakers differed with their interlocutors just as much, but had different strategies and styles to handle these moments. The second analysis presented is a conversation analytical one dealing with an interaction between two police officers who differ over the route and the benefits of a charity walk. The researchers show how the HKC user of English handles the disagreement by shifting the conversational topic back to common ground, is ready to concede, and uses ambiguity as well as praise for the NSE's ideas. At this point the NSE becomes critical of his own position and the researchers conclude, 'We have an interesting example which illustrates how contributions made by participants in discourse not only shape the contributions made by other participants but are also shaped by them' (Cheng and Tsui, 2009: 2377).

The clarity of the structure of this paper means that it would readily transfer to other language groups and could be replicated by readers in other contexts. A straightforward comparison could be made between NSE and non-NSE handling of disagreement in conversational settings where the non-NSE is from a different linguistic and cultural background from the HKC users analysed here. The point could be made that it is not necessarily 'being a HKC' user of English that is the most prominent effect, but 'being a non-native speaker speaking to a native speaker'. Replicating the study with a range of speakers from different language backgrounds and cultures would be one way to test this idea. A practitioner may wish to take the conclusions of this paper and see how students in his/her class deal with disagreement and also use the findings to raise awareness for students of the potential for cultural norms to affect how they 'come across' in a conversation. The findings may be particularly relevant to the English for Specific Purposes contexts where handling disagreement in business or professional contexts may be very delicate.

7.4.2 Potential reader project: replication and extension to an online environment

Cheng and Tsui (2009) suggest that the frequency of expression of disagreement does not differ between a native speaker of English and a Hong Kong Chinese speaker using the same language. They conclude, however, that the HKC speaker will handle the divergence of opinion differently and will use more strategies to soften and mitigate the effect. It would be interesting to probe this further and to understand more about what is inherent to the cultural background of the speaker and what may be affected by particular context and mode. One way to begin this process would be to look at disagreement in an online environment. It has been suggested that explicit markers of politeness tend to be missing or greatly reduced in, for example, chat room discourse (Carlo and Yoo, 2007). Will HKC speakers show higher incidence of politeness markers when disagreeing in this environment than NSEs? More generally, will speakers from Chinese and similar cultural backgrounds handle disagreement in online environments differently from speakers of other ethnic origin?

Stage 1: Preliminary decisions

It may not be possible to directly replicate the pairings of Cheng and Tsui (2009) and it would be necessary to make it clear to the reader how you are defining the speakers' language backgrounds that you eventually analyse. Are you going to use authentic chat room data available online, or are you going to set up structured discussions? The study described below uses the latter approach. Rich and authentic data may be available online, but the difficulty would then be checking the language background and other aspects of the users such as age, gender and so on.

Stage 2: Data gathering

If the project is being carried out by a teacher with students from a range of linguistic backgrounds and access to online resources that allow 'chat' it would be possible to set up a structured discussion and retain the 'threads' as the basis of the analysis. For instance, the students could be allocated to 3–4 different 'rooms' and a theme or a problem-solving task that will naturally generate differences of opinion set up in each. The archive of these electronic discussions together with the identity of the students involved would become the basis for findings about differences between students from the different cultural backgrounds in relation to confrontation in an online setting.

Stage 3: Analysis and findings

One of the advantages of this approach is that data are readily available in written form to be analysed without the need for transcription. It would be good practice to work with another researcher to check exactly how 'disagreement' is being defined and to code instances according to an agreed system. It would then be possible to carry out both quantitative and qualitative analysis to see whether there were behavioural patterns to the handling of disagreement across the different cultural groups. The quantitative analysis would measure the incidences of expression of disagreement in users of different language backgrounds and the qualitative work would look at whether Asian speakers mitigated disagreement more than users from different backgrounds. A comparison could be made to the finding of Cheng and Tsui (2009) and some discussion presented of the implications of what is found. Whether the same tendencies or not are perceived there will be interesting conclusions to be drawn. Either these would be concerning the strength of the cultural tendency to mitigate disagreement even in online contexts or, if these patterns were not visible, questions would arise about the interaction of cultural and pragmatic factors in face-to-face interaction versus the online environment.

7.5 A project that analyses a professional speaking genre so it can be handled in the classroom

> **Quote 7.5** From Burns and Moore (2008) 'Questioning in simulated accountant–client consultations: exploring implications for ESP teaching'
>
> This paper reports research investigating spoken accounting discourse derived from simulated accountant–client consultations. It draws on the work of Drew and Heritage (1992), in which questioning is identified as a key discursive feature in institutional talk, and also the more recent work reported in Heritage and Maynard (2006), in which the complexity of the formulation of questions and responses is revealed in doctor–patient consultations. The paper discusses the use of simulations in cases where access to actual workplace settings by ESP teachers is unattainable, as well as the usefulness of the interactional data these simulations generate.
>
> (Burns and Moore, 2008: 322)

7.5.1   Commentary and ideas for further work

This paper deals with the interface between spoken interaction in professional contexts (in this case accountancy advice giving) and the English for Specific Purposes (ESP) classroom. It is an interesting article in several respects. First, this is a little researched genre in a field that has high levels of training needs for international students. Second, the main focus of ESP has tended to be written rather than spoken discourse. Finally, it discusses a number of methodological issues raised by the approach used to gain data and gives a wide range of suggestions for further work. The authors analysed the question and answer patterns between trainee accountants on a master's programme and volunteers who role-played members of the public asking for advice about how to complete a tax form. Based on this they tentatively produce a taxonomy of question types used by advice-seekers and advice-givers in these contexts. In terms of how to transfer this idea to the classroom they suggest: 'Learners can be given opportunities to enhance their understanding of the functions of each questioning technique and the kinds of responses they are intended to elicit. They can be introduced to the questioning techniques primarily utilised by the accountant in contrast with those that clients might introduce' (Burns and Moore, 2008: 333). They also note the lack of interpersonally oriented questions asked by the trainee accountants and note that raising awareness of the acceptability of using these kinds of questions and also humour may be beneficial for the students and 'improve the overall tenor of consultations'.

The use of simulated interaction is the fundamental point in relation to the methods used to gather data. The authors are very clear that in terms of a research paper without direct reference to the classroom this source of data would be questionable. See also Quote 7.6.

Quote 7.6   Justifying a method

... [W]hile simulation may be criticised for lacking the features of naturalistic data from the authentic worksite (and given the absence of such data this criticism is itself speculative), it also offers, we have argued, a way for ESP teachers to raise their own and their students' awareness of the nature of accountant–client interaction. Given the problems of access, recording, and analysis of workplace data for most ESP teachers, such simulations, as a means of preliminary analysis and insights into discoursal patterns, present a promising alternative.

(Burns and Moore, 2008: 333)

In the research-into-practice domain, the data elicited in the simulations serve multiple functions, therefore, rather than the single function that would be the norm more generally. In other research contexts, data would be primarily elicited/captured for linguistic insight without reference to the needs of, or constraints on, the practitioner. In the current context, they are both a model on which to base preliminary assumptions about the target genre in authentic communication and to raise the awareness of the student and the ESP teacher of what may happen in general terms in these types of interactions. At the same time, they represent the product of students aspiring to be fully fledged accountants who are themselves potentially recipients of the insights in a future ESP classroom. In this sense the simulations become part of a needs analysis for the future development of an ESP curriculum (what skills and knowledge the students may lack) and provide indications of some basic input for that curriculum (the patterns of questioning that were seen and the different input of client and advisor).

The need to tackle the issue of the lack of access to authentic data and explain why there are good reasons not to be concerned about this provides a useful example for the novice researcher to consider. In terms of the dialogue with the reader an experienced researcher can explain the level of limitation clearly (hence pre-empt criticism) and show the features that add to the validity of what they are concluding. To do this well the writer of the article needs clearly to set out the frame of reference that they wish to be judged against. Crucial to this paper is the fact that it has been written from the outset with direct teaching applications in mind. This allows the multiple functions for the data to work well, permits a level of sketchiness to the generalisability to all such interactions, and generally motivates and provides a solid rationale for the defence of the use of simulated data.

The authors provide several avenues for further work. First, at a very general level they note the lack of any detailed research into accountancy discourse. They suggest that this is therefore a fruitful genre for more investigation. They also suggest widening the participants from master's level trainees to other levels to help gain a sense of what ESP students may need and may lack at these different points in their study career. In addition, they point to the work that could be carried out in terms of analysing interactions between dyads from different linguistic and cultural backgrounds. At a more theoretical level, it could be interesting to pursue the idea of the benefits and limitations of the use of simulated interactions in applied research settings. In particular it might be beneficial to explore further the idea of the student as model generator and a reflective user of the insights gained from the experience of role playing their future self interacting with others in their future career role.

7.5.2   Potential reader project: extension of approach to placement learning

The aim of Burns and Moore (2008) is to gain some insights about accountant–client interaction and to discuss the usefulness of simulated role-play as a tool for gaining these insights and in then embedding results into an ESP curriculum. This approach could also be beneficial in the context of university-level assessed placements that are commonly found in the later stages of undergraduate programmes and master's training for vocational and professional purposes. In these contexts, the advanced learner needs to handle complex spoken interaction and manage semi-professional relationships outside the educational setting. In this context, they are regarded both as a student and as an emerging 'expert' with a developing professional identity. It would therefore be interesting to investigate the usefulness of simulated role-play in preparing students for placement learning. A control and experimental group approach could be used. In this approach, two groups of students are trained in the same area but in the case of one group, the input or approach differs in respect to the research question. In this case, one group (experimental) would be exposed to simulated role-play; the other (control) would take the standard preparation. Usually some measure of performance is taken at the start and end of the training programme and differences between the two groups are evaluated in relation to the different input. In this way the approach seeks to connect the differences in achievement to the difference in experience that has been designed to link to the topic under consideration in the research. It will be clear from this that a key point is to try to match as far as possible the experimental and the control groups in all other respects such as age, gender, curriculum, teaching methodology, language level at start of experiment and so on. In reality, in the context of a 'live' teaching environment it is actually quite unrealistic to match all features of the experience of students in both groups apart from the 'intervention' (in this case use of simulation). However, the researcher will make every effort to match the conditions and the subjects and will then provide a narrative to explain any significant points of departure. For instance, if a different teacher teaches the groups they will include some discussion of the possible impact of this variable both at the outset in relation to the design of the project and then again in the discussion when they are looking at the results and giving possible explanations or reasons for particular findings.

Stage 1: Preliminary decisions

This project would work well if carried out by an ESP/EAP practitioner team in tandem with a researcher who would provide the theoretical background and design the experimental framework. Two groups of students preparing for the same professional or vocational careers would be chosen. Decisions would need to be made about several aspects. For example, there would be the question of how to embed simulated role-play into the curriculum for the experimental group, and the characteristics of students to be involved would also need to be considered in terms of benchmarking oral skills at the start of the project and consideration of their linguistic and cultural background(s).

Stage 2: Experimental phase

It would be good practice to carry out a small pilot study with a different group of students from the two that will be in the main study. This will allow the practitioners and researcher(s) to work out exactly how the simulation will be delivered and iron out possible problems that are difficult to predict before an approach is tried out in a classroom. One approach would be to create a bank of videos of simulations of interactions previewing the type of speech genres that the placement will entail. These could be used as a prompt for discussion and for further role-play in the classroom with the experimental group.

Having refined the approach on the basis of the pilot the next step would be to arrange the experimental and control groups and carry out a baseline assessment for both groups. In this particular project, it would be beneficial both to test general oral skills and to carry out an interview or survey of the students' levels of confidence and knowledge of the placement context they will be facing. The experiment would then run for the duration of the programme, say a university term, and the students would be retested. The second assessment would be a repeat of the oral skills test and an opportunity for the students to reflect on their levels of confidence and awareness of the skills needed for the placement ahead of them. Ideally, the students would then be tracked through their actual placements and their performance in the field compared to the training they had received.

Stage 3: Analysis and discussion

The results of the initial and final assessments and the reflections of the students on their confidence levels and their subsequent experiences in the actual placements would provide rich data to evaluate the usefulness of simulations and would become the basis for further refinement of the curriculum. In this approach the cycle of research into practice and practice informing research would become part of the focus of the project.

7.6   A project on speaking assessment with low education immigrant test takers

---

Quote 7.7 From Simpson (2006) 'Differing expectations in the assessment of the speaking skills of ESOL learners'

This is a study of the assessment of the speaking skills of adult learners of English for speakers of other languages (ESOL). It is prompted by a concern that participants can have differing expectations of what nature of speech event a speaking test actually is. This concern was identified during the administration and analysis of assessments carried out as part of a study into adult ESOL pedagogy in the UK. The paper employs the notions of *knowledge schema* and *frame* in discourse to draw together areas of interest in testing: whether the speaking assessment should be viewed as an interview or as a conversation; divergent interpretations of the test event by learners; and variation in interlocutor behaviour. Implications for testing the speaking skills of adult ESOL learners are discussed; these are pertinent at a time of large-scale high-stakes testing of learners who are migrants to English-speaking countries.

(Simpson, 2006: 40)

7.6.1   Commentary and ideas for further work

This article reports part of a larger project on adult language and literacy teaching and testing for English for Speakers of Other Languages (ESOL) in the UK – the Effective Practice Project – run by the National Research and Development Centre for adult literacy and numeracy. As such, it brings insights from a different perspective from the general English as a Foreign Language world and the applied linguistics world that many of the other studies in this chapter are dealing with. The students involved in ESOL classes may have very traumatic backgrounds and life histories if they are asylum seekers or refugees and they may have minimal schooling in some cases. The testing of these learners may have particularly significant impact for them in terms of ability to remain in a country, as was highlighted at the end of Chapter 4. An example of the specific needs of these students is the fact that in adapting the test to the project the designers removed the question 'Why did you come to the UK?' The reason for this was that what would have been a neutral 'warm up' question to the general English student would have had a very different significance for a refugee ESOL student. Not only would the narrative involved in the answer have been potentially very emotive for the student, it would also have been asked at the point of entry to the UK in a very different interview context in the process of achieving entry to the country.

However, the insights gained by Simpson (2006) are valuable not only for this cohort but also for the wider implications they point to in terms of how expectations on the part of examiner and examinee affect oral communication under test conditions. The ESOL community from which the subjects were drawn provided a particularly clear data set on which to base conclusions about the effects of prior knowledge of what it is to be tested – the 'what kind of oral interaction am I in and how should I behave?' question – and the ability to 'perform' in these conditions.

From 400 possible oral interviews undertaken in the wider project, 23 were selected using the following criteria: learners were taking an examination at the higher of the two tested levels and the test takers had little or no schooling. The reason for the former criterion being applied was that the lower level speaking test would only call for very basic factual responses from the examinee and the researcher wished to have data in which longer and more complex information was being asked for. The reason to limit the number of years' schooling was to be able to investigate the reaction to being tested by learners with untrained expectations about the process in order to elicit 'non-schooled responses' or similar (Simpson, 2006: 47). Extracts from five interviews were used as the basis for the analysis in the current paper. The maximum number of years' schooling of these students was four and the minimum zero.

In terms of analysis of the data selected by the criteria outlined above, a qualitative method based on conversation analysis was used. In contrast to the hypothesis-testing approach reported in section 7.4 that also used CA methods, Simpson (2006) uses a much broader questioning approach. He selects sections of data that will help him illustrate the patterns that he sees as 'not atypical of the testing experience of ESOL learners in the effective practice project'. These are motivated by an overarching research question: 'What happens when learners with little or no experience of formal schooling carry out the speaking assessment?' (Simpson, 2006: 48). Through these examples he touches on four more specific aspects: whether the test taker regards the event as a test or a different kind of speech event; what might make a student say very little in the test (under-elaboration); how speaker collaboration can help the test taker; how the examiner's stance towards the speech event may affect the test taker. The example of under-elaboration is particularly clear and interesting. In the data illustrating this feature, the candidate provides single syllable or no replies in the test but at the point when the test is over produces two extended turns. Simpson speculates whether the examinee had experienced situations where it was better to say as little as possible, or to constrain replies to what she was certain was correct, and this is what led to the mismatch between her performance in the test and soon afterwards. The extract is salutary.

Although not mentioned, presumably the lack of assessable material meant that the candidate would have failed the test. Seeing the large amount of material that could have been assessed and the clear motivation to speak that the candidate shows after the test provides a compelling indication of the need to ensure good preparation and practice testing for all candidates, and particularly those from backgrounds similar to these ESOL students.

7.6.2   Potential reader project: extension to test conclusions

There are several directions that could be followed up in relation to this project. First, as noted in the comments on methodology, the approach here uses illustrative material to make points about patterns that an expert in the field asserts are typical. The novice researcher may need to take a less 'open' approach and so one project that would be of interest would be to replicate the basic data (speaking assessments with ESOL learners with minimal schooling) and apply a different method such as hypothesis testing and statistical analysis to look for correlations between instances of under-elaboration to a variety of factors such as gender, years of schooling, age and so on. A possible criticism of the current work is that the interactive behaviour ascribed to a naiveté about what it is to be in a test of speaking could be due to a number of other factors. A project that took one of the conclusions and worked on it in detail would therefore be interesting.

Stage 1: Preliminary decisions

This project assumes that the researcher has access to ESOL learners of similar backgrounds to those described in Simpson (2006) and a comparison group with similarly low language ability, but greater exposure to schooling. Decisions would be needed as to how to define the higher and the lower thresholds of schooling and some initial work done to ensure that the language levels were comparable. The investigation would also require some expertise in oral assessment or availability of standard oral assessments for the students to undertake.

Stage 2: Hypothesis setting

According to Simpson (2006), ESOL candidates with very few years' schooling confuse an oral assessment interview with a conversation and do not know how to handle the interaction so that they perform the role of being examined appropriately. One of the features he points to as evidence of this is the under-elaboration of answers by candidates. A possible hypothesis therefore would be that ESOL learners with low levels of formal schooling ('Type 1') will produce shorter turns in response to examiner questions than ESOL learners with similar language levels in the target language to Type 1, but with adequate levels of formal schooling for their age ('Type 2').

Stage 3: Data gathering

Students in the two categories would be given some preparatory classes and then an oral assessment would be undertaken by both groups. Their interactions with the examiner during the test would be the basis for evaluating the strength of evidence for the hypothesis.

Stage 4: Analysis of results and discussion

A quantitative analysis would be made of the number and the length of turns by the two groups in response to examiner questions. Ideally, this would be carried out with a statistically significant sample and appropriate statistical techniques applied. This would allow some conclusions to be reached about the performance of the two groups that could be ascribed to the differences in schooling. Whether or not a significant difference was found between them, something of interest could be said. If, contrary to expectation, the two groups with similar language levels performed similarly there would be less support for Simpson's link between levels of schooling and effects on candidates' performance in formal tests of speaking. If, on the other hand, the hypothesis was supported there would be some grounds for suggesting that fair and appropriate assessments were not being achieved for some ESOL learners due to their incorrect understanding of what is expected in formal oral assessment, possibly based on a lack of schooling.

7.7   A project investigating the relationship between gesture and speech processing using fMRI scanning techniques

> **Quote 7.8** From Straube *et al.* (2010) 'Social cues, mentalizing and the neural processing of speech accompanied by gestures'
>
> Body orientation and eye gaze influence how information is conveyed during face-to-face communication. However, the neural pathways underpinning the comprehension of social cues in everyday interaction are not known. In this study we investigated the influence of addressing vs. non-addressing body

orientation on the neural processing of speech accompanied by gestures.... Our findings indicate that social cues influence the neural processing of speech–gesture utterances. Mentalizing (the process of inferring the mental state of another individual) could be responsible for these effects. In particular, socially relevant cues seem to activate regions of the anterior temporal lobes if abstract person-related content is communicated by speech and gesture. These new findings illustrate the complexity of interpersonal communication, as our data demonstrate that multisensory information pathways interact at both perceptual and semantic levels.

(Straube *et al.*, 2010: 382)

7.7.1   Commentary and ideas for further work

This paper presents work on speech communication that is at the cutting edge at the time of writing and is included for this reason. The technique used, fMRI scanning, is described on page 38 and is one that allows the researcher to see what parts of the brain are activated by different stimuli, in this case a combination of speech, stance, and gesture. This project shows that speakers' brains respond quite differently when someone speaks to them directly as opposed to standing as if speaking to someone else. They also respond differently when a speaker is describing an object with an illustrative gesture (such as 'The bowl in the kitchen is round' spoken in combination with a circular motion of the hands), or describing a human entity and using a commonly understood ('emblematic') gesture ('The actor did a good job in the play' in combination with a thumbs-up sign). These variables – stance and gaze, person- versus object-related message and descriptive versus culturally known gesture – were set up as four conditions to be combined with the gestures: Person-related + Frontal stance, Person-related content + Lateral stance and ditto Object-related content. These were recorded as short video clips and 30 of them in each condition were shown to 18 subjects. These were carefully chosen, as would be expected in the experimental paradigm being used, and were: all male, all right-handed, all native German speakers with no impairments to vision or hearing, had an average age of around 24 and were all between 20 and 30. The flow of blood to various parts of the brain was analysed and conclusions reached as to the differing effects of speech, content, stance and gesture in the combinations outlined.

It is not assumed that the classroom practitioner will wish to undertake this kind of neuro-linguistic research directly or that they would have easy access to fMRI equipment if they wished to. However, it is included to suggest that our understanding of spoken communication may soon be very different and that this will have an impact on how the skill is regarded and is taught. As new insights such as those reported here are gained about the complex interplay between different modes and signals – speech, gesture, social cues – that need to be taken into consideration together when understanding speaking, our understanding of spoken communication will begin to change quite radically over the next few years. In particular, the idea that speaking can be treated as a simple linear process that is similar to writing but carried to the world on breath rather than paper or a screen will become untenable. The authors of the current study conclude: 'Our findings illustrate the complexity of natural communication, in which multiple channels of information interact at both the perceptual and semantic level' (Straube et al., 2010: 393). In terms of applications in teaching, knowing that person-related information is processed quite differently from impersonal information, that believing a person is speaking to you affects how the brain is 'primed' to speak, and understanding the subtle effects of gesture in relation to speech generally will all have clear relevance to both face-to-face classroom teaching and perhaps more importantly the ability to move the teaching of speaking online.

7.7.2   Potential reader project: raising awareness of speaking as a multi-sensory skill

The findings reported in Straube et al. (2010) imply that many cues other than simply the stream of spoken sounds help us to communicate via speech. As noted elsewhere in this book, speaking is very often taught as if it is written language delivered through oral/aural channels. The cutting-edge work reported here suggests that our understanding of speaking may soon be very different. This project investigates the potential differences between listener comprehension of explanations with and without the benefit of visual cues.

Stage 1: Preliminary decisions

This project could be based on the data gathered for the study on speech rates in presentations described in section 7.3.2. The material could then be played to listeners via a sound recording only or via a video to include visual cues. A decision would be needed whether particular sections of the presentation would be the focus, for example, where a student is explaining a technical term, or whether the whole presentation would be used. The benefit of using a particular functional category such as explanation or giving examples would be that some patterns of gaze, stance and gesture could potentially be linked to the function. Another approach would be to begin from sections of talk where the speaker uses gesture to enhance meaning and extract these for the viewer/listener. Evaluating listener comprehension is a particularly tricky process and thought would need to be given to the background knowledge of the listeners on a given topic and their current listening ability in the target language.

Stage 2: Experimental phase

Two groups of listeners, matched for age, language ability and educational background, would be played extracts from the presentations under two conditions: (a) via video showing speaker plus gaze, stance and gesture; (b) via a sound recording. The hypothesis would be that comprehension levels are higher under condition (a). Ideally, there would be sufficient extracts for the listeners to be played a large enough set of samples for statistical analysis and for the same extracts to be played to different listeners to allow direct comparison by extract as well as general analysis. For each extract, the subjects would be required to indicate their level of comprehension. This could be a simple Likert scale (0 = could not comprehend to 5 = fully comprehend) or some other technique such as testing recall via a written reformulation or notes. The advantage of the former approach is that it does not depend on the subjects' written language ability that may interfere with their capacity to explain clearly what they have really understood.

Stage 3: Analysis of results

The hypothesis would be supported if there were higher levels of comprehension in listeners under condition (a). Further analysis of any trends might show correlations between language function, gesture and other visual stimuli and ease of comprehension.

IV Resources and further information

Chapter 8

Research borders and boundaries

This chapter will...

- provide indications of the relationship between research into speaking and other applied linguistics disciplines;
- situate work on spoken language in emerging trends in some other disciplines.

8.1 Introduction

As noted in many places in this book, there has been remarkably little work either in linguistics or in applied linguistics into speaking as a unified language faculty. Therefore, to a certain extent this book has needed to draw together work from different fields and at different levels within the skill of speaking to present a picture of research into speech. Any unified theory of speaking would need to both bring together, and demarcate itself clearly from, a number of interrelated academic disciplines, from pragmatics to corpus linguistics, from psycholinguistics to phonetics. Both of these are well-known and flourishing areas in linguistics and each, along with a number of others, has something to say about speaking, even if they cannot provide a unified theory of spoken discourse in all contexts and domains.

We do not yet have such a theory and the other sections of this book have, in part, been about why speaking has this ambiguous status in linguistics and applied linguistics. The growth of insights about the spoken form that are beginning to emerge from work in discourse analysis, conversation analysis, pragmatics, corpus linguistics and neuro-linguistics means that there is, however, a distinct pressure for more work on the topic, and a need to make research findings usable by the more applied and pedagogically oriented sections of the linguistics community.

This chapter reviews some of the sister disciplines which are particularly pertinent to research into the faculty of speech, and attempts to show how their insights could relate to a more holistic approach to research into speech. Initially this broadening of the scope of work on spoken data may seem to be unduly far-reaching, making the study of the spoken mode a study of global cultural and ethnographic issues, social issues, psychology, biology, as well as the more traditional aspects of research into language, such as phonology, grammar and syntax. However, I have been arguing throughout this book that there is a need to begin to tease out the differences between research into the language faculty and research into the faculty of speech. This can only be done by moving beyond conceptions of speech which remain grounded in strongly text-based approaches to the study of language and towards those that draw on emerging inter-disciplinary insights.

Secondly, the broadening of the base of research into speech does not look as extreme as it might if it is compared with attitudes to research into the written mode. Work on literacy, particularly that in the field of critical linguistics, has long acknowledged the role of social and cultural factors in writing performance. It is perhaps only the conceptualisation of speech as both natural and the primary form of language which has led to the mode being treated somewhat differently from the written form, and, paradoxically, to the detriment of our understanding of the speech faculty.

8.2   Speaking and ethnographic or cross-cultural studies

At the broadest level, research into speech needs to be informed by the cultural expectations of speakers. Our understanding not only of conversational 'rules' and norms, but also our interpretation of meaning or even individual words is coloured by our (generally unconscious) acceptance of certain fundamental cultural premises.

A better awareness of the potential differences between cultures in ways that affect language behaviour can also imbue research into speech with greater insight and sensitivity. For example, speech rate, intonation, interruption or self-correction, pauses and attitudes to silence may all be areas that a researcher interested in the spoken mode would investigate. While within one's own discourse and language community such aspects may have one interpretation, in a different setting their implications and effects may be quite different – the silence that in one culture is uncomfortable or even rude is unproblematic or deferential in another. Awareness of such issues can provide insights for the researcher into speech, but, more importantly, can raise fundamental questions about the constructs we engage with in dealing with speech phenomena in the research process. Investigations carried out via actual speech data, particularly if quantitatively based, might attempt to answer research questions via inappropriate elements in the discourse if the broader cultural and ethnographic context is not properly understood. Work in the fields of ethnography and pragmatics is clearly relevant to these broader questions about the relationship between the spoken mode, conversational action, and social behaviour.

8.3   Speaking and psycholinguistics

Psycholinguistic studies focus on the relationship between brain, language and behaviour. The tendency has been for links to be investigated between psychological processes and speech behaviour at the level of planning and delivery rather than on wider psychological motivations to speech behaviour, for example how idiolect is affected by emotional or experiential factors. Aspects of speech which the psycholinguist would be interested in revolve around both practical topics such as the relationship between grammar, memory and language processing and, at the more theoretical end of the spectrum, the different levels or hierarchies involved in language production and comprehension, or the links between the brain and language acquisition.

8.4   Speaking and neuro-linguistic studies

Neuro-linguistics differs from psycholinguistics in that the focus of research is on the biological and neurological basis of language processing. As such, research into fundamental aspects of speech such as those outlined at the end of Chapter 7 can be investigated within neuro-linguistic frameworks. It is interesting to note how little either psycho- or neuro-linguistics affects mainstream applied linguistics and language teaching, despite a long and reputable research tradition. There is, however, a strong link existing between this field and speech pathology/therapy.

8.5   Speaking and corpus linguistics

Until relatively recently the greatest part of corpus work in linguistics was based on written evidence and overall the balance remains in favour of the written mode. This is due to the labour-intensive nature of preparing transcribed speech data in comparison with the relative ease, particularly in the age of electronic documentation and scanning, of capturing written material.

However, with a growing interest in speech data and the technological advances offered by powerful personal computers and the internet a large number of projects based on spoken material is being created, and, more importantly, being made generally available to researchers.

There is also a strong relationship developing between particular publishing houses and the creation of different corpora. See for instance Collins and the Cobuild Corpus (information at *http://titania.cobuild. collins.co.uk/boe.info.html*) or Longman and the British National Corpus, or Cambridge University Press and the CANCODE (Cambridge and Nottingham Corpus of Discourse in English) project.

Research into spoken corpora is throwing up many insights about the form, but from the perspective of a unified theory or approach to speech, work on corpus linguistics will always tend to isolate the samples of speech data from the original oral/aural channel in which they were produced, and also from the overall context of the discourse. The development of multi-media corpora that is starting to emerge may begin to address this issue and is one of the most promising avenues for a model of the spoken form that does justice to its rich and complex resources for communicating meaning. Analysis of a corpus that can provide linked data on a number of factors at one time – gaze, gesture, prosody, syntax and lexis – should provide a model that goes beyond the literate.

8.6   Speaking and new technologies

A fast-moving area in recent years has been the development of new technologies that blur or alter the traditional boundaries between the spoken and written mode. There are several strands to this, ranging from text to speech software, speech recognition, to robotics, to mobile computing and telephony. The aim of much work is for the user to be able to speak to a computer in much the same way as they would to another person, and for the machine to be capable of carrying out the instruction. The major applications of human–machine speech are in automated call centres, internet searching as well as applications in the military and aid for the physically less able. Uptake by the teaching community has tended to be slow, but in the first decade of the twenty-first century mobile phone providers were starting to offer English lessons via their handsets and this was becoming particularly popular in markets where the demand for English teaching outstrips face-to-face teaching capacity, such as China.

Chapter 9

Research resources

This chapter will . . .

- provide a selection of resources for the researcher;
- provide research process summaries in tabular form.

9.1 Traditional library resources

The following central journals in applied linguistics will all contain relevant material on the diverse aspects of spoken language, if not on the spoken mode *per se*. It would be worthwhile adding these titles to an automatic alerting system and scanning the table of contents regularly for key words in relation to personal research interests in spoken language:

Annual Review of Applied Linguistics
http://journals.cambridge.org/action/displayJournal?jid=APL
Applied Linguistics
http://applij.oxfordjournals.org/
Discourse & Communication
http://dcm.sagepub.com/
Discourse Studies
http://dis.sagepub.com/
Interaction Studies
http://www.benjamins.com/cgi-bin/t_seriesview.cgi?series=IS
Intercultural Pragmatics
http://www.reference-global.com/loi/iprg?cookieSet=1
International Journal of Corpus Linguistics
http://www.benjamins.com/cgi-bin/t_seriesview.cgi?series=Ijcl

International Journal of the Sociology of Language
http://www.degruyter.de/journals/ijsl/
International Review of Applied Linguistics in Language Teaching (IRAL)
http://www.degruyter.de/journals/iral/
Journal of Applied Linguistics
http://applij.oxfordjournals.org/
Journal of Politeness Research: Language, Behaviour, Culture
http://www.degruyter.de/journals/jpr/detail.cfm
Journal of Pragmatics
http://www.elsevier.com/wps/find/journaldescription.cws_home/505593/ description#description
Journal of Sociolinguistics
http://www.wiley.com/bw/journal.asp?ref=1360-6441
Language
http://muse.jhu.edu/journals/language
Language & Communication
http://www.elsevier.com/wps/find/journaldescription.cws_home/616/ description#description
Language Learning
http://www.tandf.co.uk/journals/rllj
Linguistics
http://www.linguistics-journal.com/index.php
System
http://www.elsevier.com/wps/find/journaldescription.cws_home/335/ description#description
TESOL Quarterly
http://www.tesol.org/s_tesol/seccss.asp?CID=209&DID=1679
The Modern Language Journal
http://mlj.miis.edu/

More specifically speech-oriented journals include:

Computer Speech and Language
http://www.elsevier.com/wps/find/journaldescription.cws_home/622808/ description#description
Dialogue and Discourse
http://www.dialogue-and-discourse.org/
Gesture
http://www.benjamins.com/cgi-bin/t_seriesview.cgi?series=Gest
International Journal of Speech Technology
http://www.springer.com/engineering/signals/journal/10772?detailsPage= editorialBoard
International Journal of Speech, Language & the Law
http://www.equinoxjournals.com/ojs/index.php/IJSLL

Journal of Phonetics
http://www.elsevier.com/wps/find/journaldescription.cws_home/622896/
description#description
Journal of the International Phonetic Association
http://journals.cambridge.org/action/displayJournal?jid=IPA
Language and Speech
http://www.asel.udel.edu/lgsp/
Phonology
http://journals.cambridge.org/action/displayJournal?jid=pho
Pragmatics
http://www.elsevier.com/wps/find/journaldescription.cws_home/505593/
description#description
Research on Language & Social Interaction
http://rolsi.lboro.ac.uk/
Speech Communication
http://www.elsevier.com/wps/find/journaldescription.cws_home/505597/
description#description
Text & Talk
http://www.degruyter.com/journals/text/detailEn.cfm
Voice & Speech Review
http://www.vasta.org/publications/voice_and_speech_review/vsr.html

9.2   Societies and organisations

The special interest groups of the UK English teachers' association the International Association of Teachers of English as a Foreign Language (IATEFL) on research generally and on pronunciation can be found at: *http://resig.iatefl.org/* and *http://www.reading.ac.uk/epu/pronsig_new.htm*
    TESOL Inc is a US-based association promoting English language teaching and research and can be found at: *http://www.tesol.org/s_tesol/index.asp.* The association has a special interest section on speaking and listening at: *http://www.soundsofenglish.org/SPLIS/*
    Search terms: 'TESOL inc' and 'TESOL inc pronunciation'.
    Other societies with links to the spoken mode include those listed below. An internet search containing the full title of the association should bring the reader to the current web presence.

American Dialect Society
http://www.americandialect.org/
Institute of Translation and Interpreting
http://www.iti.org.uk/indexMain.html
International Clinical Phonetics & Linguistics Assoc
http://www.ucs.louisiana.edu/~mjb0372/ICPLA.html

International Phonetic Association
http://internationalphoneticassociation.org/
International Society of Phonetic Sciences
http://www.isphs.org/
Special Interest Group for Computational Phonology (SIGPHON)
http://salad.cs.swarthmore.edu/sigphon/
VUIDS – Voice User Interface Designers
http://www.signalprocessingsociety.org/technical-committees/list/sl-tc/spl-nl/2009-04/vuids/

9.3   Online resources

The development of the internet has meant that access to oral language data is becoming increasingly easy. As well as the corpora described in section 9.4, sound archive material is available at the following sites, most of which provide downloadable sound files, or can provide taped material for research purposes:

- The Australian Film related sound archive: *http://www.screensound.gov.au/index.html* (mainly relating to film and the arts, but including interview material)

- The (British) National Sound Archive: *http://www.bl.uk/reshelp/findhelprestype/sound/index.html* (general and oral history material, including political history) and for material on British accents and dialects: *http://www.bl.uk/reshelp/findhelprestype/sound/accents/accents.html* or *http://sounds.bl.uk/BrowseCategory.aspx?category=Accents-and-dialects*

- The Michigan State University voice library: *http://vvl.lib.msu.edu/index.cfm* (including web access to samples of all US presidents' voices of the twentieth century)

- At the time of writing the BBC were providing an excellent site on the evolution of the English language which included downloadable examples of a cross-section of British voices: *http://www.bbc.co.uk/radio4/routesofenglish/index.shtml*

- The Stanford Collection of Sound Recordings: *http://www-sul.stanford.edu/depts/ars/index.html*

- The Belfer Audio Archive at the University of Syracuse: *http://libwww.syr.edu/information/belfer/*

- A very varied and downloadable set of spoken English examples provided by: *http://www.alt-usage-english.org/audio_archive.shtml*

- The US Library of Congress provides a sound archive reached through links from: *http://www.loc.gov/index.html*

- A 'meta-site' (a site at which other web resources and links are grouped) on a variety of languages other than English can be found via the LinguistList: *http://linguistlist.org/sp/GetWRListings.cfm?WRAbbrev= LangAnalysis#wr27*
- A site which incorporates sound clip and sound archive links into an EFL context including work on the differences between US and British English is: *http://eleaston.com/*

9.4 Speech corpora

There are a growing number of access routes to spoken corpora on the web. For example, the ICAME website at *http://icame.uib.no/icame-www.html* provides sample access to and also sells CD-ROM versions of the following corpora containing speech data:

- London Lund Corpus
- Lancaster/IBM Spoken English Corpus (SEC)
- Corpus of London Teenage Language (COLT)
- Wellington Spoken Corpus (New Zealand)
- The International Corpus of English – East African component

At the Aethelstan site (*http://www.athel.com/cspa.html*) it is also possible to sample a corpus of professional and academic spoken interactions and buy related software. More general spoken material at *http://info.ox.ac.uk/bnc/* can be found in the British National Corpus.

There are many speech corpora that have been created to assist with research into speech recognition and other aspects of human–computer interaction. See for instance the 'Buckeye Speech Corpus' *http://vic.psy. ohio-state.edu/*.

The Centre for Spoken Language Understanding at the Oregon Graduate Institute of Science and Technology creates specialised corpora including children's speech and a variety of accents and languages. *http://www.cslu.ogi.edu/corpora/corpCurrent.html*. The Centre also provides a free 'toolkit' to work with these corpora.

A growing number of spoken corpora in a variety of languages are also readily available:

Chinese:
http://www.lancs.ac.uk/fass/projects/corpus/LCMC/
http://corpora.tapor.ualberta.ca/wenzhou/
Russian:
http://www.ruscorpora.ru/en/index.html (includes a sub-corpus of spoken Russian from the 1930s to 2007)

Romance languages (Italian, French, Portuguese, Spanish):
http://lablita.dit.unifi.it/coralrom/index.html
Welsh:
http://www.language-archives.org/item/oai:talkbank.org:-BilingBank-Bangor-Siarad

As a hint when searching for resources online, the search term 'speech + corpus' is much more likely to bring up results in the speech recognition field than general corpus linguistics. In terms of searching for the latter 'spoken + corpus' will be more effective and 'spoken + corpus + [name of language]' should bring up a link to a corpus in almost any language that you name, although, again, many of these will be created for automatic speech recognition rather than broader applied linguistic analysis.

9.5   Speech recognition and text-to-speech

Ideas and resources for using speech recognition to help students with disabilities can be found at:
http://www3.edc.org/spk2wrt/lab.html
A history of attempts to produce artificial speech can be found at:
http://www.ling.su.se/staff/hartmut/kemplne.htm
An example of a text-to-speech engine in seven languages is available at:
http://www.nextup.com/TextAloud/
A search on the term 'text to speech' will bring you to a large number of both commercial and free sites offering to produce spoken audio output from inputted text. Examples at the time of writing are:
http://www.voiceforge.com/
http://www.squidoo.com/text-speech-programs
http://www.talkingonline.com/
http://www.abc2mp3.com/

9.6   Online pronunciation and intonation resources

A large number of useful sites are listed at:
http://www.sunburstmedia.com/PronWeb.html
A site which provides examples of different accents of the British Isles is at:
http://www.phon.ox.ac.uk/files/apps/old_IViE/
An easy to navigate and useful site which plays sound files of common American contractions in speech is at:
http://www.spokenamericanenglish.com/

Talking dictionaries are also common such as the freely available:
http://www.howjsay.com/
http://www.fonetiks.org/
For the teacher and student alike there are a number of online discussion sites, networks and linked resources, for example:
http://www.englishclub.com/pronunciation/index.htm
http://www.bbc.co.uk/worldservice/learningenglish/grammar/pron/

A search on the terms 'pronunciation + video' will lead to a particularly rich set of resources demonstrating various aspects of pronunciation through online videos.

9.7 Miscellaneous sites for the applied linguist with an interest in spoken discourse

An excellent general website for the applied linguist is: *http://www. linguistlist.org/*
From this it is possible to search through, or join, various discussion groups; for instance, a group on discourse at: *http://linguistlist.org/lists/ join-list.cfm?List=24* or language and culture: *http://linguistlist.org/lists/ join-list.cfm?List=46*
The Centre for Information on Language Teaching and Research (CILT) provides a forum and a 'virtual language centre' at: *http://www. linguanet.org.uk/*
The Speech, Hearing and Language Research Centre of Macquarie University can be visited at: *http://www.shlrc.mq.edu.au/*
There is an online bibliography of ethnolinguistics and conversation analysis at: *http://www2.fmg.uva.nl/emca/*
Resources on speaking in a business context are to be found at:
http://www.cambridgeesol.org/teach/bec/bec_higher/speaking/index.htm
General advice on teaching and learning speaking, as well as teaching resources, can be found at: *http://eleaston.com/speaking.html*
A highly useful site of tips, techniques and news can be found at:
http://www.everythingesl.net/
A fun site with links to free games to generate talk can be found at:
http://www.englishbanana.com/

As a hint, when looking for resources online the results can be very diverse in this area, and can also produce a very high number of returned pages. It is a good idea to begin with two or three search terms in combination such as 'pronunciation + vocabulary + English' or 'pronunciation + intonation + questions', therefore.

9.8 Moving towards your own project on spoken discourse

Figures 9.1 and 9.2 present some of the complexities of relationships between practitioners, research, and researchers in applied linguistics. Issues to think about at the outset are listed below.

Figure 9.1 Information exchange between academe and classrooms

Global problems for the researcher into speech data

- Very few theories of speech *per se*.
- Very few researchers have worked on speech in its own right within applied linguistics.
- Within applied linguistic theory 'speech' has often been conflated with 'language' and this can cause difficulties in trying to pin down the exact scope of a research project into the spoken form of language.

Further issues for the researcher into speech

Problem 1 What am I investigating?
Sounds?
Structures or forms?
Discourse?

Problem 2 What theoretical background can I use?
Theories of speech production?
Theories of speech processing?
Frameworks from discourse analysis or conversation analysis?
Problem 3 For language pedagogy, what is the target spoken form?
What dialect form shall I teach?
What model of correctness, if any, will I use?
What model of pragmatic or cultural behaviour will I use?
Problem 4 What are the most appropriate research methods to investigate my data?
Quantitative and/or experimental?
Qualitative and/or integrative?

TEACHERS AS RESEARCH CONSUMERS
- Comment on/assess new ideas in public domain (star rating for usefulness?)
- Ask for specific solutions to problem areas (e.g. problems of spoken grammar)
- Adapt/test approaches
- Give frank feedback
- Put forward new ideas for research topics

RESEARCHERS AS SOLUTION PROVIDERS
- Seek specific problem topics from teachers
- Instil importance of applicability of ideas in research students
- Ensure clear distinction between 'blue sky' and more applicable work
- Think of teachers and materials developers needs

PUBLISHERS AS FACILITATORS
- Provide 'research digest' service online for teachers
- Mediate between researchers and materials developers
- Fund team research projects on basis of teacher requests

Figure 9.2   **A possible cycle of information exchange between teachers, researchers and publishers**

9.9   Sources of inspiration for research

9.9.1   Personal experience of the profession

A research topic may grow from a problem, question or challenge you meet in your working life. As a practitioner this could relate to your students' progress in their speaking abilities, the dynamics of interactions between them, confusion over who is allowed to speak at a given point, or their own questions to you about speaker dynamics or conversation.

You may find it helpful to keep a research questions notebook to hand at the early stages of a research project and jot down your queries and thoughts about these at the end of a working day. This will be a good source of practically oriented research questions and looking back at the real-world questions which prompted you to begin can help with motivation as the research project develops.

An example of the kind of research which can grow from a problem experienced in a working context can be found in Tyler, Jeffries and Davies (1988).

Quote 9.1   Tyler, Jeffries and Davies on a problem arising in spoken academic discourse

Communication problems surrounding the spoken academic discourse of teachers who are non-native speakers of English are a growing concern at US universities. This paper presents partial results of an analysis of the videotaped teaching demonstrations of 18 Korean and Chinese graduate students at the University of Florida. The analysis was carried out within an integrative discourse framework, that is, one which considers the interrelatedness of various levels of linguistic organisation.

(Tyler, Jeffries and Davies, 1988: 101)

When it comes to presenting the research to a reader, these kinds of real-world difficulties give a sense of urgency and interest to the material and can help in particular with the introduction sections of the report or article.

9.9.2   Developments in the profession

Inspiration for research topics can also be drawn from broader issues outside the classroom which are seen as influencing the profession as a whole.

A broad topic which you might want to pursue might be the changing role of the teacher in the communicative classroom and how this is reflected in teacher talk. In terms of teacher development you may wish to investigate how teacher trainers relate to novice teachers and conduct an ethnographic survey of their interactions. In general, these kinds of topics are most suited to the experienced professional teacher who wants to reflect on the skill of speaking within broader issues which they have seen alter their working lives. See also Quote 9.2.

Quote 9.2   Hoey on the teaching profession and spoken discourse

Why should a language teacher be concerned with the working of spoken discourse? Certainly not because the learner's syllabus needs to be augmented by explicit introduction to discourse analysis.... The real reason that language teachers should consider how discourses are organised is that it will help them to judge better the effectiveness of what they are doing.... If the teacher knows what a natural conversation involves, he or she will be in a better position to assess whether their learners are succeeding in developing the conversational skills that they need in order to be effective speakers of the target language.

(Hoey, 1991: 66)

9.9.3   Social or pragmatic issues

Topics for research can also arise from very general matters relating to the norms of conversation. In the early stages of a written introduction to a research paper it is quite common for researchers to relate their specific topic to a real-world issue of some kind, which even the non-specialist can understand, and then to use this as a lead into the specific more academic topic under consideration. Quote 9.3 gives an example of this approach.

Quote 9.3   Eisenstein and Bodman on cross-cultural norms of thanking

Most native speakers of English on a conscious level associate the expression of gratitude with the words 'thank you'; however, they are unaware of the underlying complex rules and the mutuality needed for expressing gratitude in a manner satisfying to both the giver and recipient.

(Eisenstein and Bodman, 1993: 64)

9.9.4   Published research and theory

A very common source of questions for the beginning researcher is existing work and theory. This is perhaps the most frequent technique by which an academic presents a topic as having relevance to fellow academics. See Quotes 9.4 and 9.5. For the novice academic, providing clear links between previous work and your own also shows that you have carried out sufficient background research into your topic to be certain that what you are doing is not simply a repetition of the work of someone else. For this reason the unproven researcher may have to insert higher numbers of references in their literature review than a more seasoned academic.

Quotes 9.4 and 9.5	Two examples of researchers linking the inspiration for their work to previous studies

Another focus of our research has been on how Americans and Japanese perform such speech acts with status unequals. This question was asked because it is generally claimed that Japanese are very conscious of social status while Americans are relatively less status-conscious. Ide (1989) for example, argues.... Similarly, Matsumoto (1989) argues...

(Takehashi and Beebe, 1993: 139)

Previous studies into non-native speaker interlanguage are dominated by a focus on the variation between correct vs. incorrect target language forms (Tarone, 1975, 1988; Tarone and Parrish, 1988; Schachter, 1986; Ellis 1986, 1987; Ellis and Roberts, 1987; Preston, 1989). We must distinguish between these studies of interlanguage *variation* and the study of target language *variability* in the discourse on non-native speakers, which is the topic of this paper.

(Haynes, 1992: 43)

Where the primary aim of research is to build on previous work the researcher has to be particularly careful to show the novelty and interest of the work being presented. That is to say, if the object of the research is not to solve a real-world problem or to investigate the impacts of developments in the profession, then the value of the work has to be established in some other way. Traditionally in academic settings the appropriacy of a piece of research can be established by showing how it grows out of previous work in the field, and is fulfilling some need or gap in relation to work done before. A good place to look for ideas for research topics is, therefore, in the discussion/conclusion sections of articles you read as background to your own work. Conventionally, the academic writer will show that they are aware of the limitations of their present work by noting what further work could be carried out in the area, and this can help you to focus on a topic of your own.

9.10 Research skills summaries

This section gives a brief overview of some practical steps in the research process and how to present findings clearly.

9.10.1 Research questions

The most common way of shaping research is to found it on a single over-arching question which summarises the main thrust of the project as a whole. Table 9.1 gives some examples of initial questions the reader might have after reading some of the articles presented in earlier chapters and which might grow into a new broad topic for further work.

9.10.2 The cycle of research

It is useful to remember that the process of research is cyclical. That is to say until the final framework is set up and the research carried out the experienced researcher will keep options open and add new knowledge to existing ideas in quite a fluid way until the steps needed start to 'gel'. Priorities and tasks will differ depending on what stage in the cycle the researcher is at, and good research is rarely a straightforward, unproblematic, linear process (Table 9.2).

Table 9.1 **Broad research questions growing out of previous work**

Article	Potential further questions
Liberman (1998)	Is there real evidence for the 'biological advantage of speech over writing/reading' which Liberman takes as a premise?
Thompson and Couper-Kuhlen (2005)	How else could you investigate what speakers and listeners regard as a unit of talk? Could you apply their approach to L2 performance and what would it tell you?
Morton (2009)	These findings were from the field of architecture and looked at student presentations. How do these differ from expert presentations by professional architects in authentic contexts? If they are very different, what does this tell us, and what are the implications for curriculum design?

Table 9.2 **The cycle of research**

Research cycles	Earlier stages	Central stages	Final stages
Think (topic)	Define scope of project for yourself	Redefine scope and topic, redraft outline	Check and review scope of findings in relation to original aims
↓	↓	↓	↓
Find	Background readings; setting up relevant research questions; carrying out pilot studies	Carry out research activity to investigate topic, conducting surveys, analysing data, detailed readings and argument	Find final references, check references, complete bibliography
↓	↓	↓	↓
Think (audience)	Consider topic, outline and scope in light of assessors of your work (supervisor, examiner or journal readership)	Draft chapters or sections aiming for consistency of style and taking into account readership – remember no one will be as familiar with the detail of the work as you are	Review final draft of research text – will it make sense to a reader who has not experienced your research processes? Are there clear linking sections showing the logic and progression of your ideas? Write your introduction and abstract
↓	↓	↓	↓
Present	Present initial ideas as a proposal or outline	Present drafts to peer review, supervisor review, conferences/ seminars etc.	Submit final draft (generally there will be a final cycle of comments and minor changes even after the submission)

9.10.3 Presenting and commenting on findings and drawing conclusions

Table 9.3 Examples of data commentary and its diverse functions

Function of findings or data commentary sections in research texts	Examples from case-study articles in earlier chapters
To locate, or direct the reader to, detailed information	'Tables 2 and 3 summarise the frequency of these different question types by participant across the four role plays.' (Burns *et al.*, 2008: 329)
To direct the reader's attention to significant information (*not* simply repeating data without any evaluative language)	'As predicted, two partners together used fewer words in the workspace visible condition than in the workspace hidden condition.... Not surprisingly, directors used over four times as many words as builders.' (Clark and Krych, 2004: 67)
To begin to draw conclusions relating directly to the data	'These results indicate that there are distinct brain regions involved in the processing of specific pairings of actor orientation and speech-gesture content.' (Straube *et al.*, 2010: 389)

9.10.4 Drawing conclusions

Table 9.4 Features of conclusions and common mistakes

Contains new ideas/information?	✗
Contains repetition of main points of argument or of findings?	✓
Focuses on the best ideas you have had to 'sell' them to the reader?	✓
Gives a broad summary of all your points, whether stronger or weaker?	✗
Links back clearly to the original research questions?	✓
Gives sense of how far the research questions were answered?	✓
Hides any problems and limitations of the research process?	✗
Expresses the limitations of the research and possible further research?	✓
Gives a clear sense of finality to the research text?	✓

Glossary

Adjacency pair This is a term from discourse and, more generally, conversation analysis. Whereas theoretical linguists might be interested in isolated sentences, discourse and conversation analysts look at utterances in relation to each other. The term 'adjacency pair' relates to two consecutive utterances which are so strongly related to one another in the conversational structure of a language that one seems bizarre without the other. In standard British conversation examples might be a greeting – greeting pair ('Hi'–'Hi'; 'How are you doing?'–'Fine, thanks') or a thanking exchange ('Thanks'–'My pleasure'; 'Thanks a lot'–'Not at all').

Avoidance Avoidance is a term used in the assessment of language ability, for example in testing or in analysis of the range of forms used by a learner. A learner may be very accurate in their production, but be functioning within a limited range of forms. By contrast, another learner may make a significantly higher number of errors, but be functioning within a more complex range of structures. The technical description of what the former is doing is 'avoidance'.

Backchannel A term from conversation analysis and discourse analysis. This refers to the verbal and non-verbal feedback which a listener gives to a speaker during an interaction (for example, 'Yes', 'Mmm' or 'I see').

Circumlocution Generally a circumlocution is an extended, long-winded or roundabout way of expressing an idea (perhaps in order to avoid a very explicit phrase that might cause offence). In applied linguistics the term crops up in the investigation of communication strategies in relation to a learner's ability to express an idea for which they do not know the word in their target language.

Discourse marker A word or phrase which is used by a speaker (or writer) to orient the audience. The word or phrase has little meaning in its own right but provides a point of reference for the listener in relation to either the structure of the talk and topic ('Right', 'OK', 'Now') or the opinion of the speaker ('Yeah', 'Sure', 'Well').

Ellipsis A feature found in both speech and writing, but which has been studied less in relation to the former. A standard sentence contains certain grammatical elements that a 'full' rendering of the sentence would show. In English we expect perhaps a subject + verb + object, given a transitive verb. Other languages standardly omit the subject element. However, when an element that you would normally expect is left out this process is called 'ellipsis'. Therefore, when a speaker says 'Ready yet?' in place of 'Are you ready yet?' and someone replies 'Coming!' instead of 'I'm coming' both are using ellipsis of subject and auxiliary verb. It is important for learners of spoken language to become able to use ellipsis naturally so that they do not sound overly formal or ponderous. However, this is much easier to teach in relation to the written form where the patterns are less complex. An issue in relation to ellipsis in speech is how far any underlying full structure is clear and available for analysis.

Face This is an expression used both as a lay term and, more technically, in the field of pragmatics. The term 'to lose face' indicates that a person has lost esteem in the eyes of others. In most cultures a considerable amount of conversational exchange is devoted to ensuring that politeness conventions are met, and that an interlocutor does not feel uncomfortable. Facework is a term used to describe the sections of conversation where this most obviously takes place. For example, in British culture, speakers may ask about health or talk about the weather before developing a conversation further. If a particularly difficult or embarrassing topic has to be raised quite elaborate facework may be engaged in to assess the situation before the subject is broached. Different cultures have different attitudes to face, and facework is carried out via very different mechanisms and resources in different languages.

Formulaic exchange/utterance One of the distinguishing characteristics of the human capacity for language is the level of creativity it allows. However, not all language is novel and completely distinctive. Many sections of conversational exchange are highly predictable, although these will vary from culture to culture and language to language. For example, the opening and closing of a conversation generally follows a pattern that speakers are hardly conscious of, but which, if breached, will cause confusion and mis-communication. In particular, the treatment of functions, such as offering food or drink (in your culture do you refuse, but expect to be offered a second time?) or giving/accepting compliments (do you automatically denigrate the object which has been admired?), tend to have strongly established patterns. These patterns are so conventional they are known as formulaic exchanges or utterances.

Interlocutor This is a more technical term for a language sender/receiver (a speaker/writer, listener/reader). It is a useful term because you do not have to specify the direction of message as the word contains a sense of two-way communication.

Intonation The aspect of the stream of speech which can be isolated in terms of pitch, combined with stress and speed, and which in many languages is meaning bearing (for example, in British English the rise at the end of a yes/no question).

L1 First language.

L2 Second (or other) language.

Metalanguage This is language used to talk about language and language processes. When speakers engage in a standard conversation they do not normally comment on the process of the conversation or discuss the language in an abstract way. Two speakers may say to one another 'Morning', 'Morning' or 'Hi', 'How are you?' but they rarely think about this as a pair of 'greetings' or two 'openings' to a conversation, or an 'exchange' or an 'interaction', 'turn' or 'move'. All these ways of describing the speaker's language are examples of metalanguage.

Phonemics The study of the meaningful sound contrasts in a language. For example, although in English there are two different /l/ sounds depending on the position of the phoneme in a word (if you say the word 'little' you will hear both the 'light' /l/ at the start of the word and the 'dark' one at the end) they are not used to distinguish one word from another. In contrast the two 'th' sounds in English /Ø/ (**th**in) and /ð/ (**th**ese) are used to distinguish one word from another, for instance, teeth–teethe, wreath–wreathe.

Phonetics The study of the sounds of a language. In this science the focus is on the flow of sounds in relation to one another and their analysis through sound spectrography and phonetic symbols.

Phonology The study of the sound structure of a language especially in the context of changes to the sounds of words through time and/or the relations between the historical developments of different languages.

Pragmatics In studying discourse analysis you will probably come across words like *pragmatic* and *cultural* and *context* quite a few times and may wonder what the difference is between 'discourse analysis' and 'pragmatics'. In the case of the former the focus is more strongly on the actual words, phrases and chunks of language produced and how these interrelate to make up typical patterns. In the case of the latter, the focus is more on the kinds of knowledge, beliefs or understandings which speakers have about the way they should behave in communication, and this is sometimes referred to as 'pragmatic knowledge'.

Prosody The parts of the stream of spoken language that carry meaning, but are beyond the confines of words and clauses, and are strictly sound based. Pitch, loudness and rhythm are all parts of the prosodic system of a language.

Service encounter A term from discourse analysis to describe spoken genres that revolve around trade and business service, such as encounters in banks, post offices or ticket offices.

Socio-linguistics The branch of linguistics that is particularly interested in the interaction between language use and social influences. Whereas a discourse analyst might be interested in patterns of interaction within a conversation, the socio-linguist is concerned with how the speech of an individual or group is affected by social, economic or geographic factors.

Speech recognition The process by which a computer or other non-human communication device understands and interacts with a human user.

Speech synthesis The process of imitating human speech via computer systems.

Speech therapy/pathology Speech which is produced with difficulty (for example, stammering), or, in a child, speech which is below the level expected for a particular stage in development may need the assistance of speech therapy. Speech pathology tends to be used for problems with the faculty of speech that are the result of accident, illness or other trauma.

Suprasegmental This is a term from phonetics. As well as vowel and consonant sounds in a language there are meaningful elements that occur simultaneously with them, such as pitch, stress and intonation. These are known as suprasegmentals because they function above or across the boundaries of the other elements that are studied.

T-Unit This stands for 'thought unit'. There are a number of different definitions of this, but the two main areas they have been used in are literacy/readability studies and the study of spoken genres. The concept is regarded as useful because it gets away from the sometimes difficult to define clause and sentence units. Within spoken analysis the rather loose definition of 'a group of words expressing one idea' is tightened by the use of intonation (downward in English) and slight pausing to mark the ends of a t-unit.

Text analysis This is the sister discipline of discourse analysis. Whereas the latter tends to be more interested in the spoken mode, text analysis, as the name suggests, is concerned with extended stretches of written language and how they cohere. Both disciplines share a common interest in patterns of language and relations between elements beyond the level of the clause.

Turn-taking The process by which speakers interact with one another. A large amount of work in discourse and conversation analysis is interested in how speakers know that they have a right to speak and precisely when.

References

Aarts, B. and Meyer, C. (eds) (1995). *The Verb in Contemporary English: theory and description*. Cambridge: Cambridge University Press.

Abercrombie, D. (1967). *Elements of General Phonetics*. Edinburgh: Edinburgh University Press.

Anderson, B. (2007). Pedagogical rules and their relationship to frequency in the input: observational and empirical data from L2 French. *Applied Linguistics*. 28(2): 286–308.

Anthony, E. M. (1963). Approach, method, and technique. *ELT Journal*. 63–67.

Auer, J. (1959). *An Introduction to Research in Speech*. New York: Harper and Brothers.

Auer, P. (2009). On-line syntax: thoughts on the temporality of spoken language. *Language Sciences*. 31: 1–13.

Bachman, L. F. (1990). *Fundamental Considerations in Language Testing*. Oxford: Oxford University Press.

Bachman. L. F. (2005). Building and supporting a case for test use. *Language Assessment Quarterly*. 2(1): 1–34.

Bakhtin, M. M. (1986). The problem of speech genres. (Trans. McGee, V. W.) In C. Emerson and M. Holquist (eds), *Speech Genres and Other Late Essays*. Austin: University of Texas Press, pp. 62–102.

Baldwin, T., Beavers, J., Bender, E.M., Flickinger, D., Kim, A. and Oepen, S. (2005). Beauty and the Beast: what running a broad-coverage precision grammar over the BNC taught us about the grammar – and the corpus. In S. Kepser and M. Reis (eds), *Linguistic Evidence: empirical, theoretical and computational perspectives* (Studies in Generative Grammar). Berlin: Walter de Gruyter & Co., pp. 49–70.

Barbieri, F. and Eckhardt, S. E. B. (2007). Applying corpus-based findings to form-focused instruction: the case of reported speech. *Language Teaching Research*. 11(3): 319–346.

Bargiela-Chiappini, F., Nickerson, C. and Planken, B. (2007). *Business Discourse*. Basingstoke: Palgrave Macmillan.

Barron, A. (2005). Variational pragmatics in the foreign language classroom. *System*. 33(3): 519–536.

Beaucousin, V., Lacheret, A., Turbelin, M., Morel, M., Mazoyer, B. and Tzourio-Mazoyer, N. (2007). FMRI study of emotional speech comprehension. *Cerebral Cortex*. 17(2): 339–352.

Benson, P., Chik, A., Gao, X., Huang, J. and Wang, W. (2009). Qualitative research in language teaching and learning journals 1997–2006. *The Modern Language Journal.* 93(1): 79–90.

Berg, T. (1997). The modality-specificity of linguistic representations: evidence from slips of the tongue and the pen. *Journal of Pragmatics.* 27(5): 671–697.

Berg, T. and Hassan, A. (1996). The unfolding of suprasegmental representations: a cross-linguistic perspective. *Journal of Linguistics.* 32: 291–324.

Biber, D. (1988). *Variation across Speech and Writing.* Cambridge: Cambridge University Press.

Biber, D. (2006). *University Language: a corpus-based study of spoken and written registers.* Amsterdam: John Benjamins.

Biber, D. and Barbieri, F. (2007). Lexical bundles in university spoken and written registers. *English for Specific Purposes.* 26: 263–286.

Biber, D. and Reppen, R. (2002). What does frequency have to do with grammar teaching? *Studies in Second Language Acquisition.* 24: 199–208.

Biber, D., Conrad, S., Reppen, R., Byrd, P. and Helt, M. (2002). Speaking and writing in the university: a multidimensional comparison. *TESOL Quarterly.* 36(1): 9–48.

Biber, D., Conrad, S. M., Reppen, R., Byrd, P., Helt, M., Clark, V., Cortes, V., Csomay, E. and Urzua, A. (2004). *Representing Language Use in the University: analysis of the TOEFL 2000 spoken and written academic language corpus.* Princeton, NJ: Educational Testing Service.

Biber, D., Johansson, S., Leech, G., Conrad, S. and Finegan, E. (1999). *Longman Grammar of Spoken and Written English.* Harlow: Longman.

Blake, C. (2009). Potential of text-based internet chats for improving oral fluency in a second language. *The Modern Language Journal.* 93(2): 227–240.

Boxer, D. and Cohen, A. D. (2004). *Studying Speaking to Inform Second Language Learning.* Clevedon: Multilingual Matters.

Brazil, D. (1994). *Pronunciation for Advanced Learners of English.* Cambridge: Cambridge University Press.

Brazil, D. (1995). *A Grammar of Speech.* Oxford: Oxford University Press.

Brown, G. and Yule, G. (1983). *Teaching the Spoken Language: an approach based on the analysis of conversational English.* Cambridge: Cambridge University Press.

Brown, H. D. (1994). *Teaching by Principles: an interactive approach to language pedagogy.* Englewood Cliffs, NJ: Prentice Hall Regents.

Burns, A. and Joyce, H. (1997). *Focus on Speaking.* Sydney: National Center for English Language Teaching and Research, Macquarie University.

Burns, A. and Moore, S. (2008). Questioning in simulated accountant–client consultations: exploring implications for ESP teaching. *English for Specific Purposes.* 27: 322–337.

Butler, F. A., Eignor, D., Jones, S., McNamara, T. and Suomi, B. K. (2000). TOEFL 2000 speaking framework: a working paper. TOEFL Monograph Series 20. Princeton, NJ: Educational Testing Service.

Bybee, J. (2006). From usage to grammar: the mind's response to repetition. *Language.* 82(4): 529–551.

Bygate, M., Skehan, P. and Swain, M. (2001). *Researching Pedagogic Tasks: second language learning, teaching, and testing.* New York: Longman.

Cambridge ESOL. (2009a). Speaking Test Assessment Focus. *http://www.cambridgeesol.org/exams/general-english/sfl/speaking-assessment.html* (accessed July 2009).

Cambridge ESOL. (2009b). Examples of Speaking Performances at CEF Levels A2 to C2. University of Cambridge ESOL Examinations Research and Validation Group.

Carlo, J. L. and Yoo, Y. (2007). 'How may I help you?' Politeness in computer-mediated and face-to-face library reference transactions. *Information and Organization*. 17: 193–231.

Carter, R., Hughes, R. and McCarthy, M. (2000). *Exploring Grammar in Context*. Cambridge: Cambridge University Press.

Carter, R. and McCarthy, M. (1995). Grammar and the spoken language. *Applied Linguistics*. 16(2): 141–158.

Carter, R. and McCarthy, M. (1997). *Exploring Spoken English*. Cambridge: Cambridge University Press.

Carter, R. and McCarthy, M. (2006). *The Cambridge Grammar of English*. Cambridge: Cambridge University Press.

Chafe, W. and Danielewicz, J. (1987). Properties of spoken and written language. In R. Horowitz and S. J. Samuels (eds), *Comprehending Oral and Written Language*. San Diego, CA: Academic Press, pp. 83–113.

Chapman, S. and Routledge, C. (eds) (2009). *Key Ideas in Linguistics and the Philosophy of Language*. Edinburgh: Edinburgh University Press.

Cheng, W. and Tsui, A. B. M. (2009). 'Ahh ((laugh)) well there is no comparison between the two I think': How do Hong Kong Chinese and native speakers of English disagree with each other? *Journal of Pragmatics*. 41: 2365–2380.

Chomsky, N. (1965). *Aspects of the Theory of Syntax*. Cambridge, MA: MIT Press.

Clark, H. H. and Krych, M. A. (2004). Speaking while monitoring addressees for understanding. *Journal of Memory and Language*. 50: 62–81.

Clark, H. H. and Wasow, T. (1998). Repeating words in spontaneous speech. *Cognitive Psychology*. 37(3): 201–242.

Conrad, S. (2000). Will corpus linguistics revolutionize grammar teaching in the 21st century? *TESOL Quarterly*. 34(3): 548–560.

Coplan, R. J. and Weeks, M. (2009). Shy and soft-spoken: shyness, pragmatic language, and socio-emotional adjustment in early childhood. *Infant and Child Development*. 18(3): 238–254.

Cornbleet, S. and Carter, R. (2001). *The Language of Speech and Writing*. London: Routledge.

Croisilie, B., Brabant, M. J., Carmol, T., Lepage, Y., Aimard, G. and Trillet, M. (1996). Comparison between oral and written spelling in Alzheimer's disease. *Brain and Language*. 54(3): 361–387.

Cross, D. (1992). *A Practical Handbook of Language Teaching*. Hemel Hempstead: Prentice Hall.

Cunningham, S. and Moor, P. (1992). *Everyday Listening and Speaking*. Oxford: Oxford University Press.

Curl, T. S. (2006). Offers of assistance: constraints on syntactic design. *Journal of Pragmatics*. 38: 1257–1280.

Darling, A. L. (2005). Public presentations in mechanical engineering and the discourse of technology. *Communication Education*. 54(1): 20–33.

Dat, B. (2003). Materials for developing speaking skills. In B. Tomlinson (ed.), *Developing Materials for Language Teaching*. London: Continuum, pp. 375–393.

Davies, A. (2008). Textbook trends in teaching language testing. *Language Testing*. 25(3): 327–347.

Derwing, T. M. (2008). Curriculum issues in teaching pronunciation to second language learners. In: J. G. Hansen Edwards and M. L. Zampini (eds), *Phonology and Second Language Acquisition*. Amsterdam: John Benjamins, pp. 347–370.

Derwing, T. M. and Monro, M. J. (2005). Second language accent and pronunciation teaching: a research-based approach. *TESOL Quarterly*. 39(3): 378–397.

DIUS. (2009). Adult ESOL core curriculum. Speak to Communicate, Entry level 3. Department of Innovation, Universities and Skills. (*http://www.dcsf.gov.uk/curriculum_esol/tree/speaking/speaktocommunicate/e3/*) accessed July 2009.

Dörnyei, Z. (2007). *Research Methods in Applied Linguistics: quantitative, qualitative, and mixed methodologies*. Oxford: Oxford University Press.

Douglas, D. (1997). Testing speaking ability in academic contexts: theoretical considerations. TOEFL Monograph Series. Princeton, NJ: Educational Testing Service.

Douglas, D. (2000). *Assessing Languages for Specific Purposes*. Cambridge: Cambridge University Press.

Douglas, D. (2004). Discourse domains: the cognitive context of speaking. In D. Boxer and A. D. Cohen (eds), *Studying Speaking to Inform Second Language Learning*. Bristol: Multilingual Matters Ltd., pp. 25–44.

Drew, P. and Heritage, J. (1992). *Talk at Work*. Cambridge, England: Cambridge University Press.

Eisenstein, M. and Bodman, J. (1993). Expressing gratitude in American English. In G. Kasper and S. Blum-Kulka (eds), *Interlanguage Pragmatics*. New York: Oxford University Press.

Ellis, A. W., Burani, C., Izura, C., Bromiley, A. and Venneri, A. (2006). Traces of vocabulary acquisition in the brain: evidence from covert object naming. *Neuroimage*. 33(3): 958–968.

Ellis, R. (1986). *Understanding Second Language Acquisition*. Oxford: Oxford University Press.

Ellis, R., Basturkmen, H. and Loewen, S. (2002). Doing focus-on-form. *System*. 30: 419–432.

ETS. (2008). *iBT/Next Generation TOEFL Test ETS Independent Speaking Rubrics*. https://www.ets.org/Media/Tests/TOEFL/pdf/Independent_Speaking_Rubrics_2008.pdf (accessed June 2009).

ETS (2009). *The TOEFL® iBT: Improving Your Speaking Skills*. http://www.ets.org/portal/site/ets/menuitem.1488512ecfd5b8849a77b13bc3921509/?vgnextoid=6328e282af178010VgnVCM10000022f95190RCRD&vgnextchannel=fcaf215790d68010VgnVCM10000022f95190RCRD (accessed 13 June 2009).

Fitch, W. T., Hauser, M. D. and Chomsky, N. (2005). The evolution of the language faculty: clarifications and implications. *Discussion/Cognition*. 97: 179–210.

Florez, M. C. (1999). Improving adult English language learners' speaking skills. Report for National Clearinghouse for ESL Literacy Education (NCLE). Washington, DC: National Clearinghouse for ESL Literacy Education.

Folse, K. S. (2006). *The Art of Teaching Speaking*. Mahwah, NJ: Lawrence Erlbaum.

Ford, C. E., Fox, B. A. and Thompson, S. A. (2002). Constituency and the grammar of turn increments. In Cecilia E. Ford, Barbara A. Fox and Sandra A. Thompson (eds), *The Language of Turn and Sequence*. Oxford: Oxford University Press, pp. 14–38.

Fowler, C. A. (2008). The FLMP STMPed. *Psychonomic Bulletin & Review*. 15(2): 458–462.

French, P. and Local, J. (1983). Turn-competitive incomings. *Journal of Pragmatics*. 7: 17–38.

Fulcher, G. (2003). *Testing Second Language Speaking*. London: Pearson Longman.

Gammidge, M. (2004). *Speaking Extra*. Cambridge: Cambridge University Press.

Gan, Z., Davison, C. and Hamp-Lyons, L. (2009). Topic negotiation in peer group oral assessment situations: a conversation analytic approach. *Applied Linguistics*. 30(3): 315–334.

Gattegno, C. (1976). *The Common Sense of Teaching Foreign Languages*. New York: Educational Solutions.

Gimson, A. C. (1978). *A Practical Course of English Pronunciation*. London: Edward Arnold.

Goodwin, C. (1981). *Conversational Organisation: interaction between speakers and hearers*. New York: Academic Press.

Grabe, E. and Low, E. L. (2002). Durational variability in speech and the Rhythm Class Hypothesis. In C. Gussenhoven and N. Warner (eds), *Papers in Laboratory Phonology 7*. Cambridge: Cambridge University Press.

Grosjean, F. (1983). How long is the sentence? Prediction and prosody in the on-line processing of language. *Linguistics*. 21: 501–529.

Grosjean, F. and Hirt, C. (1996). Using prosody to predict the end of sentences in English and French: normal and brain-damaged subjects. *Language and Cognitive Processes*. 11(1): 107–134.

Guardian. (2008). Wanted: English speakers with fluency in sarcasm. *The Guardian* newspaper, Tuesday 29 January 2008, *http://www.guardian.co.uk/education/2008/jan/29/furthereducation.tefl* accessed 15 May 2009.

Gunn, B. (trans.) (1906). *The Instruction of Ptah-ho-tep and the Instruction of Kegemni: the oldest books in the world*. London: John Murray.

Halliday, M. A. K. (1989). *Spoken and Written Language*. Oxford: Oxford University Press.

Hammerly, H. (1991). *Fluency and Accuracy: towards balance in language teaching and learning*. Bristol, PA: Multilingual Matters Ltd.

Hamp-Lyons, L. (1997). Washback, impact and validity: ethical concerns. *Language Testing*. 14: 295–303.

Hamp-Lyons, L. (2007). The impact of testing practices on teaching: ideologies and alternatives. In J. Cummins and C. Davison (eds), *International Handbook of English Language Teaching*. New York: Springer.

Hargreaves, R. and Fletcher, M. (1979). *Making Polite Noises*. London: Evans.

Hatch, E. (1992). *Discourse and Language Education*. Cambridge: Cambridge University Press.

Haynes, L. A. (1992). The development of speaking/writing variability in narratives of non-native English speakers. *Issues in Applied Linguistics*. 3(1): 43–67.

Heritage, J. and Maynard, D. W. (eds) (2006). *Communication in Medical Care: interaction between primary care physicians and patients*. Cambridge: Cambridge University Press.

Hewings, M. (2004). *Pronunciation Practice Activities Book and Audio CD Pack: a resource book for teaching English pronunciation*. Cambridge: Cambridge University Press.

Hincks, R. (2010). Speaking rate and information content in English lingua franca oral presentations. *English for Specific Purposes*. 29: 4–18.

Hoey, M. (1991). Some properties of spoken discourses. In R. Bowers and C. Brumfit (eds), *Applied Linguistics and English Language Teaching*. Oxford: Modern English Publications in association with The British Council.

Horowitz, R. (2006). *Talking Texts: how speech and writing interact in school learning*. London: Routledge.

Howatt, A. P. R. (1985). *A History of English Language Teaching*. Oxford: Oxford University Press.

Howatt, A. P. R. and Widdowson, H. G. (2004). *History of English Language Teaching ELT*, 2nd edn. Oxford: Oxford University Press.

Hu, G. and Lindemann, S. (2009). Stereotypes of Cantonese English, apparent native/non-native status, and their effect on non-native English speakers' perception. *Journal of Multilingual and Multicultural Development*. 30(3): 253–269.

Hughes, R. (1996). *English in Speech and Writing: investigating language and literature*. London: Routledge.

Hughes, R. (2004). Testing the visible, literate biases in oral language testing. *Journal of Applied Linguistics*. 1(3): 295–309.

Hughes, R. (2010). Researching speaking. In B. Paltridge and A. Phakiti (eds), *Continuum Companion to Research Methods in Applied Linguistics*. London: Continuum.

Hughes, R. and McCarthy, M. (1998). Sentence grammar and discourse grammar. *TESOL Quarterly*. 32(2): 263–287.

Hyland, K. (2009). *Teaching and Researching Writing*, 2nd edn. Harlow: Longman.

IELTS (2007). IELTS: International English Language Testing System Handbook.

IELTS (2009). IELTS Speaking Band Descriptors (Public). *http://www.ielts.org/PDF/UOBDs_SpeakingFinal.pdf*

Jefferson, G. (2004). Glossary of transcript symbols with an introduction. In G. H. Lerner (ed.), *Conversation Analysis: studies from the first generation*. Amsterdam/Philadelphia: John Benjamins, pp. 13–31.

Jenkins, J. (2000). *The Phonology of English as an International Language*. Oxford: Oxford University Press.

Jenkins, J. (2006). The spread of EIL: a testing time for testers. *ELT Journal*. 60(1): 42–50.

Johns, T. (1991). From printout to handout: grammar and vocabulary learning in the context of data-driven learning. *English Language Research Journal*. 4: 27–45.

Johnson, M. and Tyler, A. (1998). Re-analysing the OPI: how much does it look like natural conversation? In R. Young and A. Weiyn He (eds), *Talking and Testing: discourse approaches to the assessment of oral proficiency*. Amsterdam and Philadelphia: John Benjamins Publishing Company, pp. 27–51.

Kaplan. (2009). *Kaplan IELTS 2009–2010 Edition*. New York: Kaplan Publishing.

Keller, E. and Warner, S. T. (1988). *Conversation Gambits*. Hove: Language Teaching Publications.

Klein, W. and Purdue, C. (eds) (1992). *Utterance Structure: developing grammars again*. Amsterdam and Philadelphia, PA: John Benjamins Publishing Co.

Knowles, G. (1990). The use of spoken and written corpora in the teaching of language and linguistics. *Literary and Linguistic Computing*. 5: 45–48.

Komos, J. (2006). *Speech Production and Second Language Acquisition*. London: Routledge.

Krashen, S. D. (1981). *Second Language Acquisition and Second Language Learning*. Oxford: Pergamon.

Krashen, S. D. (1982). *Principles and Practice in Second Language Acquisition*. Oxford: Pergamon.

Krashen, S. D. (2008). Language education: past present and future. *RELC Journal*. 39(2): 178–187.

Kumaravadivelu, B. (2006). *Understanding Language Teaching: from method to post-method*. London: Routledge.

Kvarnström, S. and Cedersund, E. (2006). Discursive patterns in multiprofessional healthcare teams: nursing and health care management and policy. *Journal of Advanced Nursing*. 53(2): 244–252.

Lam, P. W. Y. (2010). Discourse particles in corpus data and textbooks: the case of *well*. *Applied Linguistics*. 31(2): 260–281.

Lee, Yong-Won (2006). Dependability of scores for a new ESL speaking assessment consisting of integrated and independent tasks. *Language Testing*. 23(2): 131–166.

Lennon, P. (1990). Investigating fluency in EFL: a quantitative approach. *Language Learning*. 40(3): 387–417.

Levelt, W. J. M. (1989). *Speaking: from intention to articulation*. Cambridge, MA and London: MIT Press.

Lewis, M. (1982). *Partners 3: more demanding pair work practices*. Hove: Language Teaching Publications.

Liberman, A. M. (1997). How theories of speech affect research in reading and writing. In B. A. Blachman (ed.), *Foundations of Reading Acquisition and Dyslexia: implications for early intervention*. Mahwah, NJ: Lawrence Erlbaum Associates, pp. 3–19.

Liberman, A. M. (1998). When theories of speech meet the real world. *Journal of Psycholinguistic Research*. 27(2): 111–122.

Liberman, A. M. (1999). The reading researcher and the reading teacher need the right theory of speech. *Scientific Studies of Reading: The official journal of the Society for the Scientific Study of Reading*. 3(2): 95–113.

Liberman, I. Y., Shankweiler, D. and Liberman, A. M. (1989). The alphabetic principle and learning to read. In D. Shankweiler and I. Y. Liberman (eds), *Phonology and Reading Disability: solving the reading puzzle*. Ann Arbor: University of Michigan Press.

Lindquist, H. and Mair, C. (2004). *Corpus Approaches to Grammaticalization in English*. Amsterdam: John Benjamins.

Lloyd James, A. (1940). *Speech Signals in Telephony*. London: Pitman and Sons.

Lotto, A. J., Hickok, G. S. and Holt, L. L. (2008). Reflections on mirror neurons and speech perception. *Trends in Cognitive Sciences*. 13(3): 110–113.

Lougheed, L. (2006). *Barron's How to Prepare for the IELTS*. U.S.: Barrons Education Series Inc.

Low, E. L. and Grabe, E. (1995). Prosodic patterns in Singapore English. In K. Elenius and P. Banderud (eds), *Proceedings of the 13th International Congress for Phonetic Sciences*, Stockholm, 3, pp. 636–639.

Lumley, T. and O'Sullivan, B. (2005). The effect of test-taker gender, audience and topic on task performance in tape-mediated assessment of speaking. *Language Testing*. 22(4): 415–437.

Luoma, S. (2004). *Assessing Speaking*. Cambridge: Cambridge University Press.

Lynch, T. and Anderson, K. (1992). *Study Speaking: a course in spoken English for academic purposes*. Cambridge: Cambridge University Press.

McCarthy, M. (1991). *Discourse Analysis for Language Teachers*. Cambridge: Cambridge University Press.

McCarthy, M. (1998). *Spoken Language and Applied Linguistics*. Cambridge: Cambridge University Press.

McCrum, R. (2006). So, what's this Globish revolution? *http://www.guardian.co.uk/theobserver/2006/dec/03/features.review37* accessed 16 May 2009.

McEnery, A., Xiao, R. and Tono, Y. (2005). *Corpus-based Language Studies*. London: Routledge.

McLaughlin, B. (1987). *Theories of Second-language Learning*. London: Edward Arnold.

McMurray, B., Samelson, V.M., Lee, S.H. and Tomblin, J.B. (2010). Individual differences in online spoken word recognition: implications for SLI. *Cognitive Psychology*. 60(1): 1–39.

McNamara, T. (2001). Language assessment as social practice: challenges for research. *Language Testing*. 18: 333–349.

Maniwa, K., Jongman, A. and Wade, T. (2009). Acoustic characteristics of clearly spoken English fricatives. *Journal of the Acoustic Society of America*. 125(6): 3962–3973.

Marsi, E., Busser, B., Daelemans, W., Hoste, V., Reynaert, M. and Bosch., A. van den. (2002). Combining information sources for memory-based pitch accent placement. *In 7th International Conference on Spoken Language Processing* (Denver, CO, 2002), 1273–1276.

Meeuwesen, L., Tromp, F., Schouten, B. C. and Harmsen, J. A. M. (2007). Cultural differences in managing information during medical interaction: how does the physician get a clue? *Patient Education and Counseling*. 67: 183–190.

Meroni, L. and Crain. S. (2003). How children avoid kindergarten paths. *Proceedings of 4th Tokyo Conference on Psycholinguistics*. Hitsuji Shobo. Tokyo, Japan.

Meyer, C. F. (1995). Coordination ellipsis in spoken and written American English. *Language Sciences*. 17: 241–269.

Mindt, D. (2002). What is a grammatical rule? In L. E. Breivik and A. Hasselgren (eds), *From the COLT's Mouth . . . and Others: language corpora studies in honour of Anna-Brita Stenstrom*. Oxford University Press, pp. 197–212.

Moore, C. (2007). The spread of grammaticalized forms: the case of be+supposed to. *Journal of English Linguistics*. 7(35): 117–131.

Mori, J. (2007). Border crossings? Exploring the intersection of second language acquisition, conversation analysis, and foreign language pedagogy. *The Modern Language Journal*. 91(5): 849–862.

Morton, J. (2009). Genre and disciplinary competence: a case study of contextualization in an academic speech genre. *English for Specific Purposes*. 28(4).

Mushin, I. and Gardner, R. (2009). Silence is talk: conversational silence in Australian Aboriginal talk-in-interaction. *Journal of Pragmatics*. 41: 2033–2052.

Nariyama, S. (2004). Subject ellipsis in English. *Journal of Pragmatics*. 36(2): 237–264.

Nation, I. S. P. and Newton, J. (2008). *Teaching EFL/ESL Listening and Speaking*. London: Routledge.

Nelson, G. (1997). Cleft constructions in spoken and written English. *Journal of English Linguistics*. 25: 340–348.

Nelson, G. L., Mahmood, A. and Nichols, E. (1996). Arabic and English compliment responses: potential for pragmatic failure. *Applied Linguistics*. 17(4): 411–432.

Nestor, M. and Vogel, I. (2007). *Prosodic Phonology*. The Hague: Mouton de Gruyter.

O'Connell, D. C. and Kowal, S. (2009). Transcription systems for spoken discourse. In S. D'Hondt, J. Östman, and J. Verschueren (eds), *The Pragmatics of Interaction*. Amsterdam: John Benjamins, pp. 240–254.

Oller, J. W., Jr. (1983). Evidence for a general language proficiency factor: an expectancy grammar. In J. W. Oller, Jr. (ed.), *Issues in Language Testing Research*. Rowley, MA: Newbury House, pp. 3–10.

O'Malley, J. M. and Valdez Pierce, L. (1996). *Authentic Assessment for English Language Learners: practical approaches for teachers*. New York: Addison Wesley.

Ono, T. and Thompson, S. A. (1995). What can conversation tell us about syntax? In Philip W. Davis (ed.), *Descriptive and Theoretical Modes in the Alternative Linguistics*. Amsterdam: John Benjamins, pp. 213–271.

O'Sullivan, B. (2000). Exploring gender and oral proficiency interview performance. *System*. 28: 1–14.

Özçalışkan, S. and Goldin-Meadow, S. (2005). Gesture is at the cutting edge of early language development. *Cognition*. 96(3): 101–113.

Paltridge, B. and Phakiti, A. (eds) (2010). *Continuum Companion to Research Methods in Applied Linguistics*. New York/London: Continuum.

Partala, T. and Surakka, V. (2004). The effects of affective interventions in human–computer interaction. *Interacting with Computers*. 16(2): 95–309.

Pickering, L. (2006). Current research on intelligibility in English as a Lingua Franca. *Annual Review of Applied Linguistics*. 26: 219–233.

Pike, K. L. (1945). *The Intonation of American English*. Ann Arbor, MI: University of Michigan Publications.

Prabhu, N. S. (1987). *Second Language Pedagogy*. Oxford: Oxford University Press.

Prodromou, L. (2008). *English as a Lingua Franca: a corpus based analysis*. London: Continuum.

Quintilian. (2006). *Institutes of Oratory*. L. Honeycutt (ed.), (J. S. Watson, Trans.). Retrieved Jan. 19, 2010, from *http://honeyl.public.iastate.edu/quintilian/* (Original work published 1856).

Richards, J. C. and Rodgers, S. T. (2001). *Approaches and Methods in Language Teaching*. Cambridge: Cambridge University Press.

Riggenbach, H. (1998). Evaluating learner interactional skills: conversation at the micro level. In R. Young and A. Weiyun He (eds), *Talking and Testing: discourse approaches to the assessment of oral proficiency*. Studies in Bilingualism, 14. Amsterdam and Philadelphia: John Benjamins, pp. 53–67.

Rignall, M. and Furneaux, C. (1997). *Speaking* (English for Academic Study series). Hemel Hempstead: Prentice Hall.

Rivers, W. M. and Temperley, M. S. (1978). *A Practical Guide to the Teaching of English as a Second or Foreign Language*. New York: Oxford University Press.

Rost, M. (2002). *Teaching and Researching Listening*. Harlow: Longman.

Rühlemann, C. (2006). Coming to terms with conversational grammar 'dislocation' and 'dysfluency'. *International Journal of Corpus Linguistics*. 11(4): 385–409.

Salter, C., Holland, R., Harvey, I. and Henwood, K. (2007). 'I haven't even phoned my doctor yet,' the advice giving role of the pharmacist during consultations for medication review with patients aged 80 or more: qualitative discourse analysis. *British Medical Journal*. 2007 May 26; 334(7603): 1101.

Samuda, V. and Bygate, M. (2008). *Tasks in Second Language Learning*. Basingstoke: Palgrave Macmillan.

Sarwark, S., Smith, J., MacCullam, R. and Cascallar, E. C. (1995). *A Study of Characteristics of the SPEAK Test*. RR94–47. Princeton, NJ: Educational Testing Service.

Schegloff, E. A. (1981). Discourse as an interactional achievement: some uses of 'uh huh' and other things that come between sentences. In D. Tannen (ed.), *Analysing Discourse: text and talk*. Washington, DC: Georgetown University Press, pp. 71–93.

Schegloff, E. A. (1987). Recycled turn beginnings: a precise repair mechanism in conversation's turn-taking organisation. In G. Button and J. R. Lee (eds), *Talk and Social Organisation*. Clevedon: Multilingual Matters, pp. 70–85.

Seidlhofer, B. (2001). Pronunciation. In R. Carter and D. Nunan (eds), *The Cambridge Guide to Teaching English to Speakers of Other Languages*. Cambridge: Cambridge University Press.

Sheridan, T. (1781). *A Rhetorical Grammar of the English Language* (reprinted 1969). Menston, UK: The Scholar Press.

Shin, D. H. (1989). Effect of formal vs. informal environments and Krashen's Monitor Model. Unpublished Master's thesis, University of Birmingham, Birmingham, West Midlands.

Shohamy, E. (2001). *The Power of Tests: a critical perspective on the uses of language tests*. London: Pearson.

Simpson, J. (2006). Differing expectations in the assessment of the speaking skills of ESOL learners. *Linguistics and Education*. 17: 40–55.

Sinclair, J. and Coulthard, M. (1975). *Towards an Analysis of Discourse: the English used by teachers and pupils*. London: Oxford University Press.

Skehan, P. (2007). Language instruction through tasks. In J. Cummins and C. Davison (eds), *International Handbook of English Language Teaching*. New York: Springer, pp. 289–301.

Snedeker, J. and Trueswell, J. (2001). Unheeded cues: prosody and syntactic ambiguity in mother–child communication. Paper presented at the 26th Boston University Conference on Language Development.

Snedeker, J. and Trueswell, J. (2004). The developing constraints on parsing decisions: the role of lexical biases and referential scenes in child and adult sentence processing. *Cognitive Psychology*. 49(3): 238–299.

Speer, S. J. and Ito, K. (2009). Prosody in first language acquisition – acquiring intonation as a tool to organize information in conversation. *Language and Linguistics Compass*. 3(1): 90–110.

Stenström, A-B. (1990). Lexical items peculiar to spoken discourse. In J. Svartvik (ed.), *The London–Lund Corpus of Spoken English: description and research*. Lund Studies in English 82. Lund: Lund University Press, pp. 137–176.

Straube, B., Green, A., Jansenc, A., Chatterjeeb, A., and Kircherc, T. (2010). Social cues, mentalizing and the neural processing of speech accompanied by gestures. *Neuropsychologia*. 48: 382–393.

Svartvik, J. (ed.) (1990). *The London–Lund Corpus of Spoken English: description and research*. Lund Studies in English 82. Lund: Lund University Press.

Svartvik, J. (1991). What can real spoken data teach teachers of English? In J. E. Alatis (ed.), *Georgetown University Round Table on Languages and Linguistics 1991*. Washington, DC: Georgetown University Press, pp. 555–566.

Sweet, H. (1900). *The Practical Study of Languages: a guide for teachers and learners*. New York: Henry Holt and Company.

Szczepek-Reed, B. (2007). *Prosodic Orientation in English Conversation*. Basingstoke: Palgrave Macmillan.

Takehashi, T. and Beebe, L. M. (1993). Cross-linguistic influence in the speech act of correction. In G. Kasper and S. Blum-Kulka (eds), *Interlanguage Pragmatics*. New York: Oxford University Press, pp. 138–157.

Tan, A. A. and Molfese D. L. (2009). ERP correlates of noun and verb processing in preschool-age children. *Biological Psychology*. 80(1): 46–51.

Taylor, L. (2006). The changing landscape of English: implications for language assessment. *ELT Journal*. 60(1): 51–9.

Taylor, L. and Falvey, P. (2007). *IELTS Collected Papers: research in speaking and writing assessment*. Cambridge: Cambridge University Press.

ten Have, P. (2007). *Doing Conversation Analysis*. London: Sage Publications.

Thompson, S. A. and Couper-Kuhlen, E. (2005). The Clause as a locus of grammar and interaction. *Language and Linguistics*. 6(4): 807–837.

Thornbury, S. and Slade, D. (2006). *Conversation: from description to pedagogy*. New York: Cambridge University Press.

Tribble, C. and Jones, G. (1990). *Concordances in the Classroom: a resource book for teachers*. Harlow: Longman.

Tyler, A. E., Jeffries, A. A. and Davies, C. E. (1988). The effect of discourse structuring devices on listener perceptions of coherence in non-native university teachers' spoken discourse. *World Englishes*. 7(2): 101–110.

Underhill, N. (1987). *Testing Spoken Language: a handbook of oral testing techniques*. Cambridge: Cambridge University Press.

Uppstad, P. H. and Tønnessen, F. E. (2007). The notion of 'phonology' in dyslexia research: cognitivism and beyond. *Dyslexia*. 13: 154–174.

Ur, P. (1996). *A Course in Language Teaching: practice and theory*. Cambridge: Cambridge University Press.

Usó-Juan, E. and Martínez-Flor, A. (eds) (2006). *Current Trends in the Development and Teaching of the Four Language Skills*. Berlin: Mouton de Gruyter.

Vachek, J. (1966). Some remarks on writing and phonetic transcription. In E. Hamp, F. Householder and R. Austerlitz (eds), *Readings in Linguistics*. 2. Chicago: University of Chicago Press.

Vachek, J. (1973). *Written Language: general problems and problems of English*. The Hague: Mouton.

Van Avermaet, P., Colpin, M., van Gorp, K., Bogaert, N. and van den Branden, K. (2007). The role of the teacher in task-based language teaching. In K. van den Branden (ed.) *Task-Based Language Education: from theory to practice*. Cambridge: Cambridge University Press, pp. 175–196.

Van den Branden, K. (ed.) (2006). *Task-Based Language Education: from theory to practice*. Cambridge: Cambridge University Press.

Viney, P. and Viney, K. (1996). *Handshake: a course in communication*. Oxford: Oxford University Press.

Wallwork, A. (1997). *Discussions A–Z, Intermediate: a resource book of speaking activities*. Cambridge: Cambridge University Press.

Walsh, S. (2006). Talking the talk of the TESOL classroom. *ELT Journal*. 60(2): 133–141.

Watanabe, M., Hirose, K., Den, Y. and Minematsu, N. (2008). Filled pauses as cues to the complexity of upcoming phrases for native and non-native listeners. *Speech Communication*. 50: 81–94.

Webber, P. (2005). Interactive features in medical conference monologue. *English for Specific Purposes*. 24(2): 157–181.

Wennerstrom, A. (2001). *The Music of Everyday Speech*. New York: Oxford.

White, L. (1987). Against comprehensible input: the input hypothesis and the development of second-language competence. *Applied Linguistics*. 8(2): 95–110.

Widdowson, H. E. (1972). The teaching of English as communication. *ELT Journal*. 1: 15–19.

Willis, D. and Willis, J. (2007). *Doing Task-Based Teaching*. Oxford: Oxford University Press.

Wolf, J. P. (2008). The effects of backchannels on fluency in L2 oral task production. *System*. 36(2): 279–294.

Xi, X., Higgins, D., Zechner, K. and Williamson, D. M. (2008). *Automated Scoring of Spontaneous Speech Using SpeechRaterSM v1.0*. Educational Testing Service Research Report ETS RR-08-62.

Young, R. and Weiyun He, A. (1998). *Talking and Testing: discourse approaches to the assessment of oral proficiency*. Studies in Bilingualism, 14. Amsterdam and Philadelphia: John Benjamins Publishing Company.

Yu, G. (2007). Students' voices in the evaluation of their written summaries: empowerment and democracy for test takers? *Language Testing*. 24: 539–573.

Yungzhong, L. (1985). Writing versus speech in foreign language teaching. *Wai Guo Yu*. 3(37): 12–15.

Index